GOD DAY BY DAY

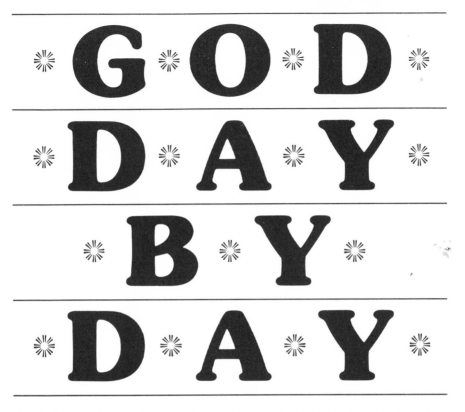

A COMPANION TO THE WEEKDAY MISSAL

VOLUME FIVE

ORDINARY TIME:

MARK

COMMENTARY ON THE TEXTS

SPIRITUAL REFLECTIONS ※ SUGGESTED PRAYERS

MARCEL BASTIN · GHISLAIN PINCKERS · MICHEL TEHEUX
TRANSLATED BY DAVID SMITH

Paulist Press • New York/New Jersey

Library of Congress Cataloging In Publication Data

(Revised for vol. 5)

Bastin, Marcel.
    God day by day.

    Translation of: Dieu pour chaque jour.
    Vol. 2 has bibliography: p. 450–451.
    Contents: v. 1. Lent and the Easter season—
v. 2. Ordinary time: Matthew—   —v. 5. Ordinary
time: Mark.
    1. Church year—Prayer-books and devotions—English.
2. Bible—Liturgical lessons, English.   3. Catholic
Church—Prayer-books and devotions—English.
I. Pinckers, Ghislain.   II. Teheux, Michel.   III. Title.
BX2170.L4B3713   1984   242'.3   84-60391
ISBN 0-8091-2642-7 (pbk.: v. 1)

Published by Paulist Press
997 Macarthur Boulevard
Mahwah, New Jersey 07430

Printed and bound in the United States of America

CONTENTS

iv

PRESENTATION

This book is the last of a set of five covering the whole of the Church's weekday lectionary. Many books have already been published containing commentaries, suggestions and prayers for the Sundays of the three-year cycle of readings, A, B and C. There was still a need, however, for a similar aid for the corresponding weekdays. Now the last of these five books has appeared and the set is complete.

The structure and method of presentation are similar to those of the first four volumes. The authors have followed the order of the days of the week, but have grouped certain days together according to liturgical seasons or within coherent wholes, each of which is preceded by an introductory note.

Under each day, the following three elements will be found:

1. A short commentary on the readings and the Psalm. A biblical scholar has drawn a clear, simple and firmly based message from the sacred texts.

2. A spiritual reflection, intended to provide material for private meditation, a preparation for the homily and other purposes outside the Eucharist itself, both by individuals and groups.

3. Suggestions for prayer, which can be used to extend meditation, for example, by thanksgiving. These prayers can also be used throughout the rest of the day. Their language and thought are strongly biblical.

The authors do not intend any of these three elements to be used to replace the texts and prayers of the liturgy itself. The very reverse is true. Because the authors' aim is to help the reader to prepare for and to extend the liturgical act, their suggestions are above all at the service of the liturgy. They have their origin in the Eucharist and their only intention is to help to make each day holy. To that end, these suggestions are an attempt to stimulate the spiritual benefits of the liturgy as from a source of life-giving water.

The Publisher

Lent and Easter
Ordinary Time: Matthew
Ordinary Time: Luke
Advent and Christmas
Ordinary Time: Mark

These books are the result of ministry and pastoral experience in the parish of Saint-Denis in Liège, Belgium. The parish church is at the center of a neighborhood that is dominated by trade, administration and leisure, and the local community that has grown up there is always in a state of movement. The church is visited every day by a very great number of people living and working there. It is that aspect of the church that the authors have also tried to present in the pages that follow.

FOREWORD

We have outlined the intentions and the possible ways of using these books in the introduction to the first volume in the set (Lent and Easter). In the present volume, we are concerned with Weeks 1 to 9 of Ordinary Time in years with uneven and even numbering. We decided to base our volumes on the reading of the three Synoptic Gospels and, as a result, this volume covers the weeks when the Gospel According to Mark is read.

The exegesis of the Gospel (which is read each year) is given in the first half of the book under the heading of "Uneven Years." For the even years, the reader will have to refer back to the relevant page in the uneven years.

The general principle underlying the spiritual reflections is the same as that followed in the volumes that have already appeared: to set the two readings as it were in parallel and let them throw light on each other, insofar as this is possible without making unreasonable demands on the texts.

The reader who finds it preferable to base his daily reflection on a continuous commentary on the Gospel may want to use the table provided at the end of this book. This table will help him to refer to the uneven or to the even year, according to the sequence of the Gospel.

He will also find two other tables at the end of this final volume. The first of these is an index of themes that will help him to use the spiritual

commentaries that have appeared in the whole set of five books. This index
has been arranged under six main headings: faith and its decision; faith, its
demands and consequences; the image of God; the image of Christ; the
Church, the believing people; the spiritual life. The second table sets out the
relationship between the Sunday and the weekday liturgies. Many of the
passages read during the week are taken up again in one of the three Sunday
cycles, and the spiritual reflections intended here for the daily liturgy can
therefore form an introduction to the Word celebrated on Sunday.

UNEVEN YEARS

ORDINARY TIME
WEEKS 1–9

Gospel According to Saint Mark
Letter to the Hebrews
Book of Sirach
Book of Tobit

A Gospel that is short, dry, sharp as a sword and as new as the revelation that it puts into words and images. Made itself in the image of the first sermon, it goes right to the heart of things and calls at once for decision: the decision of faith. It is itself enclosed within the framework of two professions of faith. At the beginning is that of the Father saying to his Son: "You are my Beloved; in you I have placed all my love." And at the end, a foreigner, a centurion serving in the army of occupation, confesses his faith: "In truth, this man was the Son of God."

The Gospel of Mark is from beginning to end dramatic. It is the drama of a man from Nazareth who, in the secret of his everlasting intimacy with God, is entrusted with a mission for all time. His task was to reveal the Father and to proclaim deeply disconcerting news. It is the drama of a prophet going to his death so that he might dedicate himself entirely to his suffering as the only Son. It is also the drama of men and women, torn between the great longing that Christ's testimony awakes in them and the force of their secular habits and stereotyped daily certainties. It is the drama of religious men who are enslaved to their withered faithfulness. It is the drama of sick people who are afraid to believe in their healing, and people who are dedicated to death and dare not hope that they are being offered life. It is the drama of the disciples who are fascinated by the astonishing words of their master, but who become discouraged by the events in his life.

Finally, it is also the drama of the women who were the first witnesses of the resurrection and who were terrified by this new reality. They were literally "outside themselves." That is how this Gospel ends. It also points in the direction of a great question mark—ours.

We are "outside ourselves." We know nothing any more. Who is this man? Let us ask God to let this Gospel touch our hearts in the weeks ahead so that this question will remain with us. It is the very question of faith itself and the dignity of our existence as believers.

The biblical texts for weekday reading during Ordinary Time provide us with an excellent opportunity to immerse ourselves in scripture. The Synoptic Gospels are read almost completely as are the most important passages in the Old Testament. This opportunity, however, is also accompanied by a very real danger, because the restrictions imposed by the liturgy mean that the texts have to be presented in small units, with the result that it is difficult to be conscious of the existence of the whole structure. If we are to avoid this danger, we have to follow the overall plan of Mark's Gospel or at least consider carefully the great themes that constitute it. We would strongly recommend the book that we have followed here: J. Radermakers' *La bonne nouvelle de Jésus selon saint Marc* (Brussels, 1974), or else B. Standaert's very rich analysis, *L'évangile selon Marc. Composition et genre littéraire* (Bruges, 1978).

First and foremost, however, it is important to remember that Mark was the creator of the literary genre that came to be known as "Gospel." The word existed before his time, of course, and was used, both in Hebrew and in Greek, with the meaning of "good news," in the sense of the announcement of a fortunate event, such as a victory over the enemy or a royal enthronement. By the time of Second Isaiah, however, it had taken on a religious coloring and pointed both to the end of Israel's exile and to God's visiting mankind. We may say, then, that the good news proclaimed by the Gospels is Emmanuel, God-with-us. The word had come to mean this on Easter morning and when Jesus was enthroned as the Son of God, but Mark gave it an even richer meaning by identifying it with the very person of Jesus.

After a prologue (which is read on the second Sunday of Advent, B), the Gospel opens with a first stage which resembles a preliminary sketch for a portrait. Mark gives two replies to the question that we have already enunciated in our introduction: Who is this man Jesus? These two replies divide the whole Gospel into two parts. The first can be summarized as follows: Jesus is the "contesting authority" (1:21-45). The second, however, shows how quickly that authority was contested (2:1-3:6).

The first answer is placed within an entirely artificial framework—that of a day spent by Jesus in Capernaum. That day, which is a sabbath, opens with an exorcism in the synagogue (1:21-28). In his confrontation with evil, Jesus calls sin itself into question. It is this that makes the demon call out: "What do you want of us, Jesus of Nazareth? Have you come to destroy us?" The healing of the man clearly causes a great stir and Jesus' popularity spreads quickly from the synagogue to the whole of Galilee.

"And immediately" (these are two words that Mark uses again and again to point to the imminence of the kingdom), the reader is taken into Peter's house, where Jesus heals his sick mother-in-law. This healing has a pronounced flavor of Easter because Mark uses a verb that is also employed for Jesus' resurrection—he *woke* or *raised her* (1:29–31).

After sunset (that is, on the day following the sabbath), "the whole town came crowding round the door and Jesus cured many who were suffering from diseases. . . . He also cast out many devils" (1:32–34). Despite its brevity, this episode forms the pivot of the whole story, because the day following the sabbath is the day of the Lord. It is Easter. We can even say that the door mentioned in the episode opens to a new week. Mark is suggesting here that a new world is established when the kingdom breaks in.

If the whole thrust of the story is summarized in this little episode, it is hardly surprising that the text that follows it should, as it were, take us back to the point of departure. Jesus leaves the town and goes into the desert where he prays, although his disciples look for him there with the intention of persuading him to return (1:35–39). So he proclaimed the Gospel throughout Galilee and contests evil again by purifying a leper (1:40–45).

From the sabbath to the morning of Easter, from the synagogue to the whole of Galilee, the Word breaks out and spreads irresistibly. New creation emerges from the door and life triumphs over the powers of death. But, if Jesus speaks with an authority that astonished those who heard him, surely he also ran the risk of being questioned by them, because he laid their hearts bare.

■

You knock on my door
and yet I waste your love.
Lord, have mercy!

You call me by my name
and yet I remain withdrawn.
Lord, have mercy!

Your breath has the fragrance of the open sea
and yet I stay where I am.
Lord, have pity!

■

It is truly right and just
to proclaim your glory, God,
you who give yourself
to the despised and rejected.

7

You look with love at the leper
and live in the heart of his misery.
Your Son's body is given
to flesh already marked by death.
That is why,
now our hearts have been purified,
we proclaim that you alone are holy.

FROM MONDAY OF THE 1ST WEEK

TO WEDNESDAY OF THE 3RD WEEK

The Mediator

Jesus is the man in our history in whom the total fullness of God lives "in his body" (Col 2:9). He is the man who discloses for us the whole of God's activity, both the action and the word of his revelation. That is the totally unexpected news presented by the challenging Gospel of Mark—that we can see in Jesus what God is in his "essential substance." When God entrusts the man from Nazareth with his mission after he had gone down into the waters of the Jordan, the words are heard: "In you I have placed all my love," although the speaker is not seen. Jesus is the human visibility of the invisible God. He is the humanity of God: God's way of existing as a human being.

Jesus' divinity is situated within his humanity. Jesus is not simply the one who expresses and communicates God's plan. He is God present as a human being insofar as he reveals himself. The word of God is his word. God had, of course, already spoken but, until the coming of Jesus, he had been deflected into the world from a distance, as it were, and had never given himself totally, but had always been measured in some way by the urgency of the questioning. With Jesus' coming, however, that distance disappeared. God became compromised with human history because he had become man. That is the scandal of the good news: God's revelation is inseparable from the man Jesus. "In you I have placed all my favor." Revelation is not simply found in the words said by Jesus—it is there in Jesus himself, in his person. He is the revelation and the revealer.

In and through his humanity, which was situated within and conditioned by history, Jesus is God's revelation for us. That is why we have to be so concerned with his life and that is the essential reason why the Gospels were written. There is no other place where we can meet God apart from the books

---

where we are told about the life of that one man. If he was to achieve a truly personal communion with man, God had to become God in a human way, by addressing himself to man. In Jesus, God's secret becomes the secret of man, because that man is God. So the person of Jesus is our living guarantee that God has given himself to the world, and that the world has been received in love by God. In the strictest sense of the word, Jesus is the Mediator. Karl Rahner expressed this very well when he said that the humanity of Jesus is the expression that God gives of himself outside of himself. And Christian Duquoc has called Jesus our mediator because he is the incarnation of the "different God." I have said that he is the visibility of the invisible God and I would go further and say that that is why we believe in the unique ministry of salvation, that Christ is the only mediator between God and men. Christ is and has always, from the very beginning, been totally and in a unique way "of God" (1 Cor 3:23).

MONDAY OF THE 1ST WEEK

THE LAST WORD

Hebrews 1:1–16. Our modern understanding of the Epistle to the Hebrews can be summarized in three negative statements. First, the Epistle is not a letter; second, it is not addressed to the Jews, but to people who had been Christians for a long time and third, its author is not Paul, even though it contains several points of contact with the Apostle's teaching.

The essential message of the Epistle is Christ, and it culminates in an affirmation of the unparalleled value of his priesthood and his sacrifice. It opens with a solemn introductory discourse recalling God's many interventions in human history. It shows how, by his work of redemption, Christ has inaugurated the last times and inherited a name that is quite different from that of the angels. The author's primary intention is to develop the theme of Christ's glorification and, with this in mind, he begins by establishing the dignity and position of Jesus Christ with regard to the angels. In this task, he has to oppose the view held in certain circles that the angels had power to save and, in support of his argument, he quotes a number of passages in the Old Testament stating that the name of "Son" was given to Christ and not to any angel.

Psalm 97 is composed in imitation of the songs of victory which were sung at the end of a campaign for the enthronement of the ark of the covenant. Later, they were used again in the temple in Jerusalem, during the Feast of

Tabernacles. Although it is a relatively late work, this psalm makes use of early material, particularly a theophanic poem.

Mark 1:14–20. A page is turned: John the Baptist is arrested and this leaves the field free for the Messiah. John had baptized in water; Jesus will baptize in the Holy Spirit. But, for the present, it is enough for him to go into Galilee and proclaim the good news of God.

Jesus invites the people he meets to become aware. His words confront them with God's plan of liberation. The kingdom will not be fully manifested until everyone has discovered in Jesus the source of the happiness they hope to achieve. Jesus therefore begins preaching in Galilee because it is the Jewish province that is most open to the pagan world.

His word is effective straightaway. He spends a little more time near the "Sea" of Galilee and invites four men to follow him. This call is very meaningful since, in the Bible, the sea is regarded as the haunt of forces that are hostile to God and men. Jesus' call, therefore, sets these four men free from the forces that are trying to extinguish God's work in them. They have been fishing in the lake, but they at once abandon everything—that is the essential condition for following Jesus.

■

For man, speaking is living! Through his words, he gives meaning to things and to the world. Through his words, he becomes a man by receiving from others the meaning of words, beings and reality itself. Man speaks and his words fashion the world. Man is born in a world in which people speak and he awakes to a world which is already a world invested with meaning, a universe in which beings and things are established in their place, because that place has been allocated to them. And throughout his life, man has to take a risk and express that life and what he is experiencing and feeling and what he is in words, without ever exhausting those words that are able to express the whole of that life. Man's life is a constant attempt to express himself. For man, speaking is living!

For God too, speaking is living! From the very beginning, God has existed speaking. The word of the Father has always begotten words that are a response to his tenderness. The Word who was born within God himself—that Word is the only Son because he is the Word who is the perfect response to the tenderness offered by the Father. God is in his very being dialogue: Father and Son are one word in such close unity that it leads to one breathing, which is the Spirit. For God, existing is speaking.

Dare I say it? It is, I am sure, the very nature of God to express himself, to speak, to reveal his name. And our Christian faith has this extraordinary and quite new aspect: When God speaks to us, his word is based not on the model of his own divine being, but on the spirit of man, with whom he enters into communication.[1] When, in his love, God takes the initiative and suggests to man that he should share his divine life, he enters into the game of the laws of love, with its fundamental rule: He, the "other," should determine my love, and the fundamental condition for the achievement of his communion with man: that he, God, should become man.

After having spoken in various ways, "God has spoken to us through his Son," who is the perfect expression of his being. "The times have been fulfilled." The good news is proclaimed because the eternal Word has been made man, the word of flesh and blood. In the words of that one man of Nazareth, in what he says of himself and in his words that have become actions and miracles, we are bound to recognize the perfect expression of God himself, his last word. God has nothing else to say— only Jesus.

To say that is an affirmation of the last word of our Christian faith and of our discovery that, to express himself, God has no more than a human life, our lives as men. Our human words, our actions as men and women, are able to express God. After saying Jesus Christ, God has no more to say since, in saying that word, he affirms that he has found a man who corresponds perfectly to his proposal of a covenant with man. And in Jesus, we have been enabled to reach God, that God who, in a unique way, declared to Jesus: "You are my Son; today I have begotten you," words that are applied to us also on the day of our baptism, words that express the meaning and fullness of my life and calling. "Be converted and believe the good news!" We shall always need to be awakened to that Word, who is our birth! And even in eternity, our last word will always be a word, pronounced awkwardly and with astonishment because it is so bold. That word is "Father."

■

God, Master of our times and our history,
  you fulfilled your promises
  by sending us your Son Jesus.
Make the Word that he proclaims
  new for us today.
Revive our will to follow him
  and let his teaching once more
  be the rule guiding our lives.

May what he says about you
  once again reveal your mystery.

It is good to bless you, God our Father!
After speaking through the prophets,
  you pronounced your single word,
  the ultimate revelation
  of everything that you want to tell us.

We bless you for your Son,
  who has kept in our own time
  the word that we have never been able
  to live truly,
  the perfect response to your covenant.

He is the only Son, the Word of tenderness
  pronounced from all eternity.
He is the first-born of a multitude of believers.
Through his Spirit who gives body to the word of grace,
  we dare to pronounce your name
  and give voice to the praise of the universe.

God of the word and the prophets,
  all that we can tell you
  are the words that you have yourself revealed.

We bless you for the Word,
  your Son whose powerful Word bears all things up.
  Only he can say of you
  what he has seen with his own eyes.

Enlightened by his word,
  we beseech you:
Let us understand what he is revealing to us
and let us carry out what he is asking us to do.

■

God of the word and the prophets,
  you reveal your face to us
  by giving us your Beloved.
He discloses your love to us
  by handing himself over to us,
  a life dedicated to the good news
  and bread broken for a world
  according to your will.
How could we hope

to live to the full measure
that you require of us
if Christ did not give himself to us,
the Word of our awkward words
and the completion of our rough sketches of brotherhood?
May our lives be brought into harmony with his
and may they give glory to you.

TUESDAY OF THE 1ST WEEK

MAN GIVEN BACK TO HIMSELF

Hebrews 2:5–12. The world to come has been subjected not to angels, but to Christ. With the help of a number of verses from Psalm 8, the author of the Epistle continues to emphasize Christ's superiority over the angels and the eminent dignity that he found through his glorifying passion. After having been "for a short while made lower than the angels," he was "crowned with glory and splendor." Death was followed by life and being made low was followed by glorification.

The next theme is also announced in today's passage from Hebrews—that of the close solidarity existing between Christ and those who believe in him. Because he became universal brotherhood and shared the life of men, he is able to lead many brothers to glory.

Psalm 8 is presented as a hymn to the glory of God who wanted man to be the most splendid of his creatures. This psalm must have originated in pious circles in the temple at Jerusalem.

Mark 1:21–28 J. Rademakers has commented: "Like wildfire running through dry grass, the whole of Galilee is set alight." In the space of a single day, Jesus' word searches out the hearts of men and lays bare the evils hidden in them. "What do you want with us, Jesus of Nazareth?" The forces that are hostile to God know how close they are now to defeat and they resist fiercely when Jesus orders them to leave the possessed man. The word of God calls into question all the values on which men build their lives. They can, in fact, only be satisfied by his love.

It is, then, a new dawn for mankind, until that time subjected to the law of evil. God has come face to face with sin and has overcome it. The evidence of this is clear to the whole of Galilee.

■

An impressive encounter! All those present in the synagogue are astonished. On the one hand, a man who is possessed by an evil spirit which holds him in its grip, a man who is outside himself, who has lost possession of himself, a man whose life reflects those of so many people: unhappy, meaningless, lost, no longer human. "What is man?" On the other hand, another man who is free, whose eyes burn like fire, a man in whom the Spirit dwells. "What is man, that you should spare a thought for him?" God has not abandoned us to our unhappiness. In Jesus, he shows us that life and hope are possible.

In Jesus, we are able to contemplate man fulfilled, man as God wanted him to be when he lovingly molded the clay on the first day in order to fashion man. A man who is part of our history and one of our race has been torn away from the forces which deprive man of his own existence: the forces of selfishness, injustice, despair, fatalism and indifference. Man is possible because one man has lived in full possession of what makes him man: love, sharing, joy, openness, freedom, inventiveness, breath and rebirth. Jesus is man fulfilled, perfected. Saint Paul called him the new Adam. In him, the infernal circle of our alienations has been broken in the perfect development of our abilities and we can now believe in man. Jesus is "the first-born of many brothers." Having shared in the adventure of all men, he is, "by the grace of God, the salvation of all." One man has followed the way of all men and now we can go forward to expand and develop fully. Salvation is above all the pledge that the initiative taken by God when he created us will come to a good end. Our world is not a place of exile, but an earth where, in a lasting process of giving birth, God inaugurates the success of his plan.

■

What is man, Lord God,
 that you should care for him?
Lovingly you fashioned him
 on the first days of the universe.
Even more tenderly you lead him
 towards his fulfilment.

May you be blessed for your Spirit,
 who infallibly leads us
 towards our full stature
 and gradually molds us
 into the image of your Son,
 the holy and perfect one,
 our Savior.

PUT TO THE TEST FOR US

Hebrews 2:14-18. Continuing his argument, the author of the Epistle places in the mouth of Christ words taken from the prophet Isaiah: "Here I am with the children whom God has given me" (Is 8:18). In this way, he emphasizes once again the solidarity between Christ and ourselves—just as what all children have in common is their flesh and blood, so too has Christ shared in man's condition. This solidarity quite naturally led him also to share in death, but in sharing this aspect of man's destiny, he also changed its meaning. Death had until then been in the hands of the devil, but Jesus made it an instrument of salvation and redemption for men.

The author uses this solidarity which unites us with Christ and this new value that Christ has given to death as a reason for giving Christ the unexpected title of "high priest." This title is very unexpected because Jesus never claimed it for himself and also because his death had not seemed to be a ritual act. But, apart from allowing the author to make a connection between the person of Christ and the cultic tradition of the Bible, giving Christ this title also points to a deeply pondered concern on his part with the whole work of salvation. On the one hand, the theology of the priesthood presupposed a clear distinction in Jewish society between the people and their priests, whose task was to attempt to approach God but, on the other hand, in their day to day experience of their priests the people were again and again made conscious of their priests' human weakness. Christ, however, was quite different in that he did not separate himself from his fellow-men, but completely assumed their human condition in an identification that was totally in accordance with God's plan to save mankind. His death on the cross bore witness to his obedience to God's will. In the words of the Epistle, Jesus became a merciful and faithful high priest, able to take away the sins of the people.

Written in the form of a highly developed hymn, *Psalm 105* gives thanks to Yahweh for the part that he has played in the history of his people.

Mark 1:29-39. And immediately. . . . In the Gospel of Mark, Jesus is always on the way. He is always pressed forward by the urgency of the kingdom. Here we find him in Peter's house. His disciple's mother-in-law has a fever, an illness that was regarded in the ancient world as a divine punishment, proclaiming the ruin of the sufferer because he or she had been unfaithful to the covenant.

Because she is sick, the woman cannot carry out the duties of hospitality, so Jesus approaches her. Once again, he is confronted with the power of evil. He does more than simply get rid of her fever—he "raises her." This was, in other words, a resurrection. Freed from her evil, she is now able to "serve" her guests.

What hope this must have brought to the poor, many of whom were gathered at the gates of the town. The sabbath was ending and the sun was rising on a new day. Easter was on the horizon! But Jesus had first to withdraw to a deserted place and his disciples had to come there to take him back to the world. Too few people were aware that the kingdom was on the way. Jesus had to set off again and proclaim the good news.

■

Put to the test! Every day we meet someone who is being put to the test. He or she is suffering. Suffering may take many forms: sickness, infirmity, separation, bereavement, loss of job or status, disappointment, failure. That person is suddenly put to the test and the situation continues. He holds out. He goes on living. He resists. His suffering may seem to be victorious but, because he has held his own in the struggle, he is the real victor. The man who is put to the test gains a new stature. He is purified by the experience and becomes like silver that has been put through fire. Purified, he becomes more human.

Put to the test—the word is synonymous with suffering and purification. But it is also synonymous with safe and faithful. A safe and faithful friend is someone on whom I can depend. Despite all the damaging effects of time, monotony and the lack of human understanding, he remains firm and faithful.

Jesus wanted to share our human condition. That is the message of the Epistle to the Hebrews for us today. And that message continues later in the Epistle. In Hebrews 4:15, we are told that he was put to the test in every way, in other words, that he shared the harsh experience of being a man. And the message of the New Testament as a whole is that Christ learned in obedience what it was to be a son. Put to the test in every way, he shared man's suffering and failures. He knew what it was to be disappointed and disillusioned. He experienced in his flesh his share of physical and moral suffering. "Father, may this cup be taken from me!" Like all his brothers, he learned from the hard experience of becoming a man. He is our companion in our ordeals and, because of this, he has something important to teach us.

But he is also more than our companion in misfortune. In being put to the test, he is more than that because he is the very incarnation of God's faithfulness. God will not let his friend see corruption. He will tear him, the one whom we have recognized as one of us, away from the power of evil and raise him up in the sun of Easter! In this way, he will show us

that our being put to the test is a giving birth, that one of us is showing that mankind is already redeemed.

∎

God our Father,
your Son has experienced our human condition.
He is at one with us,
  suffering and seeking with us.
Because you have brought him
  to the glory of the resurrection,
let us follow him to that place
  to which he is taking us—
  to eternal joy and everlasting life.

THURSDAY OF THE 1ST WEEK

CONTAGION

Hebrews 3:7–14. After having introduced the main theme of his sermon, the author now exhorts his readers. Today, as in the past, believers have to preserve their faith in Christ the priest and not stifle the word that is trying to find the way to their hearts.

Psalm 95, which serves as an introduction to the first office of the day, is divided into two parts. The first seven verses form a psalm of pilgrimage, while the last four are a fragment of an indictment which Yahweh is portrayed as addressing to his people in his sanctuary. These final verses recall the events described in Exodus 17, that is, Israel's attempted dispute with God and failure to believe in his providence.

Mark 1:40–45. A leper responds to Jesus' preaching by asking to be healed and his way of behaving anticipates the enthusiasm of the crowds which followed him everywhere. In approaching Jesus, the sick man is breaking the law, because leprosy was regarded as the outward sign of the inner decomposition of the heart caused by sin and lepers were kept at a distance so that they would not defile the towns and villages.

There was only one way by which leprosy could be cured and that was by the power of God, the only power that could raise the dead to life. So Jesus stretches out his hand and, touching the man, orders the sickness to leave him. Healed, the man can now be accepted by society and once again be subject to its laws. He goes to show himself to the priest and in this way not only testifies to his cure, but also provides official evidence of Jesus' holiness. In his own way, he also proclaims the coming of the kingdom, by speaking about God's search for man, whom he lures out into the desert to reveal himself to his heart.

(According to some manuscripts, Jesus responds in verse 41 to the leper's appeal with a feeling of irritation. This reaction expresses his hostility towards the power of evil.)

■

He was a leper!
At the time of Jesus, the leper was excluded from towns and cities and especially from the holy city of Jerusalem. He had to cover his face with a veil and avoid all contact with his fellow-men. He was no longer a man! The contagion was too dangerous for those in good health. The leper was also treated as an outcast in order to preserve the religious purity of the people. He was regarded as impure because he was thought to be marked by sin and his leprosy was seen as God's punishment. He was excommunicated—excluded from communion with his fellow-men and with God. Only God could cure him. It was thought that all lepers would be purified and therefore able to take their place in the society of the new people of God in the days of the Messiah. But in the meantime, they had to remain outside.

Jesus comes, however, and the laws at once begin to change. They are suddenly swept aside by a tidal wave. The leper forgets that he has to remain at a distance. He takes a risk and throws himself at Jesus' feet. He is angry and says things to Jesus that can only be said to God: "If you want to, you can cure me!" Then the incredible thing happens: Jesus touches the leper! And his words are even more incredible: "Of course I want to! Be cured!"

Now it is Jesus who has to remain at a distance from towns and villages, as though he were leprous. The man, however, is no longer excluded and untouchable. His life has been renewed by contact with Jesus. He is saved. His disfigured face has been restored to normality and, after dragging himself painfully along under the weight of his contagious disease, he has experienced a resurrection, because the Holy One of God has come close to him and touched him. From now on, it is no longer leprosy, but love that is contagious. Sickness, evil and desolation no longer have the last word. Monsignor Etchegaray has written: "The

Church is the special place of the heart, where people know that they are not labelled, but recognized as human, forgiven and loved madly. Some of the joy of Christ the Savior is lacking if the tenderness of God is not revealed to all men. And surely it is Christians themselves who are saturated with that tenderness who must make it available to others."

From now on, then, it is love that is contagious.

But what will the Church, that is, you and I, dare to say today to all those who are excluded, excommunicated, rejected by those leading a moral life with a clear conscience and condemned by the holy laws of traditional faith? Will we have the courage to tell all those present-day lepers: "We are the place where people know that they are not labelled, but recognized as human, forgiven and loved madly?"

It is dangerous to come into close contact with Jesus. It is contagious! It is perhaps better for you—and for all of us—to keep him at a distance, to exclude him, to keep him outside our towns and out of our lives. Let him die outside the walls, the God who is mad enough to love us, who are no more than the leprous shadow of our original beauty. Anyone coming into contact with him risks contagion! And if we are touched by his love, we risk being regarded as leprous by a world that protects itself from tenderness by calling it weakness. Yes, protect yourself from contact with Jesus. He is dangerous. He is contagious.

■

Everything we do is disfigured
 by our need to make a good impression.
If you want to, you can purify us.
 Have mercy on us, Lord!

Our good will towards others is eroded
 by our longing for prosperity and privilege.
If you want to, you can purify us.
 Have mercy on us, Lord!

Fatalism and our mistaken common sense
 make us dead people among the living.
If you want to, you can purify us.
 Have mercy on us, Lord!

In this section of the Gospel, the evangelist provides his second answer to the question: Who is Jesus Christ? He shows that Jesus' authority was contested. Jesus only had to be in Capernaum for a single day to upset very many people and to set almost everyone in the place against him. Five controversies took place in Capernaum and their arrangement in the Gospel makes an interesting study.

The first thing to notice is that the pretext for each of the conflicts between Jesus and his questioners becomes increasingly slight, whereas the opposition to Jesus becomes more intense. So, in the case of the controversy about the paralytic, he is criticized for having forgiven the sick man's sins. The last controversy, on the other hand, is concerned with conflicting interpretations of the meaning of the sabbath. What is particularly striking, however, is the attitude of the scribes in these two cases. At first, their opposition to Jesus is unobtrusive but, after he has healed the man in the synagogue on the sabbath, the Pharisees withdraw to plot his death.

A systematic analysis of the parallel elements in this section makes it possible for us to see how it is constructed. As in the section on the day in Capernaum, it is constructed within a clear framework (M.-E. Boismard). This construction has the aim of drawing attention to a central text which provides the key to our interpretation of the whole section. It is obvious, for example, that the passage about the paralytic (2:1-9) is parallel to that about the man with the withered hand (3:1-6). In both cases, Mark again uses the word pointing to resurrection: "wake up" or "rise." Both cures also form the framework for Jesus' twofold claim to the title "Son of man" as a means of affirming his authority and his privileges. He claims, as the Son of man, that he has power both to forgive sins (2:10-12) and to legislate with regard to the sabbath (2:27-28).

Two other passages give prominence to Jesus' disciples. In the first (2:13-17), the setting is a meal that Jesus eats in the company of sinners. The scribes react to this with indignation and they question his disciples. In the second text (2:23-26), it is an action performed by the disciples themselves that makes the Pharisees angry. In this case, they question Jesus.

This construction, then, focuses attention on the central text—the passage on fasting and the bridegroom (2:18-22). It is in this passage that we can find the hidden force behind the conflicts between Jesus and those opposing him. It is that Jesus' opponents simply reject the new reality of the kingdom. They cling so firmly to the letter of the law that they have forgotten man, the man for whom Jesus is fighting. In God's thinking, after all, the sabbath is made for man, not man for the sabbath. Jesus will go the whole way to defend man's rights—as far as the supreme sacrifice. And the Church will fast when her bridegroom is taken away from her.

REST

Hebrews 4:1–5,11. The author continues with his exhortation, telling his readers that they must persevere in faith in Christ and trust in him as the great and merciful high priest. He then recalls, in the form of a lesson, the example of Israel's ancestors. God behaved towards them as a very caring Father. He brought them out of Egypt and never left them throughout the whole of their long journey in the desert, even providing them with food. His loving care did not, however, prevent them from quarrelling with him at the waters of Meribah, when they were tormented by thirst.

Do present-day Christians listen any more attentively to the words of their Lord? To that word which leads to the meal prepared by God even before the creation of the world for those who are faithful to him?

Psalm 78, which is very long, seems to be directed against the priests of the temple at Shiloh, who favored the cult of the golden calf (1 Kgs 12). The psalmist has used the form of an indictment, but the divine discourse is replaced in this psalm by a sacred legend recalling the difficulties in Israel's relationship with Yahweh.

Mark 2:1–12. The call of the disciples and the first cures—Jesus' ministry begins under the most favorable auspices, but evil is watching for a chance to catch the new prophet out.

In this passage, Jesus heals a paralytic. Lying on his stretcher, he is very similar to a dead man. Jesus tells him: "Get up! Your sins are forgiven" and he gets up and walks. But Jesus' words have burst like a bomb among the people in the house, who believe that only God can forgive sins. In speaking in that way, Jesus has made himself guilty of the sin of blasphemy. The scribes complain among themselves.

Jesus goes on: "Which is easier: to say to the paralytic, 'Your sins are forgiven' or to say, 'Get up, pick up your stretcher and walk'?" In this way, he discloses the origin of his authority. He is more than a simple healer. He is the Son of man to whom God has given power over all the nations of the earth (Dan 7). At the same time, he also unmasks the weakness of the judgment of

---

the scribes, which is revealed in their complaints. By their attitude, they prevent God's word from acting as a force that sets man free.

■

God has promised that he will let us enter the place of his rest! Once again, the author of the Epistle to the Hebrews bears witness to the central element of faith: God is on man's side and his will is to make us happy.

Just consider this scene: a paralysed man on a stretcher carried by four men into Jesus' presence. The stretcher makes us think of a courtyard full of miracles, full of all those who are crippled because of the absence of love. Lying there and unable to rise are those who are without hope, who are imprisoned within their own loneliness, and whose hearts are dry and withered. The ancient world is not so remote from our modern world, aging, faded and at a dead end.

Jesus bends over the paralytic and tells him: "Get up!" What is happening? It is that the Son is not looking at the past. He is not in the grip of a world of misery. But he is also not clinging to his glory. He leaves it behind and plunges into the mess made by man. It is true, only God can forgive sins, but what is the price he has to pay for this? God has identified the one who is three times holy and who cannot abide evil or man's sin, thus man may be saved. God will let us enter his rest, but what is the price he has to pay for this? The Son will carry our burden and his yoke, he has told us, is easy and his burden is light.

God has given us his rest. But we have placed burdens that are impossible to carry on the shoulders of our fellow-men. We have preferred the casuistry of rules and laws to the task of loving sinners. We have opted for the security provided by good organization rather than risk being burnt by missionary fervor. We choose sophisticated medical treatment and turn away from such bold and simple words as "Get up!"

"I will give you rest!" Rest is, of course, peace. Not the peace that comes from a good conscience that is easily satisfied, but the peace that comes from forgiveness sought and recognized. Rest is also freedom, not the freedom of passivity or easy excuses, but the freedom of those who have discovered for themselves the dynamism of the kingdom. Rest is also trust—not the trust that makes us rely on our own strength, but the trust that has its origin in bold faith in God's power to act.

"Get up and walk!" That is the dynamism of the kingdom. And rest is a time of going forward, with God as our companion.

■

Your word expresses the severe demands made by your kingdom.
But it also expresses the power of your forgiveness.
Blessed are you, God,
*   for not taking back your word!*
Give us the strength
*   to try to understand how deeply*
*   our response to following your Son commits us.*

SATURDAY OF THE 1ST WEEK

GOING TOWARDS GOD

Hebrews 4:12-16. The author of the Epistle ends his exhortation by affirming that the word of God is essentially life itself. It penetrates to the deepest level of man's soul and uncovers his heart. If, however, we welcome it with faith, we will taste the rest that God has promised us.

We are not simply left to our own devices in this. We have with us a high priest whom we can trust. Jesus was put to the test again and again throughout his life and this experience has brought him very close to us, without putting him at a distance from God. The fact that he never sinned enabled him to share in God's glory and that exaltation gives him total authority.

The second half of *Psalm 19* is in the form of a confession of faith in God's law.

Mark 2:13-17. Once again Jesus goes to the shore of the lake where he has already chosen his first four disciples. This time, he calls on Levi to follow him. Levi is a publican, a profession that the Jews regarded as the prototype of a sinner. In Israel, experience had shown that tax-collectors took advantage of their position to make themselves rich.

But Jesus calls on a publican to follow him and invites sinners to eat with him. It is difficult to grasp how revolutionary this gesture was; so revolutionary, in fact, that the Pharisees believed that they had to protest to his disciples. Taking sinners into his intimate circle was also a blessing in the form of an action—he was telling them that God forgave and loved them. Finally, inviting a tax-collector to follow him was also a gesture that set Levi free. Levi who became Matthew was a sinner who became an apostle.

23

■

When we enter a Byzantine church, we western Christians are often disorientated by the strange architecture and the darkness with its thousands of points of light from flickering candles, the profusion of icons and the heavy smell of incense. If we pause for a moment and look around us, however, we soon become aware of the direction in which everything points—to a presence that unites the many parts, Christ enthroned in majesty in the apse.

The same applies to the Epistle to the Hebrews. We may have been disorientated by the words and images used in the author's sermon, but in today's text we are, on reflection, made aware that the whole is united within the framework of a single thought: the author's longing to see God. And to see God, we must go towards him.

Salvation is a movement, but we have made it static by identifying it with a great number of truths that have to be believed. But surely the Gospel always demands to be treated as something new! Salvation is a journey, but we have transformed it into many patterns of behavior that have to be respected. Salvation is an encounter with God, but we have made God an idol without a face and without a heart.

On the journey of salvation, we are not left to ourselves. Jesus himself said, after all: "I am the Way, the Truth and the Life." The way is open and, if we follow in the footsteps of the Beloved, we shall arrive at the end of it.

■

Call us together by the words of your Son.
Keep us outside ourselves, Lord,
*   and free us of our fears and anxieties.*
Give us back to the freedom of our dreams
*   and to the fascination of your light.*

May we be strengthened by your mercy
*   and saved by your grace.*

Then we shall once again be astonished
*   by what your Spirit can achieve in us.*
We shall be made new
*   and become your Son's disciples*
*   and sons of your tenderness.*

■

To whom should we turn, Lord Jesus?
   —You have the words of eternal life!
How could we go forward,
   if we were not following him?
How would we ever come into the Father's presence,
   if we had no share as sons in his inheritance
   —the table where you hand over your Body
   for our salvation?

Call us and we shall become your disciples.
Support us and we shall, in due course, receive
   the reward given to those who have believed in your Word.

MONDAY OF THE 2ND WEEK

HE IS OUR SALVATION

Hebrews 5:1-10. This famous text forms the end of the first part of the
Epistle. It evokes in a very impressive way the suffering and exaltation of
Christ. The comparison with Moses in chapter 3 has shown that Christians
have in Christ a great high priest who has a recognized standing with God.
Still wishing to emphasize the solidarity that exists between Christ and men,
the author here considers another aspect of the Jewish priesthood: the offering
of sacrifice.

The Jewish priest was chosen by God "to offer gifts and sacrifices for sins."
First and foremost, he made offerings for his own sins, because, as a man
among men, he was as much a sinner as others were. Jesus, also, did not
claim supreme glory for himself or a rank equal to that of God. On the
contrary, he simply fulfilled the will of his Father in deep humility. In
suffering, he learned what it was to be obedient. The face of man had been
disfigured by Adam's disobedience. Jesus restored man's dignity. Having been
made perfect, he became the savior of mankind and was proclaimed "high
priest in the order of Melchizedek."

Christ, the Epistle to the Hebrews, Melchizedek and Psalm 110. Not so long
ago, little banners used to greet the new priest "in the order of Melchizedek"!
It strikes us as strange that a ministry in the Church should be identified with

an Old Testament hero, but then, the figure of Melchizedek is itself particularly enigmatic.

The name "Melchizedek" appears only in Genesis 14 and it means "the legitimate king." He was the "king of Salem," a town that has been identified with Jerusalem, and a "priest of God Most High," that is, the highest god of a pagan pantheon. In Genesis 14, Abraham gives him the tithe of all his possessions and, in return for this, receives his blessing. This is clearly a very evocative passage, because it shows the patriarch himself being consecrated as a forerunner of David on the throne at Jerusalem.

Psalm 110 is regarded as a royal hymn. It is possible to distinguish two sources in it. Verses 1–3 speak of an oracle in favor of the king whom Yahweh had really "begotten in the womb of the dawn like the dew." Verses 4–7, on the other hand, contain a different oracle, addressed to a priest who is said to be "in the service of the legitimate king" (E. Lipinski). In our text in the Epistle to the Hebrews, then, the author uses both the prophetic figure of Melchizedek and the solemn promise made in Psalm 110 to attribute to Christ, who was not of levitical descent, the title of a "priest in the order of Melchizedek."

Mark 2:18–22. This is the third controversy with, on one side, the members of the Pharisaical party and the disciples of John the Baptist and, on the other, the bridegroom's disciples. The former impose a twice-weekly fast on themselves, whereas the law only insists on one fast day each year—the Day of Atonement. The latter are the groomsmen who are celebrating with the bridegroom at his wedding.

The young bridegroom is God himself. He found a young woman abandoned in the desert and, after clothing her and covering her with jewels, made her his bride. This is how the prophet Ezekiel describes Israel's origin (16:8–14). The young bridegroom—he is also God when he goes back into the desert of his youth to cover his unfaithful bride with kisses and rediscover the way to her heart (Hos 2:16–18). And the young bridegroom is also Jesus Christ, giving his life for the Church (Eph 5:25).

And when God falls in love with his people, then obviously it is a time for happiness and dancing. When Jesus comes, the old world breaks open to make way for spring and the festive season.

"But the time will come" when the bridegroom will be rejected and condemned to death and "then, on that day, they will fast," waiting until he returns.

When God falls in love with his people, then it is a time for happiness and dancing—not of mourning and fasting! It is the festive season—the time of suffering and tears will come. It is the festive season because the time of messianic salvation has been inaugurated. With Jesus, something quite new has happened, something that cannot be reconciled with the old order. His coming, his life, his preaching and everything that he did divided history into two parts: "he became for all who obey him the source of eternal salvation."

What is the origin of this division between the old order and the new era? It comes from the union in this one man from Nazareth of God's call and man's response to the offer of the covenant. For the first time in the history of the world, one man responded perfectly to God's plan. For the first time in history and for the whole of eternity, there was, in the man from Nazareth, perfect harmony between God's grace and man's freedom. For the first time and for eternity, the covenant was fulfilled in the obedience of sons.

Obedience—for us the word has echoes of authoritarianism and infantilism. In Jesus, however, it unites the most radical call to the most committed freedom. Jesus is the Savior because he is the Son from all eternity. In other words, he is the one whose entire happiness consists in doing his Father's will and whose life has its origin in God's eternal longing. Jesus is the Savior because in him is manifested that which unites the Father and the Son in the Trinity: adoption of each other. The great division that has taken place in our history with the coming of Jesus came about because what is manifested in him is an obedience that I would describe as "natural." In his human condition, he is still the only Son of God and he is that only Son because he was destined to become the word of God's tenderness manifested in the flesh. In Jesus, God and man ceased to be in competition with each other.

So the new order is this: God and man are no longer in competition with each other and the obedience of sons is made "natural." The spirit of the Son has been poured out into our hearts and Jesus has become "for all who obey him the source of eternal salvation."

And Jesus assured us that anyone who loved him would keep his commandments and that he and his Father would make their home in him.

SACRALIZATION

Hebrews 6:10–20. "Having been made perfect, Christ became for all who obey him the source of eternal salvation and was acclaimed by God with the title of high priest in the order of Melchizedek" (5:9–10). This solemn statement not only introduces various developments but, most important of all, leads directly to the author's central argument. This explains why he is so careful to hold the attention of his readers. "We have many things to say," he points out (5:11), "and they are difficult to explain." So we are warned!

He puts us on our guard by reminding us of God's promises that are guaranteed both by his word and by his oath and especially of his commitment to Abraham (Gen 22:17). That commitment can only serve to strengthen the faith of Christians, who have given up everything in order to rely entirely on God. They are like sailors in a storm who trust in the anchor that they have cast. This comparison may strike us as rather forced, because the anchor is not fixed in the seabed, but in heaven! C. Spicq has shown, however, that this image was a valid one for Jews, who believed that there was a great expanse of water above the vault of heaven which was the source of rain. The author's anchor is clearly Christ himself, who "before us," that is, as the "forerunner," and as the one who has "become a high priest of the order of Melchizedek," has already entered the Holy of Holies. This last verse of our text introduces one of the first of the developments referred to above: an explanation of 5:9–10.

Psalm 111 is not easy to classify. Despite its alphabetical structure, it is generally regarded as a hymn. It invites us to contemplate God's work and formulates principles of wisdom.

Mark 2:23–28. The fourth controversy is presented here. The disciples pick ears of corn as they are walking through the fields. What they were doing was quite compatible with the letter of the law, the sole aim of which was to protect private property (see Deut 23:26). It was the scribes who later forbade gleaning. We should also note that the disciples were conscious of being in Galilee, where they had grown up and where people were less fastidious than in Jerusalem.

Jesus defends his disciples by taking up a position that was often assumed by the rabbis themselves. He contrasts their demands with the behavior of David who, when he was hungry, did not hesitate to eat the loaves that were reserved for the levites. And is he not more than David? If David was able to take advantage of his dignity as king to break the law, surely the Messiah, his heir, is master of the law!

■

After having spoken "at various times in the past and in various different ways, . . . in our own time, the last days, God has spoken to us. . . ." This is how the Epistle to the Hebrews begins. If there is a break in the course of human history, there is also a logic that runs through it without a break. God cannot lie. What runs through the history of man is a promise that becomes a reality.

All our tentative seeking and all our activities, our adventures, our successes and our failures are marked with the same indelible seal. They are not simply our own work. They are the incarnation of God's covenant with man. Our history is a holy history. God fulfils his promise and Jesus is that fulfilment. His promise is not simply superimposed on the fabric of history. It is woven into it and inseparable from it. Divinity and humanity are interwoven in Jesus.

With this in mind, it is possible to understand why Jesus reacted so violently to the Pharisees' criticism that his disciples were breaking the law of the sabbath. He was opposed to the dichotomy between the sacred and the profane, the religious and the human. Man and the sabbath are not in competition with each other! There is not a special sacred time on the one hand and an ordinary time on the other. The fulfilment of what the author of Hebrews is speaking is a break in the order of things. From now on, the whole of time and all things and all beings are sacred. In other words, the whole history of man is a holy history, the place where God is manifested and where men are obedient to his covenant. God no longer keeps himself apart in special places. No longer is he available only at special times. He is closely involved in the daily lives of men and women. Life in common with God—and that is the meaning of the word religion—is now based on human structures that are physical and spiritual, individual and collective, historical and forward-looking. If we want to find God, we should look for him in the future of man.

■

God, your faithfulness is unfailing—
  may your name be blessed!

You work at the plan of your covenant
  until it is fulfilled
  and the last days are already here for us.

Make our everyday lives holy
  and let them be the first-fruits of eternal life.

ANOTHER RELIGION

Hebrews 7:1-3, 15b-17. We have already seen that, according to a very early tradition, the words of Psalm 110 can be applied to Christ: "You are a priest of the order of Melchizedek, and for ever." To justify his application of this title to Christ, the author of the Epistle to the Hebrews turns to the famous passage in Genesis 14, where Melchizedek is presented as the "man from nowhere," an enigmatic figure who appears briefly on the historical scene and then returns to the silence of God. This was a favorable situation for rabbinic exegesis, with its aptitude for turning gaps in the Bible to good account.

According to scripture, then, Melchizedek had neither a father nor a mother. His lack of genealogy is all the more astonishing when we recall how rigorous the law was with regard to genealogies and especially priestly genealogies. Nor is anything said in Genesis 14 about his birth or his death. He seems to share in God's eternity and the Epistle to the Hebrews says that he is "like the Son of God." For the author of the Epistle, the most characteristic aspects of the "new order" of priesthood seem in fact to be the absence of levitical descent and the perpetuity of that priesthood.

But Jesus was also not a priest and, according to the genealogy that opens the Gospel of Matthew, he was descended, through Joseph, from David and the tribe of Judah. So, when God, raising him from the dead, consecrated him a priest for ever, this was not "by virtue of a law about physical descent, but by the power of an indestructible life."

Psalm 110: See Monday of the 2nd week.

Mark 3:1-6. The scribes surprised Jesus' disciples in the act of picking ears of corn on the sabbath and criticized him for it. Jesus, then, is forewarned. A second offence against the law would place him in flagrant contradiction with the traditions of his people. In the meantime, he is closely watched.

Going back to the synagogue, Jesus finds a man whose hand is withered by paralysis. He invites him to stand up, but it is the sabbath. The theme of this controversy, the fifth, however minimal it may be, is at the level of life itself. "Is it against the law on the sabbath day to do good or to do evil; to save life or to kill?" For Jesus, the sabbath rest is only meaningful if it is in the service of man and, if it is indeed a divine institution, then it can only be in the service of human beings.

Jesus, then, heals a man on a sabbath day and at once the scribes join forces to find a way of killing him. So, precisely when the power of life sets man free, the forces of death are fiercely opposed to it and strive to silence it and reduce it to nothing.

■

Religion "binds together." That is what the word means. Religion is life together with God. It brings about an encounter between God and men, between heaven and earth, between eternity and life here and now. It goes beyond the contingencies and the particular forms that it assumes in different periods of history and the investigations and discussions of theologians. Its lasting and universal task is to bind man to God.

Religion binds together. In view of the fact that he enters into a relationship with the deity, man venerates, fears, invokes and longs for the God who, so it seems to him, controls his destiny just as he has created him and formed his being. His needs, his aspirations, his hopes and disappointments—everything takes him in the direction of God and religion tends to win God's favor.

But what a very ordinary religion we have made of our Christian faith! How tragic it is that we should have to ask ourselves whether it is "against the law on the sabbath day to do good or to do evil." Our faith is characterized by the fact that it overturns the established order. Man no longer ascends to the deity. On the contrary, God, a God who is a person, acts on his own initiative and enters into communion with man. It is God's coming to man that is so revolutionary an event.

The man who is paralyzed by his fears and failures cannot be set free by religion. But, with Christ, that old order of religion breaks down altogether because of the newness of the word that gives life: "Stretch out your hand!" Christ tells him and us: "Take hold of life now with both hands!"

The religion that is founded on our faith binds us to God because it is a joyous proclamation, a revealed word and good news. Jesus is the great high priest of that religion not because he is the intermediary between men and God, but because he is the only Son. He is the way we have to follow because he is the first-born of this new world. In him, we see the covenant fulfilled in a perfect obedience that is the most radical development of man's freedom. In the new Christian order, we are no longer in the sphere of mediations, attempting to take us to the divine level, nor are we in the sphere of sacralization, separating us at our human level from the divine world. No, we are at the heart of a revolutionary event. God speaks to us. His word is a word of freedom taking us into the kingdom of peace.

■

You are the priest of a new covenant.
Tear us away from the narrowness of our existence
  and have mercy on us.

You are the priest of a new covenant.
Break the chains of our pettiness
  and have mercy on us.

You are the priest of a new covenant.
Be the door that opens on the peace of the kingdom
  and have mercy on us.

READING AND UNDERSTANDING MARK (3:7-35)

Mark's first way of replying to the question: Who is Jesus Christ? is to list a series of acts of power performed by Jesus at Capernaum during the course of a typical day. The second stage in his reply takes the form of a series of words and actions within the framework of five controversies. We come now to the third stage, which can be summarized in the words of Jesus himself: "Anyone who does the will of God, that person is my brother and sister and mother."

This third stage can itself be divided into three consecutive steps, each of which is concerned with defining the frontier between Jesus' true disciples and those whom Mark calls those "outside." It is certainly not in any way fortuitous that the first passage, which follows a summary of Jesus' activity (3:7-12), is principally concerned with naming the Twelve (3:13-19). Jesus chooses his disciples on the basis of a single criterion: doing the will of God.

In the first of the three steps, a very sharp contrast is made between the community of the disciples and Jesus' blood-relations, which makes it quite clear that ties of blood cannot be the source of special privilege. Indeed, the evangelist himself makes Jesus' kinsfolk appear as the symbol of opposition to Jesus (3:20-21 and 31-32). For them, Jesus is no more than a man possessed. In fact, however, whether he is a man of the Spirit or the instrument of Beelzebul, no one can doubt that he is driven by a power. There is, however, real disagreement about the origin of that power (3:20-30).

■

You have said, Lord,
  that the one who looks back
  is not made to be your disciple.

32

Make us live for the present and future,
enthusiastic for new times.

Let us work with you, building your Church,
full of laughter and sunlight
and a source of peace and wonderment.

THURSDAY OF THE 2ND WEEK

THE "IDEAL HIGH PRIEST"

Hebrews 7:25–8:6. Looking forward to a priesthood that was not dependent on the temple, Psalm 110 pointed to the provisional nature of the levitical priesthood. It is true that the consecration of Jewish priests did not radically transform them. They continued to be sinful men and, because of this, were not able to act fully as mediators between God and men.

The consecration of Jesus Christ as high priest was, however, quite different, because he offered his own person as a sacrifice in order to pass through the glorification and transformation of his own being and thus reach the perpetual high-priesthood. When he was established as the Son of God, the prophetic figure of Melchizedek was completed and the promise expressed in the Psalm was fulfilled.

The author shows in chapters 8 and 9 of his Epistle how Jesus Christ arrived at his present position of mediator. He also tries to bring out the contrasts between the earlier form of cult and the "liturgy" of Christ. His first important affirmation is to stress the imperfection of the Jewish sanctuary as no more than a pale reflection of God's dwelling and the defectiveness of the cult that took place there. There was, he insists, a need for radical change.

Psalm 40, which has clearly undergone certain changes, contains both a psalm of thanksgiving (verses 1–11) and a lamentation (verses 12–17). It is also obvious that the liturgy has retained one important fact—that Yahweh has inspired the one who believes in him to come in person to the temple and express his gratitude. In the same way, Jesus later paid with his own person the cost of ensuring the salvation of mankind.

Mark 3:7–12. This passage brings us back to the lakeside which is exactly the same place where Jesus has already encouraged and called four fishers of

---

men. This time, there is a great crowd. People have come from every area inhabited by Jews. It is worth noting that the evangelist has mentioned seven. That is equivalent to saying that the whole of humanity was gathered around Jesus.

There is also a boat ready to take the Master and his disciples away. Gradually the distance between them and the crowd increases. The people are always quick to become infatuated with Jesus, but they are very slow to perceive the deep significance of his person. Already he is alone with his disciples.

■

Jesus is the "ideal high priest." The author of the Epistle to the Hebrews calls him this because he has carried out his ministry in the true sanctuary. He is the ideal high priest because his ministry went as far as the sacrifice of the cross. The cross is the moment, the act which makes manifest in the most explicit way that Jesus was seeking to do and what he chose to do throughout the whole of his life. It is the cross that reveals his true face to us, the face that was fashioned in its details by the choices and decisions that he made throughout his life.

Jesus crucified, then, is the ideal high priest. When I look at Jesus on the cross, I see a man with his feet nailed, so that he cannot move a step to come close to the people whom he was always approaching throughout the whole of his life. Looking at the cross, I see a man with his hands nailed, so that he cannot stretch them out to those to whom he offered them again and again in his life as a sign of his tenderness and in order to heal their illnesses, overcome their fears and give them peace. I see a man whose eyes are closed under the sway of suffering, so that he can no longer look with kindness, as he had always done during his life, at the faces around him.

Jesus crucified, then, is the ideal high priest, the man with his hands and feet nailed and his lips and eyes closed, the dying man who said: "I am the Way, the Truth and the Life." He said: "I am the Way"—a path leading towards the future, a road offered to us, one that we can follow. He said: "I am the Life"—life given to us in abundance, a life of resurrection. He said: "I am the Truth." That is a word full of meaning, revealing the meaning of our existence! He said: "I am the Light"—light transforming everyday things by giving them their true illumination. He said these things and I believe him.

Confronted with this man, Jesus crucified, seeing only a way that seems to lead nowhere and a life apparently broken by suffering and conscious only of hesitant words and love obscured, I believe that here life springs eternally.

Jesus is the ideal high priest. In him, I know that an indissoluble union has been established between the poverty of our love and the richness of God's love for us, between our death and life itself. I know that there is an indissoluble union between the men that we are and God himself.

Jesus is the ideal high priest who meets our needs because, by his life and his death, he has consecrated our life and our death. Since Jesus, they are both filled with the living seed of God's promise.

■

High priest of the new covenant,
Jesus, the only Son and first-born among the dead,
*   we revere in you the fulfilment of man.*

By your life and by your death,
*   we know that the meaning of life is life itself.*

Recognizing, in our lives as men and women,
*   the mysterious fulfilment of your passion,*
we ask you:
*   Let us cross to the other side—*
*   to the new world*
*   that you have opened for us*
*   by your obedience.*

FRIDAY OF THE 2ND WEEK

THE INITIATOR
Hebrews 8:6–13. The author has just shown how incomplete the sacrificial cult of Israel was. That cult was the cult of the old covenant and we may conclude from this that the first covenant itself was also incomplete, assuming that the covenant and the cult to which it gave birth were of the same nature. For the author, the fact that the first covenant was made null and void is proved by the need to replace it. In support of this argument, he quotes a long passage from the prophet Jeremiah (31:31–34). The old covenant had been engraved on the stone of Sinai but, although God intended it to lead to man's

conversion, it ended in failure, because it resulted in a purely external and legalistic obedience.

Jesus was the mediator of the second covenant which, from the very beginning, was entirely interior. This is because, in Jesus, God's will coincided with man's longings. Consequently, his commandments were no longer inscribed on stone. They were written in the heart of the man who, according to Psalm 40 said, when he came into the world: "Here I am! I am coming . . . to obey your will." Jesus, then, inscribed the image of God into his flesh.

The whole nation of Israel implores God in *Psalm 85*. In the second part, the people are expecting a favorable oracle in response to their public lamentation. This psalm is used in the Christian liturgy during Advent to express the Church's hope.

Mark 3:13–19. Jesus' historical activity forms the point of departure for the life of the primitive Christian communities. Mark draws attention to the parallel that exists between the history of the founder of the Church and the birth of that Church by recalling the beginnings of Jesus' ministry in Galilee. His intention is clearly reflected in the emphasis that he places on the appointment of the Twelve.

Jesus has already initiated a movement towards his own person, but now he has to go a step further. On the one hand, it is necessary to respond to the increasing needs of the people and he does this by calling fellow-workers who will share his authority as Master and his responsibility as a preacher. On the other hand, it is also necessary to set over and against the crowds who follow him a community that is less anxious to make a spectacular impression and that is more conscious of the inner life. Remembering the twelve tribes of Israel, Jesus therefore appoints twelve disciples.

The list of these disciples bears witness to the Church's concern to authenticate its foundation. Jesus acts here as Yahweh acted in the case of the patriarchs Abraham and Jacob, by giving Simon a new name. From the time of his appointment onwards, this disciple is to be known as "Peter," in other words, the "rock." The twelfth disciple is Judas. He is to betray Jesus. This is suggested by his surname Iscariot, which may mean "the one who hands him over."

■

Our vocation has become a reality! Our task has been accomplished! "I will put my laws into your minds!" "Your will be done!" The covenant that God wanted to establish has become incarnate in the only Son. Our ministry has been accomplished, because Jesus is the mediator of the new covenant.

Our vocation has become a reality. And yet peace is still not triumphant, justice does not yet rule on earth, doubt still troubles our minds and sin is still present in every sector of our lives. Where, then, is the new order mediated by Jesus Christ? How can we say with confidence that, thanks to him, our world has embraced life and gone over to God's side?

We can say this, not because our faith is a dream or an illusion, but because it is like our heart listening to the friend's footsteps, even though their rhythm can only wake the one who is asleep. We can say this because our faith is like our heart listening to music, although our ears are only aware of silence. Faith is like our heart opening long before the warmth of the summer sun, even though our body only feels the biting cold of winter. Jesus is not only the mediator, but also the initiator of a new order, the full measure of which only our heart can grasp.

Jesus is the initiator of our lives. He awakens our lives in order to make them conform to God's order. He awakens them like music that takes us up in its rhythm, like heat that overcomes us and like a presence that reveals itself to us. This happens spontaneously when our spirit is in tune and our heart resonates with the right emotions.

Our vocation has become a reality because our lives have become caught up in the impulse of the one who has gone ahead of us on the way towards God's world. Jesus is that one taking us in the direction of the new world. "I am the gate," he said. He is the gate leading to eternity.

■

Your Son, God our Father,
  is the way that leads to a new world
  and the fullness of life.

We ask you, Lord,
  to let us follow him to where he is taking us.
Put your Spirit in us
  so that we may enter into your covenant for ever.

SATURDAY OF THE 2ND WEEK

SACRIFICED FOR OUR EASTER
Hebrews 9:2-3, 11-14. The author of the Epistle to the Hebrews is above all critical of the value of the mediation of the ancient cult. He was convinced that the temple could not lead men to God and that, on the contrary, it led

into a dead end. The sacrificial liturgy of the old covenant did not call for personal commitment on the part of the officiating priest, with the result that the cultic act proved to be ineffectual in transforming the lives of those who offered the sacrifice.

Christ, however, has gained access to God by "passing through the greater, the more perfect tent, . . . taking with him . . . his own blood." His sacrifice of his own person is essentially different from the sacrifices made by the Jews. Whereas theirs was an external and ritual cult, his was a total and profound offering and, whereas their cult was separate from life itself, his offering was made real in the dramatic events of his passion. "Destroy this temple and in three days I will raise it up." The new tent through which Christ passed to have access to God was the temple of his own body, radically transformed by his own personal commitment. The cult of the old order was external. In the new order we "worship in spirit and truth."

Psalm 47 calls on us to praise Yahweh, the king of Israel and the whole world. Here it accompanies the return to the glory of the Father of Christ, whose greatness has been inscribed for ever on the cross.

Mark 3:20–21. These two verses set the scene. On the one hand, we see Jesus and his own and, on the other, there is the crowd. Among the crowd are his opponents and his family. His relatives do not understand the prestige enjoyed by the Master. Like the scribes, they judge him with ill-will.

■

"Christ offered himself as the perfect sacrifice to God." It is not difficult to understand how important it was for a Christian who had come from Judaism to make use of Jewish cultic images to define the irreplaceable position occupied by Christ in the lives of men. But the fact remains that the word "sacrifice" has become for us an obstacle rather than a way through which we can gain access to the meaning of the mystery.

The profane use of the word is not without significance. It hardly arouses enthusiasm! If prices are reduced in a store and the manager "sacrifices" his goods, we all know that it is not his best wares that he is selling off. And many of the religious practices of the previous century led to so many distortions of Christian feelings and attitudes that the word sacrifice is viewed with suspicion today.

Should we, then, abandon the word and risk losing an essential dimension of our faith? It is surely preferable to try to find out what sacrifice really means.

The everyday use of the word is a great help here. "I have given up salt. I had to choose, but I made the sacrifice for the sake of my health." To give another example: "I had to choose between promotion to a position that would have kept me away from home and my family for even longer periods. I decided in favor of the happiness of the family. It was not such a great sacrifice after all."

These two examples are a long way from the traumatic meaning of sacrifice. In both, the word is almost synonymous with choice or life. Growing, spreading, gaining new freedom. . . . When it is born, a baby has to sacrifice the well-being of its mother's womb for a life of its own. Later, the child has to sacrifice immediate satisfaction of its needs if it is to reach adult life. Sacrifice is not for its own sake; it is for life itself.

"Christ offered himself as the perfect sacrifice." The cross is not the ransom paid to obliterate God's anger, nor is it a tribute paid to pacify a vindictive or jealous God whose good fortune has been scorned. No, Jesus' supreme sacrifice or renunciation is a source of life and the cross is the ultimate and decisive act of freedom offered totally. As a total dispossession of self, the cross opens the way to a life received in superabundance, a life that cannot be measured. The other face of Good Friday is Easter. "Christ offered himself . . . and his blood will purify our inner self from dead actions." His sacrifice, which opens out into lordship, saves us from death. He is the Way, the Truth and the Life.

■

God our Father,
  your Son consecrated himself
  to bear witness to your loving kindness.

Consecrate us by your Spirit
  and his Easter will flow
  as a source of eternal life.

■

The cup is passed from hand to hand
  and everything is fulfilled in an act
  that is the sacrament of life handed over.

Father of Jesus, our Father,
  because we have had communion
  with the sacrament of the new covenant,
let us enter the sanctuary
  in order to sing of your glory eternally.

CHOOSING

Hebrews 9:15, 24–28. Jeremiah, in chapter 31 had prophesied that there would be a new covenant, not engraved on stone, but written in the hearts of men. This covenant of the heart presupposed a man totally purified from sin and totally dedicated to the love of God. It presupposed man's death to himself so that his whole being might be totally renewed.

This demand was fulfilled in the sacrifice of Calvary. The death of Christ, rooted in his voluntary offering of himself, established him in a new relationship with God. His offering, which was personal and perfect, enabled him to enter the new tent and be with God. At the same time, it took away men's sins.

Psalm 98 is hymnic. Here in today's liturgy, it is used to sing of the glory of the dead and risen Christ.

Mark 3:22–30. Jesus' family are ill-disposed towards him and now it is the scribes' turn! They come from Jerusalem and accuse him of driving out demons with the help of, yes, the demons' prince. In other words, they are claiming that Jesus' healings are the result of magic practices. This is certainly not a harmless accusation! If it is proved true, Jesus can receive the death penalty.

Jesus "called the scribes to him and spoke to them in parables." These words are not simply a statement about Jesus' vivid manner of expressing himself in imagery. What is involved here is in fact the kingdom, and Jesus often makes use of the language of parables when he discusses this theme, because the kingdom can only be known by the heart. Parabolic language discloses and conceals at the same time, and only reveals the mystery of the kingdom to those whose hearts are open to it. It hides the kingdom from those who reject it.

Jesus' opponents refuse to admit that the kingdom is made manifest in his person. They do not regard his healings as a sign that the reign of Satan has ended. They see them only as demoniac practices. Their sin is unforgivable because they have placed themselves outside the kingdom.

Has it ever been known for a kingdom to survive internal divisions? If it is true that Jesus cured with the help of demons, that would mean that their power would be self-destructive. But Jesus has no need of such help. He drives out Satan, the powerful man, because he is, according to John the Baptist (1:7), "more powerful."

40

■

There is an obstruction in the lives of some people because they have refused to do something or have rejected something—an attitude, a career, a call—that would have given them peace. But it would have called for a sacrifice and they have not agreed to that. They continue to carry, perhaps for the rest of their lives, which may even seem to be externally successful, the weight of that denial which resulted in a betrayal of their true destiny.

Everyone's life is marked by a number of critical moments when, confronted with a necessary renunciation or with the need to consent to or to reject, his future is secured or undone. Nietzsche observed that "whatever we may do, sacrifice is always necessary." Life always compels us to make decisions. We cannot want everything, do everything and embrace everything. We have to choose and we are judged by that selection, because it reveals what we prefer and what we relinquish as less important. Sacrificing is never gratuitous. It is the other side of choosing. And ultimately we choose to be more or to be better. Countless sacrifices are woven into the fabric of our lives, but they are really only the scars left by the choices on which those lives are founded.

"Jesus brings a new covenant, as the mediator. . . . His death took place to cancel sins." We are justified by the cross not because it is a sacrifice washing away our sin in blood, but because it is the fulfilment of a life marked by the sign of a gift.

We are saved by the way and the life of the one who continued until the end to be the Son. The cross is the ultimate and decisive manifestation of the choices made by that only Son. Jesus decided in favor of a certain life-style and it was that choice that cost him his life.

Christ is the great high priest of the new covenant who "does not have to sacrifice himself again and again," because he consecrated his life once and for all time to the Word of the Father. The cross is the last signature that he places on a plan that had already been signed a long time previously. It is not an accident encountered on his way, but the voluntary and resolute manifestation of a deliberate choice. That decision was to be the witness to God's eternal mercy. The cross fills the whole of Jesus' life. When he was in Galilee, he was already following the way to Golgotha. The accusation made by the scribes: "It is through Beelzebul, the prince of the devils, that he casts devils out" corresponds to Caiaphas' accusation: "He is a blasphemer."

■

God our Father,
put your Spirit into us
and let the Word of your Son be the choice of our life.

In that way we shall do your will
  today and for ever.

TUESDAY OF THE 3RD WEEK

"GOD, HERE I AM! I AM COMING TO OBEY YOUR WILL"

Hebrews 10:1–10. The last part of the central exposition in the Epistle begins here, in chapter 10. The author has already shown that Christ's priesthood is superior to the levitical priesthood and has emphasized Jesus' personal offering of himself. In this passage, he concludes from this that, because Christ's single sacrifice was total, it alone is effective and able to lead to eternal salvation.

The old law was incapable of saving man. It called sin to mind, but did not abolish it. The prophets of the old covenant had already shown how useless external sacrifices were for man. The author of the Epistle speaks at an even more radical level, declaring that only a personal offering can find its way to God's heart. Jesus' sacrifice of himself was of this kind and the author cites a text from Psalm 40, which he sees as summarizing the life and work of Jesus: "God, here I am! I am coming to obey your will."

Psalm 40 applies to Jesus the cry of the believer whom God has inspired, not to offer a sacrifice, but to express his gratitude personally.

Mark 3:31–35. Here is the clan again! "They are asking for you," Jesus is told. They remind one of those groups that are always trying to possess God for their own profit. "They are asking for you"—but they have in fact gone to all that trouble for nothing. "Who are my mother and my brothers?" His reply seems to be straightforward, but an obvious interpretation does not take into account the kingdom, which overturns all realities. "Here are my mother and my brothers!" Jesus says, and the evangelist adds: "looking round at those sitting in a circle about him," in other words, at the crowd listening to him. In the kingdom, then, Christian fellowship is not based on family bonds, but on a shared spirit, that of doing the Father's will.

■

According to the psalmist, Christ said, when he came into the world, "God, here I am! I am coming to obey your will." What Jesus has taught us is that we cannot give anything to God to recognize that he is God unless it is ourselves. Jesus has told us that life can only be orientated towards and given to God. What we offer to God is not a destroyed and "sacrificed" personality, but a personality built up of many onerous choices.

"Here I am! I am coming to obey your will." The sacrifice that God can accept is: "I lay down my life. . . . No one takes it from me; I lay it down of my own free will." Similarly, when the Christian reveals himself among his fellow-men in order to grow and become more fully himself, he is offering himself to God.

"Anyone who does the will of God, that person is my brother and sister and mother." Those who bear Christ's name are those who experience in their hearts Jesus' reason for living. "By the love that you have for one another, everyone will know that you are my disciples." It is not simply a question of becoming followers of an excellent man or of accepting as our own a very exalted way of life. It is rather a question of becoming "Jesus' people." The disciples did not really become such people until the day of Pentecost, when they received the fullness of the Spirit of the Son. "Here I am! I am coming to obey your will": That is the Christian's way of life. Even more than that, it is also the prayer of the Spirit given on the day of our baptism.

■

Here we are, God our Father!
We are coming to obey your will!
Accept our desire
    and, through your Spirit, support our prayer.

May the promise made at our baptism
    become a daily reality—
    that we may belong, day after day,
    to your family
    until the end of time.

■

Father of Jesus and our Father,
    you make us his intimate friends.

43

Let us, through your Spirit,
do your will and imitate Christ,
who was obedient until his death on the cross.

■

Thanks to you, God our Father,
we have been admitted to the family meal.
Through your mercy,
your Son has handed over his body for our salvation.

May this Eucharist,
in which we have taken part in his Easter victory,
mean that we shall be included
among his people for ever.

READING AND UNDERSTANDING MARK (4:1-34)

The scribes have accused Jesus of having acted with the power of Beelzebul. This points clearly to the division among those who surround him. On the one hand, there are his disciples and, on the other, "those who are outside." Now, in this chapter, the author describes the "day of the parables," in which he emphasizes the vital importance of the Word. This sequence of parables acts as a warning: the kingdom breaks into human history and questions men's consciences without doing violence to them. The fate of each individual depends on his or her response to this. Jesus' opening word: "Listen!" also serves as the keynote for the whole series.

The first parable that Jesus tells the crowd is that of the sower. This provides a magnificent illustration of the relationship existing between the growth of the seed and the quality of the soil on which it has fallen. The disciples reveal themselves to be good soil because they are obviously interested in what Jesus is saying and question him about it. His reply to them is also quite clear: "The secret of the kingdom of God is given to you, but to those who are outside everything comes in parables" (4:1-12).

Leaving for a moment the explanation of the parable of the sower, let us now turn to verses 21-25. The image of the lamp illustrates the responsibility of those to whom revelation has been given. They in turn have make the kingdom manifest. They will, however, only have sufficient "measure" to do this if they have listened to the word. But will their listening be equal to this task? Is it not true that the soil is more often bad rather than good? We can only think exclusively of the quality of the soil if we fail to be aware of resources of the kingdom. The sower has a completely different attitude. He is not ruffled, because he is conscious of the quality of the seed that he has sown. What is more, even if the seed is as small as the mustard seed, it can still grow into a great tree (4:26-34).

Here too a central text can be seen to emerge from a comparison of the various structural elements. What is most clearly revealed in the explanation of the parable of the sower (4:12-20) is that the different soils symbolize the different ways of listening to the word. In addition to this, however, this explanation also draws attention to the fact that the parable of the sower conceals within itself another parable. This second, true parable, from which the explanation of all the others can be derived, is Jesus himself. We can therefore say that any attempt to understand the others will fail if this parable has not been understood.

WEDNESDAY OF THE 3RD WEEK

THE FIRST-BORN

Hebrews 10:11-18. The history of the people of Israel certainly points to man's reluctance to be converted. But at the same time, it also reveals God's great patience. God has never ceased to write his laws in our hearts. And indeed, he has been successful in that task! It is true that Adam's sin resulted in man's disintegration, but it is equally true that his unity has been restored by Jesus' obedience. Jesus' personal immolation was sustained exclusively by his longing to do his Father's will and, because of this one sacrifice, man can once again be truly man.

It was in his flesh that Christ experienced the event of Calvary and it was his humanity that was radically transformed by the resurrection. Neither his obedience nor his exaltation separated him then or separates him now from his fellow-men. His salvation reaches man in the depth of his being and in his totality. Unlike the consecration of a Jewish priest, which separated him from other men, Christ's glorification concerns the whole of humanity.

Psalm 110: See Monday of the second week.

Mark 4:1-20. A sower and seed and soil of different quality. . . . The theme of the divine seed was very familiar to those who heard Jesus. The prophet Zechariah, for example, said that where he is, there would be sowing and

---

45

growing. The word of God, the seed, does not come back without achieving a result. On the contrary, it has extraordinary vitality and, if it falls on good soil, it can yield a hundredfold. But not every soil is good; there are also bad soils.

Just as the roots growing from the seed go deeply into the soil on which it has been sown, so too does the word of God search men's hearts. But it only reaches those who really want to listen to it. The hearts of Jesus' disciples are revealed as pure and, even though the Spirit may find that they, like the hearts of all men, contain obstacles, that does not mean that they listen less attentively. On the contrary, those who are outside offer a stubborn resistance to the action of the Spirit. God, however, respects human freedom and does not try to force the door of men's hearts open. So, because the deafness of some people cannot be overcome, the message contained in Jesus' parables, however accessible it may be to men of good will, is transformed for them into an insoluble enigma. Did not Jesus' relatives treat him as mad when he was teaching at Capernaum?

A sower and seed and soil of different quality. . . . Taking its point of departure from life itself, each individual parable leads us to a more intimate knowledge of God. But the great parable of history is surely Jesus himself, the man "who went about doing good and curing all who had fallen into the power of the devil" (Acts 10:38). And the one who listens to him can therefore understand all his parables.

∎

"By virtue of his single sacrifice, Jesus has achieved the eternal perfection of all whom he is sanctifying." The great mission of the high priest of the new covenant is to give us access to the sanctuary. In other words, he enables us to enter an order that is different from the one here on earth. We have access to holiness.

Christ is not simply a model to imitate. He is also the obedient man who is, for his brothers, the type of their life. He is the first-born of a world which he enables us to enter following him. His appearance in the world and the fulfilment in him of the Easter mystery have really introduced something new into the human condition.

This new element cannot be defined simply by the appearance of grace, as though that had not existed before Christ's coming. It can, however, be defined by the word "glory," since this is the new quality of specifically Christian grace.

By dying on the cross and in this way taking to the very end his life as a man that was totally open to receive the power of God, Jesus received, in his resurrection, the power to communicate what he had—

paradoxically—abandoned: the glory that had been his from eternity with the Father. From then on, Jesus has been communicating not simply his grace, but also his glory. In the risen Christ we have become "capable" of receiving God. We no longer belong simply to this earth. We are made citizens of heaven. We are no longer just those who have been saved, redeemed and forgiven, those on whom grace has been bestowed. We are saints, sons, those who have been born again and glorified. Humanity can no longer be satisfied with being simply human. We are divine.

The grace that has been done to us transcends all our hopes. The seed thrown on the ground has borne fruit that goes far beyond all our expectations. It has yielded a hundredfold. The mission of the high priest Jesus Christ is not simply functional. In other words, it is not purely to restore us to full communion with God or to reconcile us. No, his mission is more than this. It is ontological. In other words, with Christ we enter a new order of existence. He is the one who has come to teach us how we can enter into Glory.

■

In raising your Son from the dead,
*   you consecrated him, God our Father,*
*   and appointed him Lord of all the living.*

We give you thanks for the glory
*   that you have given him.*
We bless you too for your mercy.
In your Beloved,
*   the first-born of the new world,*
*   we know already, even now, the glory*
*   that will be our inheritance in eternity.*

FROM THURSDAY OF THE 3RD WEEK

TO SATURDAY OF THE 4TH WEEK

Deciding to Believe

Confronted with the "fact" of Jesus, it is quite possible for man to refuse the ultimate meaning of that event. That is precisely the drama that is presented by the evangelist Mark.

We may regard the New Testament as an interesting and even edifying document that is well-worth reading. We may think that the man of Nazareth is likable, fascinating and moving. And even though we may believe that he is the true Son of God, we may still not include him in our way of life, our plans or our relationships. Even when we are confronted with the good news, we only come to faith when its message becomes the reason for living.

For the next ten days, the readings from the Epistle to the Hebrews encourage us to make that journey. If Christ is the only mediator, it is because we have access to the Father in and through him and because we become ourselves a "living sacrifice" and are consecrated in and through him. If we say "no" to faith, it is not because we doubt the saving facts to which the New Testament bears witness. It is because we do not want to respond to the demand that God expresses in Jesus, the norm of our life.

■

God our Father,
let us express the longing
that urges us towards you
and let us sing in praise
of the power of your Word.

It penetrates our silence
and we can give you, Father,
the response your Son inspires in us.
Blessed is the man
who is at one with the good news.
Blessed is the man
who is immersed in the grace of your revelation!

God, you have told us your name—
strengthen the faith of your Church
and let her proclaim the Gospel now
and make incarnate today
the grace of your presence among us.

THURSDAY OF THE 3RD WEEK

WITH CONFIDENCE
Hebrews 10:19–25. "We have confidence." Under the old covenant, the temple priests had to make the sacrificial offering an indefinite number of

times. The separated Qumran brethren sought a purity that they could never obtain in the ritual baths. Christians, however, simply "have confidence to enter the sanctuary"! Their victorious optimism is based on Christ's gift—a gift that does not have to be returned.

Entry into the kingdom is no longer dependent on human effort. It depends on faith. We are saved as long as we believe in the mediation of Christ. The doors of the heavenly sanctuary are opened by his blood to those of us who approach "with our bodies washed by pure water." Received in faith, the sacraments of Christian initiation make Jesus' personal offering present here and now.

Psalm 24 forms part of a liturgy for entry into the holy place. The conditions required for entry are detailed by the ministering priest.

Mark 4:21-25. "The secret of the kingdom of God is given to you." God's word is given, however, not to be locked away in a safe, but to be proclaimed and to resound throughout the world. That is the responsibility of the disciple, who must not act like the scribes who, after they had been given the "key of knowledge" (Luke 11:52), "prevented others going in who wanted to." If the disciples were to do that, they would receive the punishment promised to the bad shepherd by the prophet Ezekiel.

But only those who have listened attentively will be able to proclaim the good news. "Take notice of what you are hearing!" Jesus says again and again. Your understanding of the mystery of God depends on your ability to listen!

∎

Because Jesus has given us access to the world of God, we have confidence to approach him filled with faith. In and through Jesus, we have the power to encounter God. And the God of Jesus is not an idea of pure but empty austerity, or an idol with an illusory prestige, but a presence that is disarming because it is without weapons, the presence of love: a child born at Christmas, a man washing his friends' feet before the passion. Not power, organizing ability, abstract certainty, violence or repression, but the weakness of the Creator, disturbed in the depths of his being when confronted with the man he has created. Only Jesus, and Jesus crucified, his holy face raised up in the heart of the world, has made it possible for us to suspect that God's face is unique and like no other face.

We have confidence to approach God filled with faith. We do not have to satisfy any precondition before encountering God. We do not have to pass any test. We have only to welcome a face, because he alone is the perfect reflection of the glory of the Father. We have only to

---

49

contemplate a mystery, because the Son knows the way that leads to the Father. We have only to receive a life, because Jesus alone is the mediator of the new covenant. We have only to hear a word, because he alone is the eternal Word.

The face that we welcome is the face of the crucified Christ. The mystery that we contemplate is the mystery of a man bending over us in our weakness. The life that we receive is given to us in a body handed over, bread broken. The word that we hear is a question addressed to us: "Do you want me?" It is not courage, a critical spirit or culture that enables us to approach God. With Jesus' eyes, he is in search of us. And, because he has followed the way that separates us from him, we have confidence to approach him.

■

Lord Jesus, you are the reflection of God's glory.
  Have mercy on us!
  Reveal your face to us!

You are the royal highway leading to the Father.
  Become our way!
  Have mercy on us!

You are the eternal Word expressing God's tenderness.
  Be our prayer!
  Have mercy on us!

■

A little bread helps us on our way.
A word of grace strengthens our hope.
  God our Father, may your goodness be praised!

Lead us to where we shall meet you!
Take us to the dwelling-place
  that your Son has prepared for us
  for endless ages.

FRIDAY OF THE 3RD WEEK

ALL THE SAME
Hebrews 10:32–39. "Let us keep firm in the hope we profess, because the one who made the promise is faithful" (10:23). For the first time, the author says a

few words about the situation of those for whom the Epistle is intended. They are being harassed and even persecuted and their initial impetus has slowed down. So they are invited to hold on. If they persevere as Christ persevered in his final testing time, they will be seen as "the sort who keep faithful until their souls are saved."

The structure of *Psalm 37* is alphabetical. It is a little anthology of different texts, contrasting the situation of the righteous with that of the wicked man. The verses chosen here invite us to trust in God, the protector of those who "take shelter in him."

Mark 4:26–34. Two parables, but only one lesson. In the first, the peasant's work when he is sowing seed and harvesting the crop is contrasted with his inactivity while the seed is growing. This parable calls to mind the confusion of Jesus' compatriots, to whom he proclaimed the imminence of the kingdom of God without revealing the judgment that they expected would precede it. Jesus invites his listeners not to doubt that his ministry is important. It is the time to be converted and that hour is the last one offered to men.

The apparent shortage of time in the present does not, however, put the flourishing of the kingdom in the future in any way at a disadvantage. However lacking in brilliance Jesus' ministry or the Church's beginnings may be, God's word has an irresistible power which "does not return without watering the earth, making it yield and give growth" (Is 55:10). What God decides one day, he always realizes.

■

"Remember the earlier days when you had just received the light of Christ." There is always a great risk that faith will be weakened with the passage of time and when it is put to the test by adversity, contradictions and mediocrity. The author of the Epistle to the Hebrews therefore invites us to go back to the point of departure of our faith.

"Remember: you believe!" When I think about believing, I prefer to think about the act of faith rather than about faith itself, because that seems to me to be an abstract term, whereas believing is an active verb which at the same time includes the act of thinking, living and acting on the part of the person at grips with its mystery. So, whenever I think about that act of faith, I always come back to this: believing is living and acting and entering into the life and activity that the word of God is suggesting to me in order to experience his presence and be united with his life. Believing, then, "all the same" is living all the same, hoping all the same and loving all the same and in spite of everything.

Our experience, which does not have to be very long, makes us feel and recognize that life is a promise that is not kept. It gives us no more than a very few of the many hopes that we have placed in it. It never achieves completely positive results. Even when it offers us really satisfying creative achievements, these always contain within themselves the seeds of death and destruction. These seeds are so threatening, in fact, that they make us question ourselves. Is what we are doing advisable? Will the results not be disappointing? And we are led to conclude that all our attempts to love will never succeed, because we can only love badly and this will always end in disappointment for us and others. If our attitude towards ourselves were completely logical, we would know that the wisest and most reasonable decision would be not to undertake anything! After all, every commitment to live and to love makes us aware—often in a very painful and cruel way—of the limits of our actions and the fragile nature of our hearts.

In the light of this experience, believing is ultimately living all the same and loving all the same, because we are urged on by the word of God that we regard as true.

Hold on, then! This life, to which we are committed each morning, makes the kingdom of God rise up again and again and makes infinite and eternal bonds as well as links of human existence which are limited, weak and disappointing and which, because they are so limited, seem to be no more than signs and appeals. But, rooted in the experience of the resurrection of the Lord, we go on living all the same. We are not fleeing in disorder! We are not defeated! We are people of faith fighting to safeguard hope and for the future of the world.

■

Increase our faith, Lord our God.
In the light of your Son's word,
*   we have to continue in the battle of life.*
May it not overcome our hope
*   and may we, strengthened by your promise,*
*   come to peace for ever.*

READING AND UNDERSTANDING MARK (4:35–6:6)

The parables, and now several acts of power! This third step gives us another insight into the solid structure that forms the framework of the text of the Gospel. This section begins with a particularly impressive miracle story: Jesus "wakes up" and calms the storm (4:36–41). Towards the end, there is another equally impressive miracle: Jesus "wakes" a girl from the sleep of death (5:35–43). The question arises even more urgently: Who is this man?

Two people can help us to find the answer to this question. Both of them have in fact met Jesus on their way: first the Gerasene demoniac (5:1–17) and then the woman with a hemorrhage (5:25–34). The healing of the demoniac plunged him into a kind of holy fear which led him to throw himself at Jesus' feet (5:18–19), just like Jairus in the next incident, when he was mourning for the death of his daughter (5:21–23). Jesus goes with the leader of the synagogue to his house, but he does not, however, agree to the suggestion made by the Gerasene, who is a pagan. He gives him another mission: to proclaim "throughout the Decapolis all that Jesus had done for him" (5:20). What follows this account shows just how important this mission was to be. The country inhabited by the pagans was to become increasingly a priority.

Before examining this question, however, we must conclude our consideration of the three steps that we have outlined in these attempts to read and understand Mark's Gospel. The first step (3:7–35) stressed submission to the Father's will, which is what characterizes the true disciples of Jesus. The second (4:1–34) emphasizes openness to Jesus' teaching. In this third part, we have seen how the pagan demoniac submits to Jesus' words and actions. It is not difficult, then, to distinguish a single theme that is common to all three stages. According to the way in which they receive Jesus' words, people are divided into two groups: Jesus' disciples and those outside. Quite naturally, then, Mark concludes this section of his Gospel with a passage on the attitude of Jesus' contemporaries (6:1–6).

■

Lord Jesus, you came into the world
  to shine your light
  on those who walk in darkness.
Have mercy on us!

O Christ, you were sent by the Father
  to liberate man
  imprisoned by too many hostile forces.
Have mercy on us!

Lord, you were raised to the glory of the Father
  to give us a share in the Kingdom.
Have mercy on us!

SEEING THE UNSEEN

Hebrews 11:1-2, 8-19. "Faith possesses without holding; it knows without seeing." That is one translation of the opening words of this text. Supported by hope, faith gives birth to unseen realities in man and turns his gaze in the direction of God's future. Faith made Abraham leave for an unknown country. The patriarch and his descendants carried that faith like a title-deed, their eyes fixed on the Promised Land. The faithfulness of the living God is the guarantee of our faith and that guarantee transforms it into a power of life that is able to make the future open. It was therefore by that faith that a man who was already marked by death was able to give birth to countless believers who knew how precarious their stay on earth was, but who hoped for a better homeland.

The *Benedictus* (Luke 1) praises Yahweh's faithfulness to the promise that he made to the patriarch, Abraham. That promise is fulfilled in Jesus Christ.

Mark 4:35-41. The "day of parables" ends "with the coming of evening that same day." Mark, however, goes on to narrate four miracles. He clearly wants to show that the power of the kingdom is made manifest not only in Jesus' preaching, but also and equally in his actions.

The story of the calming of the storm is very christological. To interpret it, it should be borne in mind that, in the Old Testament, God alone was seen as having power over the wind and the sea and that the evil powers found refuge in the waves. In imposing silence on the sea, then, Jesus was acting like God. Hence the disciples' question: "Who can this be? Even the wind and the sea obey him!"

At the same time, Jesus' action lays bare the disciples' hearts. They are afraid because they still do not have total faith in him. The distance that has, up to this point, separated Jesus from "those outside" would seem to begin here to set the Master over and against his disciples.

■

**Living all the same, believing all the same and in spite of everything!
Our hope is not based either on smug human optimism or on stern
human courage. It is a God-orientated and God-given hope which has its
origin in God's grace, not in human power. We live all the same and
believe all the same because we are open to a another word, one other
than our own, because our eyes are open to another reality, one other
than the reality within our very limited vision and because we respond**

to a call that goes beyond the calls made by purely human hope—calls that are very courageous, but ultimately very restricted. We hold on because of an inner conviction that we can see today what is still unseen.

Is it possible to discern, at the heart of all the powers of death that assail us, a power of life? In a work of art, it is always possible to detect something other than what is immediately perceptible. Before a concert begins, there is always a time of silence. That silence is not empty or arid. On the contrary, it already contains within itself the rhythm and the music that will be heard and interpreted. Our task is to uncover. We have to remove the veil that covers the concealed reality and proclaim the deep and hidden meaning of the events. That is our vocation: to watch.

We stand at the end of a long line of watchers who have examined the unfolding of the human adventure, while at the same time being turned towards the coming of God's gift. We also stand at the end of the line of men and women who have taken life by the handful and have, perhaps only slightly, changed the course of history. We stand there because, if God is at all tender, he must in his tenderness take us seriously and find a way through the darkness that still holds us prisoner.

Sometimes, confronted by the uncertainties of the present time, we cry out in fear. Or we find ourselves violently opposed to the incomprehensible achievements of our century. But, because we go on believing all the same, we know that, in the ship of our adventures, there is a man at the helm who will steer us into the harbor. That is what God has promised!

■

In the uncertainties of time
  and the vicissitudes of history,
  be our help and have mercy on us.

When our confidence is threatened by so many failures,
  be our hope, Christ,
  and have mercy on us.

When we doubt if we shall ever reach the harbor,
  strengthen our weak faith
  and have mercy on us.

■

God of Abraham and of the fathers of our faith,
hear our prayer:

illuminate our history by your promise,
make our future fertile by your power,
overcome our fears and strengthen our will.

Make us stand up
so that, seeing the unseen,
we can welcome the day of your coming.

MONDAY OF THE 4TH WEEK

THE POWER OF FAITH

Hebrews 11:32–40. "Many prophets and kings wanted to see what you see, and never saw it; to hear what you hear, and never heard it" (Luke 10:24). Like David they conquered kingdoms, raised the dead to life like Elisha, were sawn in two like Isaiah, or were persecuted like all the prophets—but none of them heard the words of the Son. God kept for the witnesses of the new covenant the fulfillment of his promises and the achievement of his plan, which was "to bring everything together under Christ, as head" (Eph 1:10).

Psalm 31 is the prayer of a man in distress. The verses chosen for today express the quite legitimate trust that the righteous man places in his Lord, who is the protector of weak and insignificant people.

Mark 5:1–20. In his attempt to edit his very complex story of the man from Gerasa who was possessed, Mark has combined two traditions. The first was a report of one of the many exorcisms attributed to Jesus. The second was a reinterpretation of this miracle in connection with the accidental death by drowning of a herd of pigs in Lake Tiberias. Their drowning was attributed to the activity of the demons driven out of the possessed man.

Mark's account contains one very important fact, namely that Jesus was in territory that was pagan and therefore impure. The references to the tombs and the herd of pigs give emphasis to this fact. Further emphasis is provided by the fact that, after having confronted evil in its watery den, Jesus pursued it on land where it reigned supreme. What is more, when the possessed man was freed from his alienation, he asked Jesus to grant him the privilege of being admitted to the circle of his disciples. Jesus, however, refused. This is a clear illustration of the fact that the initiative to choose disciples was his alone. He sent the man back to his own people. His mission was to make the mercy of God, which he had just experienced himself, known to his compatriots, who had seen the episode as nothing more than a confirmation of folklore. For the first time, the good news was to be proclaimed in pagan territory.

Another important datum in the story is that the man was possessed by an impressive number of impure spirits. This shows how divided the man was. When Jesus follows the usual practice of exorcists and asks him his name, the man replies that a "legion" of demons lives in him. Then he only gradually surrenders his weapons, as the spirits are driven out of hiding. Jesus is therefore really the "more powerful" one, who is able to achieve such a striking victory in the kingdom of Satan. Only a little later, he would be celebrating the Eucharist on this land that was regarded as pagan (see 8:1–10).

■

"Is there any need to say more" about the power of faith? Yes, there is! What are we to say when, after centuries of Christianity and prayer to God for the coming of his kingdom, we are forced by the bitter reality of our situation to admit that no more than a glance at the world around us and at our history must inevitably silence the words of the *Our Father* before they cross our lips. Where, after all, can we see the will of God being done on earth? Where are the hungry receiving their daily bread? Where is temptation being overcome? Where is evil disappearing? Is there any need, then, to say more about the power of faith after we have looked honestly at the harsh reality of our life?

And if we observe what happens to that basic power that drives our lives forward, the power that we call love, to those positive impulses that sometimes succeed, to those passions that support our more generous efforts and our more risky undertakings, then we are bound to recognize that the results are not encouraging. So many projects abandoned and so many failed plans! We can only feel shame and distress.

Is there any need to say more about the power of faith?

Perhaps just this: Despite all the evidence to the contrary, we go on praying that the petitions of the *Our Father* may be answered. Faith, after all, takes us into another world. Grace has already taken the deepest part of our being to where God's kingdom has already come, to where God's will is fully unfolded, to where hunger is satisfied and to where evil no longer exists. And it is that part of ourselves that is already living there which arouses in us the longing to make the whole reality of our human existence cross over into that other world and which prompts the movement of prayer.

Is there any more to be said about the power of faith?

Perhaps only this: We do not, in fact, accept with resignation the meager evidence of our attempts to love that have ended in disappointment or misunderstanding and our passionate and risky impulses that have come to nothing. We are astonishingly persistent! To our own suprise and in spite of everything, we go on all the same with our search. Why is that? Perhaps because the power of faith has already taken the deepest part of our heart into that other world which is the realm of love and it is the call that comes to us from that realm which gives birth unceasingly and again and again and in spite of all our fears, our weakness and our failures to that irrepressible longing to love.

We are anxious to find the trace of that other world in the movement of our prayer and the longing of our heart. We do not want to be at the stage of having succeeded in that prayer and of having fulfilled that love. That is the condition imposed by our present status as believers. And we should not be surprised if, because of weakness or even cowardice, we do not in fact fulfil that longing as we would like to or as we ought to. It is present in us as the trace that the power of faith is at work and as the sign of what it is in the process of achieving in a veiled but an undoubtedly victorious way.

■

God of our fathers in faith,
may your name be blessed!
  In the trials of our present time,
  your Word is the promise,
  the longing that takes us to you
  and the mark of your faithfulness.
May the power of faith be active in our life
and may we not find it too painful
  to move towards the fulfilment of the centuries.

TUESDAY OF THE 4TH WEEK

NOT LOSING SIGHT OF JESUS
Hebrews 12:1–4. The final chapters of the Epistle are an exhortation to Christians to persevere. They should "not lose sight of Jesus"! He, too, experienced adversity, but he "leads us in our faith and brings it to perfection."

The greater part of *Psalm 22* is in the form of a complaint, but the verses selected for today's liturgy only speak of the promise to celebrate the good things done by Yahweh. The final verses form a series of wishes addressed to God himself.

Mark 5:21–43. Jairus is "the one who wakens" or "the one who enlightens." In this story, Mark makes us swing between life and death. He introduces us to a woman who has "suffered from a hemorrhage for twelve years." Because of this, and all the more so because her illness excludes her from society, she is slowly moving towards death. While this is happening, a little girl is growing up and is experiencing life to the full. Then, quite suddenly, the woman is healed and the girl is dead. What we have here is a parable, a discovery of the kingdom through an event, but it is reserved for those who are not outside.

The woman wants to touch Jesus' garment, believing that contact of this kind can heal her. Her faith is clearly mixed with superstition, but it goes further than the faith of the crowd that is pressing Jesus on every side. He does not, however, want a stealthy cure. The woman, he insists, must emerge from her barren anonymity and have a personal relationship with him. When he heals her for the second time, he does it openly.

There is also a crescendo in the way the leader of the synagogue behaves. Jairus is moved by a deep faith that is obviously put severely to the test by the lack of faith of the people in the crowd, who are already celebrating the girl's death. But, Jesus says, "the child is not dead, but asleep." This is a kind and euphemistic way of describing the tragedy that has descended on the whole family, of course, but what faith when that "sleep" becomes an expectation of resurrection! The woman with a hemorrhage is cured of her illness and the girl is delivered from death. "If anyone believes in me, even though he dies, he will live."

We have, then, to believe in Jesus in spite of all the evidence against that faith. In the storm on Lake Tiberias, when they were very frightened, the disciples discovered the power of life dwelling in Jesus. They have, however, still to experience the light of Easter. When that happens, they will be able to decipher the secret of his parables completely.

■

"Keep running steadily in the race we have started. Let us not lose sight of Jesus, who leads us in our faith and brings it to perfection." Surely there can be no better way of describing the dynamism of our faith!

"Let us not lose sight of Jesus," because we have no other name by which we can be saved and no other face on which we can contemplate the face of God. We must not lose sight of Jesus, because his face tells the story of his life and bears the mark of those thirty silent years spent in the workshop at Nazareth, and the three years devoted to travelling the length and breadth of the country. We must not lose sight of Jesus, because his face reflects not only terror. Those who have seen it have testified that it has always been the face of the only Son who, nourished by the glory of the Father, bore witness to that glory. Finally, we must not lose sight of Jesus, because he "invents" God, creates him and gives him a face that is different from the one we are used to. With what he says and does, Jesus draws a different picture of God.

If we do not lose sight of this revelation, we can certainly "keep running steadily in the race we have started," since one man, Jesus, has been a man until the end and has, in that way, revealed that he is the only Son of God. One man has loved perfectly and has, in that love, saved the love of men. One man has called God his "Father" and has therefore enabled us to say with him the prayer of sons who are loved passionately. There may be countless obstacles and difficult conflicts on the way, and the end of the road may seem to be a long way off, but we can go forward in the light of the revelation of the Word as though we were seeing the unseen.

"Do not be afraid; only have faith!" Confronted with the scandal of death, the intolerable evidence of our many failures and the calamities of fate, the only remedy that we have is in Jesus' words to the girl: "Get up!" We must dare to believe, hope and live. Jairus has only one recourse: to go back to the house where he was put to the test, where he will discover that death has been overcome.

"Do not be afraid; only have faith!" That is our only chance and our salvation is contained in those words.

■

Be steadfast in faith,
  God, our recourse and our power,
Do not let those who believe in you
  be overcome by despair!
Be our future,
  let your promise be fulfilled
  and be our happiness for ever.

BE CAREFUL!

Hebrews 12:4–7, 11–15. "Suffering is part of your training." The prophets often compared God's attitude to that of a teacher who leads his people to adulthood, not only by his teaching, but also by reprimanding and even correcting them. This way of speaking, which is that of the deuteronomistic writers, is often misunderstood nowadays. Yet it does contain an important element of human experience! On the one hand, being put to the test is a common fact of life and, on the other, is it not true that the experience makes us mature?

Christians' experience of being put to the test is not just arbitrary. It calls for steadfastness and builds up "the perfect Man, fully mature with the fullness of Christ himself" (Eph 4:13).

Psalm 103 is in the form of a hymn and praises Yahweh's concern for the righteous.

Mark 6:1–6. "The secret of the kingdom of God is given to you, but to those who are outside everything comes in parables" (4:11). With these words, Mark takes into account the questions raised for Christians by the incredulity of the Jews and the difficulties of evangelization. How is it possible for God, who is omnipotent, to tolerate that state of affairs? The evangelist goes to the trouble of showing that God has created each individual free and therefore able to make his own response to the Word. There is in fact a secret between God and those who believe in him and the world knows nothing about it.

In particular, the evangelist wants to stress the bad reception of Jesus in the village where he grew up. He and his family were too well-known there. As a result, he was labelled and reduced to a certain image. This lack of belief meant that he was prevented from working miracles there. They would in any case have served no purpose in view of the fact that the hearts and minds of the people were closed.

■

"Be careful that no one is deprived of the grace of God." Believing is being careful! Not being on the defensive, but being watchful. Keeping a vigil throughout the night, watching for dawn to break, or like the look-out man, watching the horizon from the top of the mast for the first sight of land.

"Be careful"—God is very disconcerting!

"He came to his own domain and his own people did not accept him."
He spent thirty years in Nazareth. Thirty years in a village a long way
from the main roads, thirty years among ordinary people, thirty years
living with them and being ordinary like them. Thirty years being so
much like them that they saw no difference between him and any
"James and Joset or Jude and Simon"! Thirty years altogether and then,
at the hour of the manifestation, the judgment which was to have a
dramatic echo on a certain Friday. It is surely impossible—God cannot
be so close to us! He was obviously unfortunate on this occasion. He had
been much more remote at other times, as, for example, when he
appeared wrapped in thunder and lightning on the mountain. The people
had been unfaithful to him then (Psalm 78). But now it is necessary to go
back to early traditions to express the impossible: "When the Messiah
comes, no one will be able to say from where he is."

"Be careful!"—God has deliberately chosen not to be welcomed. It is
obvious that, in following the plan to make his kingdom come among us
and, to make it come, in behaving in the way that we want him to
behave, God never thought of coercing mankind which was submerged
in spite of itself. No, he always depends on man's free response to his
initiative. The risk that God is prepared to take in his revelation is in
direct proportion to the quality that he values most in man: the free
response of a heart that abandons itself in complete trust.

There are, of course, many Nazareths that remain within the walls of
their refusal to respond. When that happens, Jesus leaves. But he goes
away "amazed," Mark tells us, in pained surprise, the surprise of a love
which is offered without wanting to wound or to be a burden, but with
the aim of making us happy and free and which suffers if it not received.
If we reject it, then, Jesus leaves, but he goes away in order to "make a
tour round other villages," because Love does not accept refusal.

■

You forewarn us, God our Father,
  but your disconcerting word
  and your coming amaze us.
Let us be careful
  so that we shall not miss
  the encounter with love.

The cattle know their herdsman
  and all creatures know their creator,

but we know you so imperfectly,
  God of mercy and tenderness!
Keep our hearts watchful,
  disclose your mystery to us
  overturn our habits
and let us be surprised by your astonishing presence!

The one you have sent to us
  has come back to his own country.
Here he is in the midst of us,
  his face always made new by your love.
God our Father,
  open our hearts to your presence,
  so that we shall be taken unawares
  by the mystery that we have glimpsed.

READING AND UNDERSTANDING MARK (6:7-29)

In our continuous reading of the Gospel of Mark, we have so far been able to distinguish two major stages. In the first, the evangelist shows how the Word breaks in on the roads of Galilee (1:14–3:6). The second stage reveals the effect of that Word on the hearts of those who hear it: it lays them bare (3:7–6:6). Confronted by such unyielding adversaries, Jesus finds himself increasingly isolated. But the painful question still remains: Who is this man?

The third stage (6:7–8:30) shows that, to reply to this question, it is necessary to be armed. J. Radermakers has written, "For faith to begin to grow in our hardened and defiled hearts and for our ears to be opened to understand the mystery of God that gives itself to us, we need an added strength: food that is more substantial than the bread and the fishes distributed by men. We need food which satisfies us without ever being exhausted. We need to eat at God's own table."

This third stage is of fundamental importance. It has often been called the "section of the loaves" and it can be divided into three steps. We shall deal with each of these in turn. For the moment, however, we shall confine ourselves to the fact that these three steps are introduced by a preamble which includes firstly, an account of the mission of the disciples (6:7–13) and secondly, a report of the death of John the Baptist (6:14–29).

■

How good it is to give you thanks,
  Lord our God!

You do not leave us alone
  in tears in the darkness.
You show us the way
  and throw light on it
  and your Son leads us forward.
He came so that the lame might walk,
  the deaf hear
  and the blind see.

We bless you,
  God of the promise that never fails.
Your Son sets the table of mercy
  and we know your faithfulness.
Let us celebrate
  with all those who are filled with your love.
Let us praise you
  with all those who share in the joy of the good news.

THURSDAY OF THE 4TH WEEK

NOTHING BUT POOR PEOPLE

Hebrews 12:18-19, 21-24. It is important to bear in mind the author's insistence on the need for Christ's sacrifice of himself. Only that personal offering could open the doors of the kingdom. The final exhortation begins in chapter 12 of the Epistle and its sole aim is to make Christians more zealous in their imitation of Christ, especially when they are put to the test. "Always be wanting peace with all people, and the holiness without which no one can ever see the Lord" (12:14). Sanctification, being made holy: This is the key concept of the ethos of the Epistle.

Following his argument, the author contrasts the attitude of the Jews towards God's revelation with that of Christians. He clearly regards the Christian position as superior to that of the Jews. This superiority is based on the inner experience of Christians. For the Jews, there were terrifying but limited cosmic phenomena on Mount Sinai—so terrifying that even Moses was deeply disturbed and afraid. The initiation of Christians, on the other hand, is the work of the Spirit. The Jews climbed an earthly mountain, whereas Christians enter the sphere of Mount Zion and the heavenly Jerusalem. They come "to Jesus, the mediator who brings a new covenant."

Psalm 48 is a canticle in honor of the holy city, which is made impregnable by the presence of Yahweh within its walls. In verse 9, there is an echo of the procession of the ark of the covenant that took place in Jerusalem. During their stay there, the people were able to admire the ark, which was the visible sign of God's protection of the city.

Mark 6:7–13. Jesus calls his first companions, chooses the Twelve and sends them out on their mission. The first stages in the Gospel are marked by the relationships between Jesus and his disciples. They are always with Jesus. They see the Word come close to men and women, as J. Rademakers noted, "like seed on astonishingly different kinds of soil." One day, however, Jesus will speak to them about his passion and they will be troubled in the depths of their being.

Now, however, they have to follow Jesus in proclaiming the good news of God, not only in words, but also in signs. They "anointed many sick people with oil." This was a practice in the early Church that accompanied the breaking in of the kingdom.

■

The Master's instructions clearly stress the need for great austerity on the part of the Twelve and the removal of all obstacles standing in the way of their mission. Their dress is to be that of pilgrims who expect everything of God and who are no longer going up to the temple, but are going out to meet their fellow-men, who are the image of God. They will, in many places where they preach, encounter hostility and they should not linger there. Jesus worked no miracles in Nazareth and they, too, should break with every town or village that they recognize as unworthy of the kingdom. The encounter between God and man is always an encounter between grace and human freedom.

When you came to God, there was nothing to attract you!

We may, of course, have lost our first ardent enthusiasm because we have forgotten how foolish we were to be attracted in the beginning. But why did we ever believe in Jesus? Not even his youthful companions, after all, those with whom he was intimate, were really convinced by him and his arguments! A wandering preacher who was not even able to keep as his followers those who had for a little while been influenced by his preaching! A man who was condemned to death and mocked on the cross! He really has nothing to attract us to him.

And what about Christians who appeal to him? Men and women who are no different from any others! The history of their Church has some glorious pages, but others that cause great scandal. Some members of the Church have been generous and even holy, while countless others have been weak and mediocre. There is really nothing to attract us!

A God who has no other words but those of men and nothing to show but the life of a man. A Church whose history is entirely human and therefore a fabric woven of sin and grace. Faith has no other object and it cannot rely on a decisive argument, an overwhelmingly convincing manifestation or a history without histories. Believing is something done by poor people. When you came to God, there was nothing to attract you!

The disciple has no other certainty than words exchanged with his companion on the road, than a face to discover and to love and a history to share in a fellowship. When he sent his disciples out on their mission, Jesus had only this to say to them: You will have nothing to support you but the faith you share with each other.

■

God our Father,
at this time that is so testing,
* we cry out to you:*
* our faith is insecure*
* and we are hesitant*
* in our response to your call.*

Have pity on us
* and attract us by your mercy.*
Let us contemplate your grace!
Let it be good for us
* to come to you*
* today and every day.*

■

With nothing but your grace
* to give us security,*
we ask you, God our Lord,
* that the word of your Son*
* may be the foundation of our faith*
* and the source of our hope.*
Grant that we may go forward in life
* with nothing but your promise to help us.*

PERSEVERANCE IN FAITH

Hebrews 13:1–8. "Continue to love each other as brothers." The author concludes his Epistle with some advice on communal ethics, at the base of which is charity. Paul's emphases in his Letter to the Romans can be found in this part of the Epistle. All of Paul's instructions in his Letter, it will be remembered, can be traced back to the practice of a spiritual cult. The author of Hebrews gives a very similar meaning to the Christian's way of behaving. According to him, the cult that is really pleasing to God is nothing but our imitation of the personal gift of Jesus Christ.

Psalm 27 is a combination of two poems. The first six verses express trust. This confidence is particularly striking in verse 3, which speaks of an army and of war. This part of the psalm was probably spoken by a king who was certain of victory in the end. Verses 7–14 comprise an individual lamentation.

Mark 6:14–29. Tongues are wagging in Galilee! People are talking about Jesus and also about John the Baptist, whom Herod Antipas has just arrested. According to the Jewish historian Josephus, the reasons for this action were political. According to the Gospel, they were religious.

People are also forming hypotheses about Jesus. His preaching leads them to think that he is the eschatological prophet, probably Elijah. Jesus himself will, a little later, ask the same question about his identity.

Elijah, John the Baptist and Jesus—there is a striking parallelism between them. The prophet of Carmel had been persecuted by Queen Jezebel. In the same way, John was the victim of Herod's anger. John's execution anticipated that of Jesus.

■

The sermon preached to the Hebrews ends with some final suggestions by the author to ensure that faith will bear fruit and therefore be fulfilled. He urges his brothers to persevere in faith. Faith is action and believing is living the law of the Gospel. This is not a law in the usual sense. In other words, it is not a set of commandments imposed on us from outside under threat of punishment. It is, on the contrary, a law in the sense that the law of the tree is to bear fruit or in the sense of a law that is the unfolding of a life given to us and dwelling within us.

The author concludes his advice with the disconcerting statement: "Jesus Christ is the same today as he was yesterday and as he will be for ever." From the point of view of purely literary logic, these words are quite astonishing. But, according to Christian logic, the law of the Gospel extends itself into the sphere of contemplation. According to the new law of Christ, life is the fruitfulness of a life that is given, a life that is Christ himself. Because Christ has entered my being as reconciliation and forgiveness, he urges me, from within me, to be reconciled with my brother. Because he has entered my being as faithfulness and unreserved love, he keeps me, deep within my heart, faithfully loving. Because he has entered my being as absolute grace, he urges me, from within me, to live for gratuity rather than for profit. Because he has welcomed me unconditionally into the Father's house, he calls me to live hospitably.

The Gospel contains both a radical demand made by a law that has been fundamentally renewed and a revelation of the secret life that urges us forward. God has put a new heart into us. Any attempt to experience the demand made by the Gospel is valueless if we do not receive Christ himself as the only one who can enable us to practice what he has said. Any attempt, in other words, to make a morality out of the Gospel is valueless if we do not at the same time make a mystical reality out of it —the mystical reality of our union with Christ.

■

You are a priest for ever, Christ and Lord!
  Consecrate us in your Easter
  and have mercy on us.

You are a priest for ever, Christ and Lord!
  Transfigure us into your image
  and have mercy on us.

You are a priest for ever, Christ and Lord!
  Take us into the glory of the Father
  and have mercy on us.

■

God our salvation,
may your Spirit be the strength of our faith,
  the perseverance of our faithfulness
  and the breath of our life.
And may the Gospel of your Son
  bear in us fruit that will last for ever.

This section on the loaves has a very complex structure. The simplest analysis consists in dividing it into three parallel steps, each of which has a practically identical beginning. The first opens with the words: "The apostles rejoined Jesus" (6:30); the second with: "The Pharisees and some of the scribes who had come from Jerusalem gathered round him and noticed some of his disciples" (7:1) and the third with: "And now once again a great crowd had gathered. . . . So he (Jesus) called his disciples to him" (8:1). These three groups of people—Jesus' disciples, the Pharisees and the scribes and finally the crowd—have been moving around Jesus since the "day" in Capernaum. In addition, this section is also characterized by the fact that, in each of these three steps, the disciples are in the foreground or, if not, they are either sharing Jesus' concern for the crowd or are being attacked by the scribes.

The disciples play a very important part in the Gospel of Mark and the evangelist again and again mentions their presence with Jesus from the time of his preaching in Galilee onwards. Now, however, something has changed in their situation. They have been sent on a mission. They have become "apostles." More than ever before, they are part of Jesus' ministry. From now on, they have to try to understand their Master at an increasingly deep level and to answer the question: "Who is this man?"

This question has just been asked by Herod and Jesus will ask it himself at the end of this stage (8:27-30). In the meantime, however, an extremely important event will have taken place; the disciples will have moved from unbelief to faith. So, in a very subtle way, emphasis is placed in this third stage on the fact that opposition to Jesus has not been the exclusive prerogative of his declared adversaries, but that even his closest companions and friends have been troubled by doubts. From now on, then, the personal attacks to which Jesus subjects those close to him become even more pointed. There are several examples in this section: "They had not seen what the miracle of the loaves meant" (6:52); "Do you not understand either?" (7:18); "Do you not yet understand?" (8:17).

The section closes with the question that is fundamental to the Gospel: "But you—who do you say I am?" (8:27-30). Peter replies, but, confronted with the ambiguity of his reply, Jesus feels obliged to make a clear statement at once about his future passion, presenting himself to his own as the suffering Messiah. With this in mind, it may be possible to understand the importance of the introduction to this section on the loaves—the execution of John the Baptist. The disciples' mission gave them an insight into the questions that would be asked about Jesus' person, but the execution of the Baptist had already provided them with the answer.

SATURDAY OF THE 4TH WEEK

REVELATION

Hebrews 13:15-17, 20-21. After reminding his readers how pleased God is by man's obedience and his sharing of his resources, the author ends his epistle-homily in solemn words that briefly recall the contents of Hebrews and its consequences for the Christian way of life and are a blend of invocation, aspiration and doxology.

Psalm 23 was originally a psalm of trust. The Church, following the synagogue, has used it as a song of entry into the Promised Land, which is called to mind by the "green grass."

Mark 6:30-34. The lectionary is really annoying in that it does not give us the first account of the miracle of the loaves. In my opinion, it would have been preferable to continue today's reading to verse 44. What has been called the "section on the loaves" leads to the question: "Who am I?" and prepares the way for an answer to this question within a clearly eucharistic context, in that it shows Jesus as the new shepherd gathering his people together, teaching them and feeding them.

The whole narrative in this section is constructed around the two accounts of the breaking of the loaves. It is important to note that the recipients of the two miracles are not the same in each case. The first miracle takes place on exclusively Jewish territory, whereas the second occurs in Decapolis, where the majority of the people were pagans. This would point to a desire to bring not only the Jews but also the pagans to salvation. The aim of the other accounts that are inserted between the two stories of the sharing of the loaves is also to prepare the way for the inclusion of the pagans in the plan of salvation. The lesson on cleanness, for example, understood in the sense of moral uprightness, indicates that a pagan is as clean as a Jew and can therefore take part in the eucharistic banquet, as long as he recognizes that Jesus is the one who gives life to the world. It is clear from this section, then, that as soon as Jesus is ready to ask the question: "Who am I?", both the Jews and the pagans are invited to reply to it.

The apostles—they can certainly be given this new name because of their mission—have come back and Jesus invites them to share a well-earned meal.

But the crowd is left to its own devices! Is there nobody to look after these people, organize them and make them into a real people? Later in the Gospel, Jesus criticizes the religious leaders for their lack of concern and for doing nothing but placing unbearable burdens on their backs. In the meantime, however, he continues to teach them, since the first task of the shepherd or pastor is to say words that are able to call the people together.

■

Jesus' contemporaries were preoccupied with an intense longing to become a nation again. They looked back nostalgically to the time of Israel's origins. They idealized the past.

Each Passover they told stories about the great things God had done in favor of their ancestors; how, for example, he had protected the scattered children of Israel in the land of slavery, and how he had made a people of what was not a people. Later, of course, they had become divided again into two kingdoms—two hostile brothers. And during the time of the Diaspora, Israel had once again been scattered in a foreign land.

And now a man arises in whom the people recognize the fulfilment of their expectation—the sheep always recognize the voice of their shepherd. Once again, they are gathered together in the desert—"the Lord is my shepherd." Only God knows where to lead his people and he has placed everything in the hands of his Son. But only the shepherd who has become a lamb so that he can be one with his flock can claim to be the shepherd. Only the one who goes to the very end in giving up his life can take them to the source of life.

The prophets had foretold his coming. In the fullness of time, God would send the shepherd who would gather his flock together. Ezekiel prophesied: "I mean to raise up one shepherd and to put him in charge of them; he will pasture them and be their shepherd." That shepherd would have mercy on the scattered sheep. "I shall look for the lost sheep, bring back the stray, bandage the wounded and make the weak strong. I shall watch over the fat and healthy." Jesus was that shepherd of Israel and his word of total power was to bind the people together.

You who are waiting with great longing for the day of renewal— recognize the water that can quench your thirst! You who are blessed by your poverty and that of the world—abandon yourself to the love of the one who can heal you! You whose heart is full of humility and tenderness —know the voice of the one who is gentle and humble in heart! You who are longing to love passionately—hear the cry of the one who calls on you to follow him to the cross! He calls you out into the desert and makes a holy people of you! You need have no fear of mirages, because he is the way and the truth and the life. Can you not hear him inviting you to join him on God's way?

■

God, you are faithful to your promises.
Let your Spirit
open our minds to your plans,
  so that the hidden taste of our present life
  may be revealed to us.

■

God our Father, your love for us is sovereign.
Let your Spirit
enlarge our hearts to contain your tenderness,
  so that the greatness of our calling
  may be revealed to us.
And may your grace be manifest
  for ever and ever.

FROM MONDAY TO SATURDAY

OF THE 5TH WEEK

Creation

The creation account enables us to understand God's fundamental appeal to man. The God who is at the origin of all things is a God who is trying to encounter man at the deepest level of his being and is asking him: "Do you love me?"

The more we read the Bible, the more we discover the truth that lies at the heart of our creed, namely that the one who is the creator is the one who is love. The one who created man in his image and likeness is the one whose love is expressed in the patience and faithfulness that he showed in his dealings with Israel, his people. The creator is also the one whose love was poured out in the man who died on the cross in an obscure province of the Roman Empire. He is also the one in whom the beloved apostle believed, the author of the words: "My dear people, let us love one another." The true and only creator is the God of Jesus Christ.

Only Love, the Love of God, is truly creative. Only that Love can make man truly human and arouse and set free in him the powers that lie dormant in him. Only that Love can enable something to happen in the depths of men's hearts and in the depths of human history. Only that Love can ensure that something rather than nothing happens. If we are sensitive, we can be conscious of that happening every day.

Power can make buildings arise, and violence can change the course of history, but only Love can make the most valuable element of all exist, that element for which we would give all the rest, that which even death cannot reduce to dust—only Love can make man exist.

Saying that I believe in God the creator cannot throw any special light on the past history of the world, on those immense periods when the world was begotten in the darkness of time. It cannot throw any light on the gradual appearance on our earth of that curious species that came to be known among biologists as "homo sapiens." We do, however, have a light that shines on our present and our future.

Who are we? Why do we exist?

Because of that infinite Love.

And we only truly exist in our response to that infinite Love of God.

■

At the dawn of the world,
when your light was rising,
    your word, God the creator,
    expressed itself in a tender refrain.
When what was not yet organized was organized,
when what was not yet living came to life,
when all beings and all things were fashioned
    and you were yourself astonished
    by the work of your hands:
    "How beautiful it is!"

Blessed are you for our brother the sun:
    how clear and warm it is!
Blessed are you for the trees and the flowers,

the fruits of the earth
and the waters teeming with life!
Blessed are you for the animals
and the birds of the sky!
But above all we bless you for man,
that child of the earth, the son of your love!
You have breathed into him your breath, your Spirit!
He has been born in your image and likeness!

Blessed are you for the love that sings in his heart
and the knowledge he has of your tenderness,
the will to serve you
and the desire to know you.

Blessed are you for the future you have promised him
and the covenant you have made with him:
you have made him your partner in your plans
and the communicator of your word.
Blessed are you for the name that you have given him:
Adam, the one of earth.
Blessed are you too for the other name
that you had already destined him to have:
Jesus, Son of man and Son of God.

What is man that you should bear him in mind?
You have given him your breath
so that he should aspire to live still more.
You have fashioned him with your hands
and clothed him with unexpected glory and splendor.

What is man, God our Father,
that you should make him pass from death to life
in your Son Jesus Christ, the new Adam,
the Lord before whom heaven and earth bow down?
We beseech you today:
recreate our world that is marked by death
and restore all things to their original beauty.
Transform your Church,
people of poor men and women,
that we may bear witness
to the marvels that you accomplish
and that we may sing in praise
and astonishment of all your creation:
"How beautiful it is!"

Then, with all the living
who have been born of your love
and recreated by your tenderness and for ever,
we shall be able to bless you,
Father of heaven and earth,
through the first living being,
your Son, our Savior,
the Man of your heart.

∎

The Book of Genesis and the Yahwist

Readings taken from the first eleven chapters of the book of Genesis, covering the period from the history of the origins to the tower of Babel, begin in the fifth week. Almost all of these readings form part of what has come to be known as the Yahwistic document.

This document appeared during the time of King Solomon, that is, about 950 B.C. It relates the sacred history from the point of view of Jerusalem. The Yahwist's text was also merged together, in Jerusalem, with another sacred history that originated in the north. This is the Elohistic document. To this can be added the complex book of Deuteronomy and a third document, the priestly text, which was for the most part elaborated in Babylonia during the exile. Together, these documents constitute the Pentateuch, that vast historico-religious encyclopedia dating from the return from the Babylonian exile. Some scholars have not hesitated to attribute this fresco, which was built up very gradually, to the scribe Ezra. The mere fact that it was elaborated over such a long period of time points to the very essence of the Pentateuch, namely that it bears witness to the life of a believing community of people.

The same can also be said of the different texts that constitute the Pentateuch. If we confine ourselves simply to the Yahwistic document, we can see how it reflects the details of the period in which it originated. It is the work of scribes who experienced the good life at the court in Jerusalem. Their training was based on the model of their Egyptian counterparts and they cultivated the art of discernment—the Wisdom literature provides us with ample evidence of this—and occupied positions in the nation's political administration. The Yahwist's work is above all a national work, dedicated to the king, who was regarded as inheriting the promises made to the patriarchs.

Just as the Elohistic tradition is characterized by the theme of the covenant, blessing is at the heart of the Yahwistic document. A summary of the Yahwist's profession of faith can be found in Genesis 12:2: "I will make you a great nation; I will bless you and make your name so famous that it will be used as a blessing." The opening chapters of Genesis show how this blessing given to all the nations corresponds to the curse that fell on Adam, following the original error. Later, this blessing was, after countless vicissitudes, to be made incarnate in the one who inherited the throne of Judah. The distance between the Yahwist and the prophet Nathan, then, is not very great: Israel's hope was always to be found in the Davidic monarchy.

Another characteristic of the Yahwist is his critical attitude. In this respect, he is an excellent witness to the spirit of his age. A careful reading of his account reveals the extent to which he constantly demythologized the Mesopotamian data of which he made considerable use. Although we are sometimes less aware of it, he also distrusted everything that came from Egypt. An example of this is the cunning serpent of Genesis 3, which may be a symbol of Egyptian power, just as Joseph is the wise man par excellence.

Finally, it should be noted that the author of the Yahwistic account was preoccupied with two closely related questions. The first is: Who is the supreme god in the universalist pantheon of the time? The second is: Who is his authentic representative on earth?

MONDAY OF THE 5TH WEEK

IN THE BEGINNING
Genesis 1:1–19. "In the beginning was the Word" (Jn 1:1). The priestly account, which opens the book of Genesis, bears witness to the scientific knowledge that was current at the time. The vision of the cosmos that emerges from it was shared by most people in the ancient world. The earth was seen as a disc at the center of that cosmos, surrounded by the sea, placed on the primordial waters and surmounted by the dome of heaven, which separated the waters above it from those below.

The Genesis story, however, is much more than an anthology of the knowledge of the priests who wrote it. It is also a theological reflection about the origin of the world and the existence of man. In the first place, it strictly defines the essence of creation. The universe, it claims, is not of divine nature. It is only the product of God's personal will. Creation only came about and only continues to exist through the grace of a Word. In stating that it is surrounded on all sides by a shapeless mass of water which might swallow it up at any moment, the opening verses of Genesis also stress the extremely precarious nature of the created world. This fundamental affirmation has very important eschatological consequences, because it suggests that the world is dependent on the Word, which maintains it in existence.

The description of the successive steps in the process of creation also contains many teachings. The first conclusion points to the part played by light as a very special element in the process, without which the whole of creation would return to darkness and therefore to chaos. The introduction of the vault of heaven is also very suggestive, because it preserves a trace of one of the two conceptions that underlie the account. According to the first, the universe was created by the Word, but according to the second and undoubtedly earlier conception, God is presented as a sheet-metal worker who beats the heavenly vault into shape with a hammer: "God made the vault" (verse 7). The description of the creation of the plants draws attention to the part played by the earth in the creative act: "Let the earth produce vegetation" (verse 12).

Finally there are the stars and planets. Detailed analysis of the text has shown that the author has adapted his source to make their creation occur on the fourth day; in other words, on Wednesday, which was the first day of the year in the priestly calendar. The task of the stars and planets was to preside over feasts, days and years. They were not to do what was generally believed throughout the rest of the ancient world, namely, direct the personal destiny of individuals. A deliberate decision, then, is clearly made in the priestly account of creation to reduce their importance. The stars and planets are simply called "lamps" or "lights" and are regarded as no more than humble servants. The Bible refuses to be in league with those who sell horoscopes.

Psalm 104 makes use of elements taken from various hymns to call to mind Yahweh's act of creation. It is the Pentecostal psalm par excellence.

Mark 6:53–56. Jesus has given the loaves to the people. He has given them food for eternal life, but no one has understood the meaning of what he has done, neither the disciples, whose "minds were closed" (verse 52), nor the people in the crowd, who could not see further than the signs. They come from everywhere, bringing their sick to Jesus and asking him for cures, but they make no progress in recognizing his person.

■

In the beginning . . . . The image touches our heart. Deep within us is a secret longing to rediscover our origins, because they tell us who and what we are. A longing to find ourselves, to discover the meaning of our life and why the world exists. To find an answer to the question that man has asked throughout his history. Many different answers have been provided by myths and religions which live on highly colored images.

In the beginning . . . . In the Bible, the story of God's adventure with man opens with a fresco which expresses God's intangible will. The creation story fascinates us with its ordered regularity. It allows one figure after another to pass in front of us, as spectators, in solemn procession and we just have time to greet each one before it gives way to the next. In the beginning of the word of God, the cosmos was organized. Light came first as a joyous appearance in the darkness. At once a pair is given a precise place and function as day and night. Next come the waters and the ground; in other words, the earth. Life is given a suitable framework. The sun and the moon are reduced to the status of street lamps. There is, after all, more than enough light already! What is to become an ordered universe, divided into days and years, enters in stately procession. God creates by bringing order into what is in disorder, by separating. In ordering his creation, what he has in mind is the end towards which he is working. He is presented here as being alone, but even at this point what he continues to reveal throughout history is repeated like a refrain: "God saw that it was good!"

Yes, in the beginning God saw that his creation was good.

That is our origin: life is good and God is already able to express his astonishment in song. He is still alone, but we already feel that, as soon as there are men and women, he will look for a murmur of approval.

Everything is good. It is even very good, the song of Genesis tells us. It is a deliberate act of faith. Everything is firm and solid. Everything comes from God's hand: days and nights, sun and moon, minerals and vegetables.

Everything will be good for you, so long as you take it with a word of thanksgiving and know how to recognize that God has, from the beginning, been on the side of man and life. A long history commenced with that beginning—the history of God's covenant with man. In the beginning, God trembled with happiness, because he is Love. And in his hands, with which he was preparing everything for man's happiness, was born the gift of love that begets and gives, yes, life.

TUESDAY OF THE 5TH WEEK

LOOKED FOR

Genesis 1:20–2:4a. After the creation of the stars and planets, a new day dawned on the world. With the animals, life first emerged in the waters before spreading over the earth. The creation of the sea-monsters is in accordance with a theological notion. The author points out that these beings (which are taken directly from eastern mythologies) were created directly by God and are simply ordinary creatures. What is new, however, is the blessing that the animals are given—they receive from God the ability to maintain life and reproduce themselves.

With the creation of man, the scene takes on a new and more solemn note. For the first time, God discusses the matter with his heavenly council. The decision to create man comes from the depths of his heart. "Let us make man in our own image; in the likeness of the *elohim* he created him" (verses 26–27). The author is very discreet in his claim that man was made in the likeness of God. What he says, in fact, is that God took as his model for his last work, man, what was found in the heavenly world (the *elohim* were the heavenly court; this is a polytheistic survival). However necessary it was to look outside the sphere of creatures for the likeness of man, there still had to be an infinite distance between man and God. In addition to this, the words used—image and likeness—indicate, as G. von Rad has observed, that the whole of man was created in the image of God. It was not just in his spiritual nature, but also and perhaps primarily in the glory of his bodily aspect that he was created in God's image. Finally, man's sexual difference is also part of the order of creation. Man was not created in isolation; he is called to encounter the other sex. According to the plan of creation, then, the full notion of man is not just the male, but the couple.

The nature of man's image and likeness may be intentionally vague in the Genesis story, but the aim is quite clear. Man was created by God to tread the animal world under foot and trample on the earth. Made in the image of God, man is the link between him and the cosmos. Just as in the ancient Near East kings had statues of themselves erected in their provinces, so too had man to defend God's rights on earth. He had been given this mandate by God, as his representative in the world.

The priestly author ends his account by saying that God completed the "work" of creation. This is not so much a statement about the institution of the sabbath as an affirmation of a rest that had existed before man. On the one hand, the world was no longer being created by God; it had been "completed" by him. On the other hand, Yahweh "blessed" this rest and "made it holy," that is to say, he set it apart as something between himself and the world, as a supreme good. Later, the people of Israel were to see in it the sign of their belonging to God.

By making the creation of heaven and earth the first of the "generations" or *toledoth*, the priestly author, as it were, added his signature to his work, which is, in fact, entirely constructed on the basis of these *toledoth*, which follow one another as far as Numbers 3:1, where the priestly descent is given to Aaron.

Psalm 8 is a natural choice to follow this reading from Genesis because it praises God for creating man.

Mark 7:1–13. The behavior of Jesus' disciples gives rise to a new controversy! The actors in this scene are Jesus himself, the Pharisees and their scribes. The communities of the Pharisees, which were real schools of perfection, included laymen from every level of the population. The scribes imposed on them rules of purity that the law reserved for priests, in this way favoring the holiness of the whole of the chosen people.

This gives us an insight into the indifference of Jesus' disciples, who, because of their Galilean origin, were hardly alert to the ancient tradition, namely that these zealous men might well find their behavior shocking. So Jesus decided to criticize the scribes for having so often forgotten the purely human origin of their laws, which therefore could not have an imperative character. And what was even more serious, this ritual practice frequently turned attention away from the Decalogue itself. This was the case with the *corban,* which consisted in giving one's fortune to the temple treasure. Some men took advantage of this to escape from the more fundamental laws of filial piety. In his reply to the scribes, Jesus' interpretation of the Mosaic law is much more radical.

■

God was sick. He was sick because he could not find a counterpart, a being who could respond to his offer of love.

We have made God a completely satisfied being of sovereign independence. This is because we think of dependence as being an imperfection. So we have made God a solitary and perfectly autonomous being. We think of relationship as revealing contingency. Yet, from the very first page of the Bible, we are in contact with a God who is impatiently looking for an opposite, someone to talk to. We like to imagine that God is impassive. Being without desires is being in a state of perfect equilibrium. But the God of the Bible is not like that. From the very beginning of the history of salvation, we find a God who identifies himself with his feelings. God is Love and Love is asking, appealing, poverty. God is infinitely poor and he is always asking, because he is longing. Because he is Word, God cannot live if he has not found someone who can become word for him and opposite him. God calls the one who responds to him in this way a being made in his own image and likeness.

Man does not exist for himself. He exists for God. We are created as God's "opposites." We were not made in the first place to love God, but so that God could love us and invite us to enter into this sharing which is a gratuitous exchange that is as without reason as the expression of joy reflected in two people's eyes, meeting and recognizing each other in the astonishment of the discovery.

We may imagine that we are looking for God, but that is not the case. He is looking for us. From the first day of the universe, we have been sought by someone. . . .

Sought by someone . . . . If you have met and longed for someone, if only for a moment, you will know what I mean when I call to mind the lover looking for the loved one with a passion that gives meaning to his life. He only lives for the one he loves. He only thinks of that person. He only exists in reference to the other's thoughts, experiences and life as a whole. Being sought by someone—that is the great happiness of the one who is loved.

From the beginning, we have been sought by God. Impatiently and passionately. Yes, we are the fruit of God's passion. A philosopher who was an atheist once wrote, very truthfully: "God also has his hell—man." God has always known the hell of lovers, because he has need of man.

"Let us make man in our own image, in the likeness of ourselves."

God gave the best of himself in that act of creation, like a lover giving everything. The greatness of that act is beyond the power of our imagination. We are everything for God and God has given us everything. God modelled us on his own image and, when Adam left his hands, they were trembling with love, and Adam had the face that God had loved from eternity, that of his only Son. Adam was already called Jesus.

God was able to look at what he had made and recognize himself in that beautiful work. "Indeed it was very good." Those are the words of astonishment with which the act of creation closes. And, as Paul Claudel wrote in his *Le Soulier de satin*, God added the first words of tenderness whispered to the man he loved so passionately: "The force with which I love you is no different from that by which you exist."

■

God, Father and Creator,
   blessed be your name.
   You have made us in your own image
   and fashioned us in your likeness.
We already have those glorious names:
   beloved sons,
   men born of a loving word.
May nothing disfigure our original beauty,
   but let it open and expand

without spot or wrinkle
in the eternal resurrection.

CHILDREN WITH DIRTY HANDS

Genesis 2:4b–9, 15–17. The author of the first chapter of Genesis was a learned priest, but the author of the second chapter, the so-called Yahwist, was clearly a man who was close to the earth. The priestly author makes a contrast between an organized universe and primitive chaos. The Yahwist contrasts the desert with the kind of park that only kings possessed in ancient society. His universe is a world that is close to man and forms the framework of his daily existence. It contains the garden from which he derives his subsistence, the familiar and the harmful animals and his beloved wife. From the very beginning, then, the Yahwist makes a close connection between man and the earth on which he lives. This vital link is expressed in his creation story in a play on words: *adam* (man) and *adamah* (earth). J. Steinmann has therefore called the man of the Yahwistic tradition "the one of the earth who has come out of the soil."

But, even though the earth produces the vegetables and the animals, it cannot give life to man. It can only give him an inert body, which can only become alive when God breathes his breath into it. Man's life comes directly from God. As X. Leon-Dufour has observed, "man is not only a stable composition of body and soul; he is also a being hanging on God by his breath, by his spirit." It is a very meaningful suggestion that man can only live authentically if he breathes with the same rhythm as God himself and similarly that, after having sinned, in other words, after having been cut off from the breath of life, he can only be saved by the Holy Spirit. There is, moreover, only one word in Hebrew —*ruah*—to describe both man's breath and God's.

Who is man? Where does he come from? Where is he going? The Yahwist tries to find an answer to these fundamental questions that have always been asked by men. This is also the case with regard to the work that has always formed part of man's destiny. The Yahwist says that the garden was planted by God, who gave man the task of cultivating and keeping it. In other words, man is called to service.

Psalm 104: See Monday of the fifth week.

Mark 7:14–23. To understand the part played by the discussion in Mark about the traditions concerning clean and unclean, it should be borne in mind that the "section on the loaves" refers to the admission of pagans to Christ's table. What is recorded in this passage was, in fact, one of the fundamental problems of the early Church. The question can be formulated thus: Did the dietary laws, to which the first Christians, who were originally Jews, believed themselves to be still subject, preclude them from commensality with converted pagans? The first Christian communities question Jesus through the medium of Mark, and Jesus gives his reply here before entering pagan territory.

His thinking is close to that of the Old Testament, with its emphasis on the goodness of God's creation. All foods are clean, he says. "Nothing that goes into a man from outside can make him unclean; it is the things that come out of a man that make him unclean." This is a parable. Finally, this repeal of the dietary prohibitions can also be explained by the coming of the kingdom and its victory over Satan.

■

"Keep yourselves clean!" That is the call made by the Gospel. But how is it possible to preserve the heart of a child, when the adult world is so hard, unjust, intolerant and evil? To be faithful to our vocation and to remain clean and pure, do we have to leave the world and wash our hands of all the inevitable compromises we have to make with it? Did not Jesus pray that his disciples should not be "of the world" when his own hour was approaching? Is it possible to share a meal with other men without losing that evangelical purity that Jesus compared with that of a dove? Surely, anyone who works at a task will inevitably get dirty hands!

"The Lord God took the man and settled him in the garden to cultivate it and take care of it." From the very first days of the existence of the universe, the world has been entrusted to man. The world is our affair and man has the task of naming the beings and things in it. The world is human and we only know a humanized earth, marked by the imprint of man. The Bible goes counter to all those tendencies that are wrongly spiritual and try to keep man in a hothouse, protected from the impurity of the world, and has always opted for the heart. "Happy are the pure in heart, they shall see God!" Happy is the man who is at the heart of the world to make the Good News incarnate in it! "They are in the world . . . but they are not of the world."

Religion does not consist in washing our hands. Uncleanness begins to stick to our skin as soon as we claim to have washed our hands of all that and try to preserve ourselves and look for God in some aseptic place of refuge. From the very beginning, God has always taken us by the hand and led us into the garden so that we should cultivate it and take care of it. He has given us charge of the earth. He has gone even further than this—in Christ, he himself became an inhabitant of the earth. In Christ, he sat at table with sinners and people like everyone else, and the bread that he shared with them was that of every day. And if we are preoccupied with our dirty hands, we should raise our eyes up to Christ on the cross and look at his hands. They are split open and dripping with blood, the hands of a man whom everyone treated as a criminal. Then let us look up to his eyes and try to see the world as he sees it. Let us contemplate our fellow-men in their wretchedness and learn to believe in them again. "Happy are the pure in heart, they shall see God!" For it is only when we seize hold of the wretchedness and suffering of the world and when our heart becomes a heart of mercy like God's heart that we shall really see God.

God has not for a single moment washed his hands of our wretchedness and suffering. That is why he is perfectly clean and pure and absolute holiness. When we take our place at the table of his Son, God does not ask us for any other kind of holiness than this. He welcomes to that table children who have dirty hands and heavy hearts because they have loved and have been responsible for the world.

THURSDAY OF THE 5TH WEEK

THE LOVE SACRAMENT

Genesis 2:18–25. The planting of vegetables in the garden, the creation of the animals and the making of woman—the Yahwist thanks God for the benevolence with which he has always surrounded man. He also tries to answer the question: What is the explanation for the attraction of the sexes? The author of the Song of Songs asked where it had come from, that love that is stronger than death (Sg 8:6) and stronger than the parental bond. Where does it come from, that mutual attachment, that attraction that knows no respite until it is made incarnate in one flesh, that of the child (von Rad)? It comes from the fact that, in the beginning, the man and the woman were only one flesh, from the fact that God took the woman from the man.

For the Yahwist, man was essentially a social being. He describes his loneliness as a lack, a form of distress. So, in his kindness, God was concerned to provide a helpmate for man, a presence of the same nature as himself. He began by fashioning the animals and bringing them to man, who gave each of them a name. This act of naming was in itself important. By naming the animals and thus determining their function, man not only established his dominance over the animal world, but also organized the space in which he was living. In the Bible, the naming of the animals corresponds to the birth of the way of speaking that names things and gives them their own form.

But man had still not found his opposite. So God made him fall into a "mysterious sleep," so that he could not see his glory, but could only observe the effects of it in creation when he awoke. He took one of the man's ribs and transformed it into the woman.[2] The man's heart leapt with joy, he looked at the woman, his companion, and said to her: "You!"

Psalm 128 is regarded as a song of ascents, but is in fact a psalm of congratulation, a kind of memorandum for the temple priests whose task was to welcome the pilgrims.

Mark 7:24–30. No sooner has Jesus done away with the frontiers between Jews and pagans than he goes to the Lebanese territory of Tyre, a district with a population that was to a great extent pagan. The serious-minded doctors of the Law called it a district of dogs.

At once a woman approaches him asking him to restore her daughter to full life. But Jesus, who has just multiplied the bread of life for five thousand Jews, challenges the woman by at first refusing to perform the miracle for her. "The children should be fed first," he says, "because it is not fair to take the children's food and throw it to the house-dogs." "That need not stand in the way," she replies promptly enough, "The dogs have their place under the table and have to put up with eating the scraps." Because of these words, her daughter is healed. The pagans have cause for rejoicing—the kingdom of God is also for them!

■

A couple—man does not exist for himself alone. He cannot manage on his own. In order to live, he needs an opposite. Created in the image and likeness of God, man cannot live alone. Love is grafted into him and he can only become himself in encounter and relationship. Because he is born of God, he is sharing. For eternity, Adam will bear the scar of his lack, his impossible self-sufficiency. He is not in himself a complete being. And Eve, born from Adam's side, becomes the living symbol of this inalienable complementarity.

Mystery of the man who needs another in order to become himself, who has to share in order to find himself and give in order to become.

Mystery of the man who needs another who says "You!" to him so that he can exist as "I." Mystery of the man who discovers himself in the other's eyes, in her way of looking at him. Mystery of man who learns about the world and its things and beings through a way of speaking received from others. Mystery of man who is society. For ever, Adam will bear the mark that he only exists with others, through them and for them. Man will not be alone. Woman will be with him. The one towards the other. The human being is a conjugal being.

And from that time, the couple becomes the sacrament of God. As a closed monad, the human being is not in the image and likeness of God, because a God in a single person is not Love. Theophilus of Antioch observed in the second century that "God created Adam and Eve for the greatest love between them, thus reflecting the mystery of the divine unity." And for eternity, God will bear in his body the mark of his passion for man: the pierced side of Jesus on the cross.

Mystery of God who is infinitely wounded. Mystery of God whose perfection is linked with the most total self-abandonment, whose power is synonymous with the greatest dependence. God is Love and Love is encounter and therefore lack and prayer. To exist, God needs man and, to exist as Love, God has to be Trinity.

Greatness of the couple. Together, they become the sacrament of God. "What God has united, man must not divide," Jesus replied to those who were putting him to the test. Marriage is a sacrament, not just because it is based on mutual tenderness, but because it is the most perfect image of what God is and of what life is according to God. In the relationship between a man and a woman, we discover and experience God as encounter, giving, sharing and love.

■

God of tenderness, be blessed!
In the love of a man for his wife
you reveal the mystery of your love!
Consecrate our encounters and bless our loving,
that they may let us experience
 what has always made you live
 and will make you live for ever.

SINNERS?

Genesis 3:1–8. Why are man, love and evil so closely linked? The Yahwist situates sin not in man's nature, but in his history, where man experiences his freedom. He also emphasizes the solidarity of all human beings in their fault. An animal like those we meet in La Fontaine's fables, a talkative woman and a weak man—these are the actors in the drama of the fall. God has just taken the world out of chaos and man plunges it back into it.

The animal is cunning. To begin with, it urges the woman to champion God's cause. "Did God really say you were not to eat the fruit of any of the trees in the garden?" But God never commanded that. He simply forbade them to eat the fruit of the tree of the knowledge of good and evil (= of all knowledge). The serpent's words are also voluntarily ambiguous: "On the day you eat it, . . . you will be like *elohim*—like divine beings—knowing good and evil." But surely it was precisely to that knowledge that man was called in being created in the "image and likeness of God"? Clearly, then, it is a question of knowing how one is authentically that image and likeness. Is it by stealing fire from heaven like the pagan Prometheus or is it by becoming "obedient to death" like Christ? Becoming gods—is that not suppressing God and, in so doing, destroying man as a created being? The legend of the jealous gods is as old as mankind itself, but the Yahwist reinterprets it here in his own way. He rids it of its mythical coloring and gives it a psychological interpretation. He confronts Eve with the image of a God who is jealous of his prerogatives and his rank, in other words, with the man's rival.

Eve is led astray, because the fruit is tasty, good to look at and "desirable for the knowledge that it could give." Covetousness of the flesh and the eyes and proud confidence in the possession of a good (see 1 Jn 2:16)! Overcome, the woman leads the man astray. Their first innocence is violated at the deepest level of their being. Their eyes are opened and they know that they are naked.

Psalm 32 is a song of thanksgiving. It contains words of welcome addressed by the priest to the faithful who have come to the temple to give thanks to God. In counterpoint to the reading, we also thank God for Christ our savior.

Mark 7:31–37. A miracle story of the kind that existed in great numbers at the time. We should note Jesus' discretion in operating beyond the sight of the crowds, as though he wanted to emphasize the transcendent nature of the event, his physical contact with the deaf man and his recourse to the medicinal properties of saliva and finally his sigh, indicating the power of resistance that had to be overcome. Mark describes the miracle as a pagan author would have described it.

It is also this pagan context which gives the event its deep meaning. The exorcism of the little Canaanite girl shows that Jesus was ready to heal the pagans of their fundamental impurity. The healing of this deaf man with a speech impediment completes the work begun with that exorcism. Set free from demons, the pagans are able to hear God's word and bless him. Like the Jews, they can benefit from what had been proclaimed by Isaiah: "The ears of the deaf shall be unsealed . . . and the tongues of the dumb shall sing for joy." In Jesus, a new mankind rises up and the crowd cries out in admiration: "He has done all things well!"

■

"They hid from the Lord God." That is the drama of man; he cannot bear the other to look at him, because he feels judged and condemned, because he knows that a fault is introduced into his life.

Original sin—Adam's sin. Original sin because every man is marked by it in his origins and it expresses the rupture that tears us all apart. Adam's sin. In Hebrew, "Adam" means "man." Adam's sin, then, is our condition as sinful men.

The sin known as "original" stares us in the face everywhere. It underlies all our institutions. It makes governments, states, the police, the judiciary system, our structures of checks and balances, our armed forces and our weapons necessary. It has taught us to count, to weigh and to measure. It has made us develop our understanding, our intelligence and our imagination. It has caused the blood of millions of people to flow. It has consumed the most precious of our resources. Countless professions have only one basic function—to go counter to it. It is so much a part of our everyday lives that we are hardly aware of it any more. It lives in us and changes as we change. Yet, although it appears in an infinite number of forms, it is still the same basic phenomenon—the same act performed by Eve when she seized hold of the apple, an act of selfishness and appropriation, the opposite of love. Sin is fundamentally connected with knowledge, but that knowledge is knowledge of oneself. It is choosing oneself, asserting oneself over others and to their detriment, looking for one's own being. There is nothing more natural than sin, but then our faith teaches us that we are not destined for the natural life.

The man and the woman tried to hide. They could not endure others to look at them and within a very short time they were no longer able to endure themselves and each other. "It was the woman you put with me;

she gave me the fruit," the man says and the woman: "The serpent tempted me. . . ." Each one of us has received his or her life from others, has existed because of and thanks to others, but sin means that everyone lives for him or herself and against others, who are competitors or objects to be exploited or manipulated.

"The eyes of both of them were opened and they realized that they were naked." They hid and discovered their distress. But are we condemned to lament our wretched state for ever? No! Lift up your eyes and look! A man has risen up and is travelling through the land of darkness and approaching his brothers, men who have become blind. "Ephphata—be opened!" Jesus looks up to heaven and sighs. He performs creative acts with the man who is imprisoned within himself, like those performed by God on man's first morning, when he gave man his breath and fashioned him with his hands. But what he does can only become saving acts through the sigh, the cry and the closed eyes of the crucified Lord. God's communion with man is very costly. God does not, however, close his eyes to the price that has to be paid. He does not draw a veil across his face. He takes our mediocrity on himself and raises it up to himself. Sin will never be the last word about our life. Where sin abounded, grace superabounded!

■

God our Savior, be praised!
You do not abandon us
   to the power of darkness.
You do not let evil imprison us.
You do not allow the evil one to blind us.

Your Son, born of our flesh,
   rises up on our behalf.
He takes us out of the power of the evil one
   and raises us up to live a new life.
He says: "Ephphata!"
   and our ears are opened.
He listens
   and our tongues are loosened to praise you.
He stretches out his hand
   and we are healed.

How much we admire your works,
Lord God, master of life!
How blessed was the fault
that merited such a Redeemer!

Our tongues are loosened to sing your praise
  and to proclaim the magnificence of your mercy.

COMPASSION

Genesis 3:9–24. Man's fault has put the whole cosmos deeply out of joint. Human relationships have been seriously impaired. This is clear from the fact that the man and the woman become aware of their nakedness and the gradual loss of solidarity between them. The man not only betrays and denounces the woman, he even goes so far as to criticize God for having given her to him. God himself is very nearly put on trial! The relationship between God and man is also spoilt, distrust and fear replacing the original familiarity. Man's fault has become his sin.

In reporting God's judgment, the Yahwist is clearly trying to find an answer to a number of important questions about evil, suffering and painful work. The condemnation of the serpent is more than simply an attempt to explain its physical structure. In drawing attention to the hostility between the reptile and man, it points to a more profound evil which is directed towards man and lies in wait for him. Man, then, is engaged in a desperate struggle with the forces of evil that will not be brought to a conclusion until both adversaries are dead. The condemnation of the man and the woman also goes to the root of the being of the two partners—to the woman's state as wife and mother and to the man's need to work. The earth that has begotten man has become hostile to him. The fellah toils in his field and the bedouin lives a nomadic life on mediocre soil.

The Yahwist even goes so far here as to make a pessimistic point. His reference to the prohibition to eat the fruit of the tree of knowledge is a criticism of civilization. The knowledge that man has stolen seems to him to be a knowledge against God, as though perfect happiness could not be combined with universal knowledge. And he describes life not only as an endless struggle against evil, but also as an experience ending in the dust and the darkness of Sheol.

He does, however, allow a glimmer of hope to appear in the woman's name. "Eve" is the "mother of the living" and the name of a goddess. It is also a profession of faith in the life transmitted by mothers, even if it is darkened from now onwards by the shadow of death. Perhaps God has not yet said his last word?

Psalm 90 was used as a public act of supplication. It not only recalls the past, but also provides an assurance for the future. It is also essentially a long exposition of human frailty.

Mark 8:1–10. The literal translation of the opening words of this passage is: "In those days" and they have an eschatological flavor that goes together with the signs of the kingdom. Mark has already provided one account of a miracle of the loaves, in which the twelve tribes of Israel had returned to the desert to be fed with bread that was infinitely superior to manna (chapter 6). In his second account, which is in accordance with the context, pagans are called to the eucharistic table. Jesus' words, which reveal his concern for those who "have come a great distance," indicate that they are not Jewish. It has been suggested that they contain an allusion to the "Gibeonites," who had "come from a distant country . . . very far away" to make a covenant with the God of Israel and his people (Josh 9:6,9). The seven basketsful of the second account (8:8), placed in parallel with the twelve basketsful of the first account (6:43), are also very significant. Did the Twelve Hebrews not give way to the Seven Hellenists, handing over to them the task of serving at table (see Acts 6:1–7)?

■

Jesus comes back from a mission in pagan territory. The people follow him and he has compassion on them: "I feel sorry for all these people."

There are so many people who do not come into our churches to taste the bread that we share there. Countless people in the world who are hungry, but who do not find in our faith any real support in their struggle. Men and women who belong to a world that is seeking and who are discouraged by our subtle claim to possess the truth. Men and women unable to escape from the closed circle of production, and who should be invited to share in the adventure of a hope that is worthy of man. An immense crowd of people, the best and the worst rubbing shoulders with each other, in an unrestrained movement towards power and the weakness to go round in circles. Jesus has compassion on them.

Poor people, wandering a great distance from the paradise of their dreams, having to produce their bread by the sweat of their brows and tear their existence out of the hard, unyielding soil. Poor people, badly treated, torn apart, accusing each other of causing the evil that they should confront together, and each one taking everything he can for himself and putting his own interest first. Jesus has compassion on them.

Salvation begins as soon as each man has compassion on his brothers, in other words, when he begins to re-establish community among others, when he discovers that he is one of them and becomes responsible for their future. Compassion is connivance, communion and passion.

Compassion is our vocation. It is not just a romantic feeling that makes those who are already wretched even more wretched. It is not a condescending concern for others that lowers their status and self-esteem rather than raises it. It is, on the contrary, based on a clear and active conviction that we all share the same history and are taking part in the same adventure, and on our experience of being bound together for better or for worse in the same process of development.

How can we celebrate the Eucharist without discovering each day new paths that we can, as the Church, take in order to go out and meet the world and share the bread with it? How can we proclaim the good news of our salvation, the Gospel, without making it incarnate in concern for our brothers, the poor of the world?

"They have been with me for three days now," Jesus said, "and have nothing to eat." Three days—as long as his own death in the tomb! Three days which sum up all our expectations as men, all our hard work on a soil that only becomes ours by dint of suffering and tears, reversals and fresh beginnings. But on the third day they will all eat their fill and Christ, the new Adam, will rise from the tomb. On that day, angels, at the entrance of the open tomb, will proclaim the good news instead of standing with flashing swords to prevent us from entering the garden of Genesis. That third day will begin with a word that is the other word of salvation and resurrection: compassion.

■

God of every genesis,
Father of all life,
  for our happiness
  you have once again opened
  the gates of the garden.
In your Son, our Savior,
  we have access to new life.
Since he has taken us out of the power of death,
let us, by our hard work,
  build up a more hospitable earth
and may our suffering stimulate our longing
  to establish a more just and caring world.

■

It is good to praise you, God our Father,
  Lord of heaven and earth,
for Jesus, your Servant,
  the Son whom you have given to us.

Because he made a perfect offering of his life
  and gave himself to the poor and rejected,
  he has justified a multitude of men.
Because he turned to the condemned
  to let them enter paradise with him,
  he can revive our hope.

That is why, together with all those
  who have recognized the power of your love,
we praise you, God most holy,
  who have, from the beginning, reserved in your kingdom
  a place for the poor.
With all those who you have confirmed by your grace,
  we bless you.

FROM MONDAY TO SATURDAY

OF THE 6TH WEEK

A Breach
A gradual deterioration in the relationship between man and God is described
in the biblical history of man's origins. At the same time, God's infinite and
unchanging patience is also emphasized. He lets man have a glimpse of a new
and better future and a possible conversion. Adam is driven out of paradise,
but he is given the promise that the serpent's head will be crushed. Cain is
protected from implacable revenge by a mysterious mark. A rainbow in
heaven is the promise of peace between men and nature, between men and
other men and between men and God.

In the history of mankind, the effects of evil are also present. Man's rejection
of love has enormous repercussions. Men treat their fellows with contempt and
indifference or dominate each other. At the same time, however, God is
tenacious in the appeals he makes to men and persists in showing mercy. He

does not leave them imprisoned in hatred and lies. He does not simply accept man's distress and the situation of evil. He goes out to meet man. He speaks to him. He invites him again and again to be saved.

Two currents run through man's history. The first is the current of distress, born of evil and guilt. The second is that of hope, rooted in a promise. At the level of faith, however, we know that the second is the right stream. Hope is a porthole that has been made in the ark in which we have sought refuge. A new world can be glimpsed in the rising sun and the dove that expresses peace flies towards it. A breach has been opened in our history and no person or thing will ever be able to close it again.

■

God, Father of men,
  it is good for us to give you thanks
  and to praise your name.
On the first morning of the universe,
  you marvelled at the work of your hands:
  it was very good.
  You had done your work very well.
And you will never be able to forget
  that cry of astonishment and tenderness.
You will never be able to abandon your creature,
  despite his sin
  and the many times he has just gone astray.
For ever and ever you are faithful, God.

Our desert seems to us to be uninhabitable,
  but your grace fills it with a word of life.
A bow of hope and light crosses our heaven
  and our journey will take us to the promised land.
A dove will bring us an olive branch,
  the pledge of peace.
We bless you, Father,
  for Jesus, the sign that you raise up in our lives,
  the sacrament of salvation
  and the covenant needing no renewal.

God of eternal tenderness,
  we want to thank you for Jesus, our Savior.
In him you have concluded with mankind
  the covenant of your first love.
Through him you have renewed a communion
  that nothing can ever break.

You took him to the desert where men live
   and consecrated him there through your Spirit
   so that our earth would be made holy by your love.

Father, we bless you.
It is so that we might be
   the messengers of life and unity
   on this earth of death and division
that your Son left us a memory of himself.
Baptized in the death and resurrection of the Savior,
   we have been consecrated for a new life.

We pray that your Church,
   the new ark of your presence in the world,
   may experience in faith
   the mystery of its union with Christ.
Make it happy in its faithfulness to that unique love
   under the leadership of those responsible for it.
Let us be the living signs of the new times
   that you never cease to prepare for our earth.
Let us also work to strengthen the covenant
   that you want to make with all men
   in your beloved Son, our Redeemer.

MONDAY OF THE 6TH WEEK

AN AMBIVALENT HISTORY

Genesis 4:1–15, 25. Two men, but two different altars. Abel is a shepherd, Cain tills the soil. Abel offers the first-born of his flock to God, his brother offers the produce of the soil. It is a difficult text, combining different traditions. To begin with, one is inclined to believe that what we have here is a conflict between two different kinds of civilization, Abel the just man representing the pastoral, nomadic way of life, while Cain is the ancestor of the settled people. But, as the story proceeds, the nomadic life is presented as a banishment. It is therefore probable that this tradition comes from an environment of settled Israelites who regarded the possession of the earth as a blessing, whereas the nomadic way of life was seen as a curse. Cain also appears as the ancestor of the Kenites, a tribe of desert marauders who were, however, marked by tattooing as worshippers of Yahweh.

Structural analysis of this text has shown, perhaps more clearly than anything else, its motivating forces, but it is still important to bear in mind the bonds that link the story of Cain to that of Adam. On the one hand, although Adam is driven from the soil that he has contributed to make "accursed" (3:17), Cain is himself accursed and driven from the soil (4:11), his curse coming from the soil itself. On the other hand, although both protagonists find themselves at the east of the garden of Eden (3:24; 4:16), Adam finds himself there as a punishment, whereas Cain settles there, provided with the mark put on him by Yahweh. He even builds a town there (4:17). Is this perhaps the light shining after the darkness of night?

In addition, although Adam disappears at the beginning of the story, Eve seems to retain an essential place in it throughout. When she cries out: "I have acquired a man with the help of Yahweh," she is acknowledging explicitly the blessing that Yahweh heaps on her again by giving her a son. (Is she not, after all, the "mother of the living"?) It is this blessing that provides the key to the whole story.

Cain begs for this blessing when he offers Yahweh the first-fruits of his harvest, but it is Abel who in fact receives it. He seems to lose it altogether after murdering his brother. The ground, which has drunk Abel's blood, can no longer feed the murderer, who is "driven from the ground" and has to "hide" from Yahweh. He has committed fratricide and has therefore to be a "fugitive and a wanderer over the earth," permanently bearing the heavy weight of his punishment. But God still has the last word and, far from abandoning Cain, he places him under his protection. On that day, the blessing that he received in his youth (as the first-born) is recognized.

Psalm 50 is presented as an indictment pronounced by Yahweh against his people, who have broken the covenant. It hands down traditions that are associated with the sanctuary at Shechem.

Mark 8:11–13. Even after the sign of the loaves, the Pharisees are not satisfied, but call for another. They belong clearly to the generation of whom the prophets said, "They have eyes that do not see." They are the living image of the generation in the desert, because they put God's patience severely to the test. There will in fact be only one sign: that of the resurrection.

■

The Bible is not a pious book provided for the edification of sensitive souls. The history that it narrates is not exemplary, serving as a model for souls on the way to perfection. It does not offer a purely spiritual religion to souls with mystical longings. It is a book that bears the scars of a history that is totally, even ridiculously human. It is fashioned out of human blood and stupidity, hope and unhappiness, faithfulness and heroism, meanness and pettiness, greatness and positive impulses. The sacred history that the Bible communicates to us is the ordinary history of everyday experience. That everyday history, of course, is composed of struggles and conflict, massacres and death, war and peace, discoveries and attempts to find freedom. Sacred history is the history of man taking place in a completely human way and following the rules of human history.

Yet the history that is presented in the Bible is still a sacred history. This is because the word of God himself forms part of the warp and weft of the human history of the Bible with its uncertainties and its failures, its tentative approaches and its successes, its conquests and its settlements. God's word is not added to the history of man. It is not superimposed on it or fixed to the outside of it. It is totally interwoven into the fabric of it. The only place where God can reveal himself is in the hesitations of man's history.

So the sacred history of the Bible is completely human and completely divine. It is a history of blood that becomes a history of the promise. God cannot abandon man to the curse that he has begotten and so he marks Cain with his protective sign. He can only speak through the history of men, which is so often dramatic and marked with evil, but he continues to carry out his plan and to work for men's happiness. However dark human history may be, it is and always will be marked by the covenant that God has concluded and is always ready to renew with his often rebellious people. He will never grow tired of offering us new opportunities to make his promise become a reality. Our history is not poised hesitantly between two equal values. We are not swinging between a blessing and a curse. No, whatever happens, God has given us his grace. We have an ambivalent history, but it has succeeded—for men's happiness and for God's happiness.

■

God our Father, you do not abandon us
*   to our failures and our misery,*
*   to our conflicts and our sin.*
You mark us with the seal of your Spirit,
*   you make a covenant with us that nothing can break.*
Through your grace
may we experience that covenant in truth
*   and may we discover the love*
*   with which you love us*
*   and live as brothers with one another.*

GOD REGRETTED . . .

Genesis 6:5-8; 7:1-5,10. To judge by the abundant literature produced by the civilizations that inhabited the Mesopotamian plain in ancient times, it would seem that there were floods of such catastrophic proportions in the Near East that they left an indelible mark on the minds of the people. But, from those ancient times to the period of the biblical story of the flood, the theme changed. The flood was no longer an expression of the caprice of the gods wakened from their sleep by the noise of men. It was the result of God's judgment of men because of the enormity of their sin.

God was dismayed by men's sinfulness. Only those who are influenced by Cartesian thinking are troubled by the anthropomorphism of the Bible. In depicting God, the biblical authors certainly wanted to stress his absolute nature, but they also gave equal importance to his liveliness. They never thought of Yahweh as cold and distant. For them, he was a God who was very close to men. The Yahwist is, however, also anxious to stress the obedience of Noah, whom he presents as building his quite extraordinary boat without knowing anything about God's intentions and only learning about them when he goes aboard the ark. Noah's faith is emphasized in the story; he "finds favor with Yahweh" as a righteous man in his generation who "walks with God" (see also Heb 11:7).

It is also worth noting that some of the animals have a lower value because they are "unclean." This classification is the result of the struggle for the purification of Israel's faith and the cult of Yahweh. The animals regarded as unclean were highly valued in pagan cultic practice.

Psalm 29 is composed of different parts that were originally independent. It is possible to distinguish a central theophanic poem celebrating Yahweh's coming in the storm and several hymnic elements.

Mark 8:14-21. After the miracle of the loaves, there is anxiety about food! The disciples get into the boat with Jesus, but forget to take bread with them. Jesus puts them on their guard against the yeast of the Pharisees and of Herod.

In the rabbis' language, "yeast" was regarded as a source of impurity (See 1 Cor 5:6-7) and symbolized man's evil propensities. Jesus is critical of the bad attitudes that the Pharisees had towards him in their refusal to believe in him and of Herod's equally inflexible attitude.

Jesus is in fact giving his disciples a serious warning here. They are acting no differently from and are just as obstinate as his opponents. In this case, they are anxious about bread. What short memories they have! Have they already forgotten how he broke and shared five loaves among five thousand people and many pieces were left over? They have not yet understood that the bread broken and shared was the bread of life! When will they recognize the greatness of the mission with which he wants them to be associated?

■

A flood that sweeps over the earth and the animals that have emerged from the primordial chaos with man on the days of creation—that is how our story begins. "God saw that the wickedness of man was great on the earth and that the thoughts of his heart fashioned nothing but wickedness all day long." There is nothing new under heaven! Men go on tearing each other to pieces while professing the same ideology. Husbands and wives make life impossible for one another. Friends again and again betray each other. One-third of humanity is dying from overeating while the other two-thirds dies because it is starved of justice and bread. The litany is endless. It can never include the full list of human evil.

"God regretted having made man on the earth." For forty days the waters of death swallowed up the last breath of life. It was a return to the desert! Man, created to cultivate the beauty of the world, found himself submerged by the dark forces of discord, selfishness, fear and death, forces that he had not been able to overcome. The world returned to chaos and the waters covered the earth. Because of man, who had destroyed life, the earth once again became a desert in which men behaved like wolves. A parched land in which no one cared for his fellow-men, a land burnt by the fire of intense rivalry between men. It is not surprising that "God regretted having made man on the earth"! He had wanted a world that was a sacrament of his tenderness and his covenant, a good and beautiful world that could be inhabited by man. He had been ecstatic about the work of his hands, but very soon the earth had become disfigured. It was no more than a very distorted image of God's dream.

Yes, it is hardly surprising that "God regretted having made man on the earth"! The violent and murderous spiral of sin had drawn, and is still drawing, the history of men into greater and deeper chaos. But does that sin always have the last word? "God said to Noah: 'Go aboard the ark, you and all your household.'" God cannot let his covenant go adrift! Love is stronger than justice!

Our history is a wretched history of men who are marked by desolation, despair, barrenness and deep wounds. We have good reason to lose heart! But, "Go aboard the ark!" Our history is also marked by a word of promise and a pledge of the future. Because of that word and that pledge, our wretched human history is able to become a history of salvation and rebirth. The promise and the covenant run through the times of distress as a manifestation of God's will. And that will is that we should be saved and live.

■

God, the Father of men,
you do not regret having created us.
  We count for more in your sight
  than our wretchedness
  and the sin of the earth.
We give you thanks for your promise
  and for the future you offer us!
Blessed are you, Creator of the ages!

WEDNESDAY OF THE 6TH WEEK

AT THE END OF FORTY DAYS

Genesis 8:6–13, 20–22. At the end of forty days, those on board the ark once more had contact with the outside world. The black raven came back with an empty beak, but the white dove brought back a branch of fresh olive. Seven days later, Noah left the ark and built an alter to Yahweh.

The reconciliation between God and men was sealed in this way. The new covenant was, however, not unrealistic. The shadowy side was not overlooked. Although man recognized the need for expiation, his heart still remained evil. But God had agreed to resume the dialogue with him. He offered him a word of grace and forgiveness, a word that was made incarnate in the definitive return to the stability of natural rhythms.

We noted the prominent part played by the animals earlier in the story. It is also worth considering the creatures that are prominent at this stage. The raven and the dove do not disappear from man's memory. The raven was regarded as unclean (Lev 11:15) and continued to be the symbol of perversity and lies. The dove, on the other hand, continued to express purity and holiness. This symbolism seems also to have been used in the synoptic accounts of Jesus' baptism, where a dove manifests the presence of the Spirit.

Psalm 116 is a psalm of thanksgiving.

Mark 8:22–26. This time Jesus performs a cure in stages. He begins by putting saliva on the eyes of the sick man—human saliva was highly valued for its curative qualities—and lays his hands first on him, then on his eyes.

But, if we see nothing but a miracle of physical healing in this story, then we are blind! The text has a further meaning. Within the context in which it is placed in Mark, it draws attention to Jesus' attempts to open the minds of his disciples. After having criticized them for having eyes, but not seeing the signs of the kingdom, he heals them and opens their hearts to his light. This story is followed by Peter's confessing the faith of the group.

■

God regretted having made the earth. For forty days the waters of death had swallowed up the slightest breath of life. Back to the desert! Left to itself, the world had returned to the original chaos. The waters had covered the earth, submerging every trace of life. But God is aware of man's complicity with death, and never gives death the right to do its work without making sure that there is a springtime, a resurrection, somewhere! "At the end of forty days," Noah was able to open the porthole of the ark and send out the dove, to discover dry land—land that was renewed and recreated.

Forty days . . . . The children of Israel wandered in the desert for forty days before discovering the land that God had promised them. They spent forty days walking in desolation before possessing the sign of the covenant. Jesus, too, retired into the desert for forty days before beginning his public ministry—forty days of prayer and intimacy with the Father in order to discover himself as the bearer of good news and the pledge of a new covenant. The dove also descended on Jesus to prove that God would sign what he would say and do. Forty days . . . . It had been valueless for the waters to be unleashed, for life was already arising once more, roused by God's smile. Another seven days, the time it took God to create and would take him to recreate the face of the earth, and the dove would bring back the olive branch, the sign of the reconciliation that God wanted.

Forty days for the new reality and salvation, liberation and fertility to appear! Forty days of giving birth to new life for, after all, that is what was happening; man's sin and distress are not the last words in his history. The flood let man inherit an earth that had been renewed by God's grace. That is where our faith originates—in that promise which, going beyond or rather through our sin, runs through our personal and our collective history. I know that there are representations, symbols and institutions in the Christian tradition which seem to prove that those who think that the religious attitude originates in the most characteristic forms of guilt, either conscious or unconscious are right. But I also know that the best of what I experience today comes from a completely different source. Our life, its most unquestionable appeals and the most worthwhile responsibilities that it calls on us to accept, are not the result of a feeling of guilt that directs our actions like a disconcerting ambivalence, an obsessive fatality or a restraining captivity. No, what runs through my life, and all our lives, is a word that bears witness to the fact that the promise is there, beyond the desert, and indeed that, even in the desert, that promise is already present. Within the order of faith, we try—sometimes without surety and sometimes succeeding in belief—to live our life as a response to the personal word that is calling us, and not as an impatient reaction to an anonymous intimation that accuses us. Within the order of faith, even if it is very often a desert existence, our life is lived in the light of a covenant which is certainly an appeal and a vocation, but which is even more grace and liberation. For, at the end of forty days, the porthole can be opened to let the dove of peace go out.

■

God, promise and life of every living thing,
you created us so that we might live.
Do not let us be submerged by fatality
or go round despairingly in circles.
Open our hearts to the power of your word
and let it be the peace of our souls
and the strength of our hope.

READING AND UNDERSTANDING MARK (8:27-9:13)

So far, Mark has repeatedly warned his readers not to come too quickly to a conclusion about Jesus' person, in this way emphasizing his transcendence. When Jesus commands those whom he has healed to be silent or calls on the people to go as it were into retreat in the desert, it is clear that God, dwelling in man's heart, can only be grasped in solitude and prayer.

With this section of his Gospel, however, a corner of the veil is lifted. For the first time, Peter gives Jesus the messianic title of Christ and the Father vouchsafes for his beloved Son. Jesus, however, hastens to add to this that, as the Son of man, he is also destined to suffer. From this time on, the order to preserve silence is even more strictly imposed.

The author has edited this section of the Gospel with great care.[3] In it, the end part of chapter 8 forms a kind of pivot. On each side of this central part (8:34–9:1), in which the meaning of human life is clearly outlined, he places one tablet of a kind of diptych with very pronounced parallel pictures. First there is a dialogue between Jesus and his disciples about Elijah (8:27–28 par. 9:11–13). This is followed by a declaration made in the first place by Peter, and in the second place by the heavenly voice, about Jesus (8:29–30 par. 9:7–10). Finally, there is Jesus' teaching, first in words and then in actions (the transfiguration), both followed by Peter's reaction (8:31–33 par. 9:2–6).

THURSDAY OF THE 6TH WEEK

THE BOW APPEARED IN THE CLOUDS

Genesis 9:1–13. Increasing sin on earth had led to disorder but, not only for the Yahwist, but also for the author of the priestly document, the important aspect is that God makes a word of grace heard in the world. Despite the disorganization introduced by violence and despite the destruction caused by the flood, order is maintained in the cosmos. But relationships between God's creatures are changed. The commandment to procreate is repeated and man's position as lord over the animals is once again stressed, but the need to kill is also recognized and the human community is given the right to avenge murder. God's sovereign rights, however, remain absolute. Life, and especially the life of man, who is created in God's image, belongs to him.

A sign is given and a covenant is concluded between God and Noah. The impossibility of a return to primordial chaos is written into creation itself. God shows the world that he has hung up his warrior's bow. He bears no ill-will towards man, "The time of God's patience began with the time of Noah" (von Rad)—God's patience because he was about to undertake his historic work of salvation not in an ideal world, but in a world disfigured by sin.

In today's liturgy, we have only the end part of *Psalm 102*, which is a poem of supplication. There is first a reference to God's protection of Zion. This is followed by the text of the favorable oracle given in the sanctuary and a promise to celebrate Yahweh with praise.

Mark 8:27–33. Caesarea Philippi . . . . This was to be a solemn confession of faith and the site is chosen with care. The Jordan has its source here. The Jews also believed that the dwelling-place of the dead was situated here. It was therefore a place for a struggle—a life and death struggle.

At Caesarea, the disciples are confronted with Jesus. The healing of the blind man has had its effect, and in Jesus Peter recognizes the Christ. The majority of the people, on the other hand, had only come to know part of the truth, seeing Jesus as a prophet. But Elijah and John the Baptist belong to the past, whereas Jesus comes from the future. For his disciples, he roughly lifts the veil and tells them: "The Son of Man is destined to suffer grievously. . . ." Jesus knows that that is his mission. He will not enter into the glory of the kingdom until he has experienced suffering.

Peter indignantly rejects this suggestion. His profession of faith is quite authentic, but it is far from complete. What does he know, after all, about the Messiah? His ideas are the same as everyone else's! And he wants to impose those ideas on Jesus. So, immediately after confessing that Jesus is the Christ, he leaves his disciple's place and walks in front of Jesus. Jesus has to put him back in his proper place: "Get behind me, Satan!" Peter's faith has to become deeper. He has to learn that it is not enough to say something true about Jesus to express the full truth. He has, in other words, to wait for the resurrection. Then he will be able to grasp Jesus' person and his message. Then he will be able to bear true witness.

■

The flood is past and the experience ends with a new promise. A "bow in the clouds" is to be the sign of a possible peace and agreement between men and nature, men and their fellow-men and men and God.

That bow in the clouds spells out in letters of many colors the word *shalom*—"peace."

A man has appeared in the history of men. "Who do people say I am?" He was submerged in the waters, like so many other poor men whom John the Baptist had called to receive a baptism of conversion on the banks of the Jordan. He was enthroned as the Messiah, a man according to God, when the dove of peace descended on him. And, in that hostile and desolate place, the desert of Judea, as dry and committed to death as a heart condemned to die, a new harmony came about: Jesus living with the wild animals. The desert became a new paradise where Adam named the things and animals he found there. A man living in harmony with his environment. A rediscovered peace between man and his earth, where he had wandered as a stranger—in the desert, Jesus was at home.

It is also a rediscovered peace between man and God. "You are my Son, the Beloved," God had said, making the bow of peace span the sky. Chaos, brought about by man's failure, had given way to a rediscovered peace and to the initial beauty of creation.

Our life is a fabric woven of the good and bad fortune of human history. Our earth belongs to us, but we behave as strangers in it. We do not really belong to one another and the mysteries of the world always escape us, however successfully we analyse its secrets. It is an earth that bears the scars of so many human failures and so much discord, death and barrenness. Floods of fire, war, injustice, fatalism, discouragement, wickedness . . . . But in the disordered sky the sign of God's covenant still appears—a name: Jesus; a hope: "You are the Christ"; a faith, which expresses the longing of so many men and women whose lives are sustained by the astonishing news that, as soon as the veil concealing the identity of the Son is lifted, the difficult way of his fulfilment, the way of the cross, is also revealed. The Church's word is a delicate olive branch among the many mutually contradictory voices naming salvation almost at random, and the love that it tries to express is as risky as the word that it gives us as a promise: *shalom.*

"Who do people say I am?" We have only a few stammered and hesitant words to guide us on our way: "You are the beloved Son of the Father, our Savior and our God." But, because God has made the rainbow of Easter appear over our lives, both men and the earth are reborn like a sacrifice with the good savor of life, gentleness, peace, forgiveness and love. A morning sacrifice praising the God of the covenant.

■

God of the covenant,
in faithfulness to your promises,
let the sign of your tenderness
     —the good news of our salvation—
     rise over us.

By the passion of your Son,
     who sets us free from all fear,
     take us to the morning of the eternal Easter.
Then we shall be able to offer you
     the sacrifice of praise,
     the song of all ages.

■

You keep your word, God,
  blessed be your name!
Your Spirit lets us hear
  the good news of your salvation.
You want to share your love
  and conclude a covenant with us.
Let us conform to what you expect of us
  and live in communion with you and our fellow-men.

READING AND UNDERSTANDING MARK (8:31–10:31)

The hour of decision has sounded. At the same time that he reveals his painful destiny to his disciples, Jesus invites them to take up their cross and follow him. The Word that has been heard in Galilee and beyond, forming a community of faith around the Master, is now calling on that same community to experience the serious fact of its close adherence to concrete human existence. The question that has been put to the disciples continues to play a decisive part. It has been asked again and again in various ways, all expressing an invitation to examine the mystery of the Messiah, from the beginning of the Gospel onwards. Now it throws light on the way to be followed by those who have decided to follow him to the end.

This new section of the Gospel is paraenetic. Its rhythm is marked by three prophecies of the passion, taking the reader from Caesarea Philippi to Jerusalem but, from the very beginning, the healing of the epileptic indicates the direction of the journey. This is a healing in fact both of the father and of the child. Both are raised up by the transfigured Christ and set on the way of life (9:14–29).

Having set out on the way of life, however, the first action required of a person is astonishing both in its simplicity and in its depth. In other words, in Christian terminology, he has to agree to lose his life, to receive it from another. He has to "welcome the kingdom of God" as a gift, as grace, "like a little child" (10:13–16). Molded into the pattern of Christ, he will regard his life as a service for the good of all and will consequently renounce whatever he needs to renounce (9:30–50). It is only then that a man and woman will be able to understand that they are called to love one another as only God can love (10:1–10). It is only then, too, that the fascination of riches will reveal to man his fundamental inability to save himself unaided (10:17–27). If only he

---

would trust God and welcome the hundredfold reward promised to those who have followed him without looking back (10:28–31)!

UNITY IS STRENGTH!

Genesis 11:1–9. "Throughout the earth men spoke the same language, with the same vocabulary." This statement expresses one of mankind's oldest dreams, a longing for toleration and mutual understanding. But the migrations of peoples have more often resulted in war than in peace, and all great civilizations have carried within themselves the seeds of their own destruction. There is a titanic element in the story of the tower of Babel. This time all the Adams of the earth rise up against God.

In Assyrian, the word *babal* means "to confuse." In the popular mind, the word was seen as a possible way of explaining the name of the proud city of Babylon, with its powerful influence. The tower of Babel thus became the labyrinth of the nations.

Now, however, the peoples have become scattered and their languages confused. An even wider gulf has opened between man and God. Once again, the powers of chaos have been victorious and the cosmic order is threatened. What kind of relationship will there be from now on between Yahweh and rebellious mankind? So far, each time that man has moved away from God, grace has abounded. Despite the fall, Adam continued to live, Cain was protected against his crime and Noah had the blessing of a new covenant. But now—will the catastrophe be final? This time, no promise is given. Yet, with Abraham, human history will recover again. In him, God finds among the confused mass of the nations a man after his own heart.

Psalm 33 lists various themes in the praise of God and especially his choice of Israel, after having eliminated the nation's enemies.

Mark 8:34–9:1. "He called the people to him. . . ." Jesus' teaching is becoming more and more emphatic. He is in fact defining in public the meaning of human life. Among the crowd there are possible followers of Jesus and it is important for them to know what conditions they have to fulfil in order to be disciples.

Mark has situated these words of Jesus at the very center of his Gospel. This indicates that he regarded them as fundamental. What is at stake is nothing less than man's salvation. Jesus presents himself as the measure of human existence. Whoever is for him will be saved, but "anyone who wants to save his life will lose it."

The full significance of the Easter event is clearly contained in this statement about saving and losing one's life. Losing one's life is consciously entrusting it to God, believing that Jesus has the power to save it and that he is the only source of salvation. Losing one's life for Jesus and the Gospel is recognizing him as the Son of man; in other words, as the eschatological judge who protects the community of believers. Jesus only calls volunteers. Deciding to follow him is therefore a free choice made with full knowledge of what is at stake.

But the disciple is not above the master. He is also "available" for martyrdom. It is important, then, that he should know that he will not taste death before the visible manifestation of the kingdom. Some authors have seen in the concluding words of this section a reference to Jesus' certainty of the imminence of the eschatological hour and have gone so far as to suggest that some disciples would not experience the suffering involved in the passion. Mark saw this as a promise of salvation made to those who would follow Jesus carrying their crosses. They would not experience eternal death.

■

We ought to be scandalized by the story of the tower of Babel! Surely God the Creator of mankind could accept that the men he had created would work together to regulate their own lives and control their own destinies, to build something that would last and to set up structures in society to make the world a place fit to live in? Did he have to come down from his eternal dwelling-place to make tribal dialects and divisive languages come about, so that, every time one crossed a river or a mountain or an abstract demarcation line, one encountered a new vocabulary? Did God have to intervene in the affairs of men so that they no longer understood and agreed with each other?

I shall be told, of course, that the same Lord God put everything right again on the day of Pentecost—several hundreds of thousands of years later. But that was for only one day, when each one heard the good news "in his own language." It was not even for a whole day—it was only for one morning in springtime. Did God perhaps make this division among men in order to govern them better?

Man was created to share. In himself, he is solidarity and communion. God made him man and woman, the Bible tells us. Man is the call of the other, who is like him and equal to him, and at the same time he is also the call of the other, the longing of God. As soon as the first men had no reason for remaining united other than pride, the urge to take God's place, then they behaved like wolves towards each other. Each man for himself and God for all of us! Man, created to share and to be in communion with his fellow-men, became imprisoned in himself. Looking for complete autonomy and independence, he put up barriers which separated him from others, cut him off from God and destroyed himself. We have become incapable of "corresponding" with God, other people and ourselves.

"Corresponding" in the widest sense means speaking, holding a dialogue and finding in the other person someone who will listen, understand and agree, finding solidarity with him. "Corresponding" is finding the equivalent relationship without which a destructurization takes place and we dissolve and break into fragments. It is finding that relationship without which we cease to exist, without which freedom becomes licence and flight forward, without which the human will no longer has any objective and without which the human heart itself ceases to beat. "Corresponding" certainly means being dependent, but it is only in sharing and communion that man can find himself. Unity is strength!

■

You call us, Lord,
  so that we may follow your Son
  on the way of the kingdom.
We ask you:
let us learn from him
and let the Spirit make us breathe your life.

■

God of unceasing journeys,
  we bless you!
Your Son followed the way of the cross
  to rouse us to life.
He took the bread of death
  to become our Bread of life.
May thanks be given to you,
who have given us the viaticum.
The road will not be too hard
that leads to the ages to come.

EXAMPLE

Hebrews 11:1–7. Conscious of the many vexations that Christians were suffering because of their faith, the author of the Epistle to the Hebrews exhorts them to persevere. The guarantee of faith is the faithfulness of the living God. The first pages of the Old Testament have preserved the memory of men whose faith was not found lacking.

Abel, the just man, continues to live in men's memory. If his sacrifice was more pleasing to God than his brother's, was that not because his faith was deeper? It was also faith that enabled Enoch to become intimate with God. Indeed, no one can approach God or share in the good things of heaven without faith. Finally, the author mentions Noah, who built the ark without even knowing anything of God's intentions. His attitude of faith was in striking contrast to the unbelieving attitude of his contemporaries.

Psalm 145 is another hymn, but it has an alphabetic structure and its composition is more individual.

Mark 9:2–13. Peter, James and John—these three disciples witnessed the resurrection of Jairus' daughter and later they will be with Jesus in Gethsemane. Agony and resurrection, death and life—these are the two aspects of the same mystery. Before entering into life, the Son of man has to "suffer grievously and be treated with contempt."

Once again, Peter intervenes. He suggests that they should make three tents. His plan can be explained by the fact that the transfiguration takes place during the Feast of Tabernacles. The building of these tents or huts, in which the Jews lived for the eight days of the feast, was one of the essential rites of the liturgy. They called to mind the Hebrews' sojourn in the desert before their entry into the Promised Land and the feast in this way anticipated the coming of the kingdom of God.

But has that kingdom not already arrived? What does Jesus' "metamorphosis" really mean? What do the white garments mean? And the presence of the privileged witnesses of the covenant? Is God finally about to visit his people? Peter thinks so, and he wants to stop the course of history by offering three tents as resting places.

But be less hasty, Peter! Listen to the voice that comes from elsewhere. What has Jesus just said to you? He is "destined to suffer grievously, to be rejected by the elders and the chief priests and the scribes and to be put to death and after three days to rise again." So do not be in such a hurry, Peter—the resurrection will come after suffering. Be intelligent! You have had a momentary glimpse of the glory of the Son of man. Now you must come down to earth and carry on in the darkness of faith. In a little while, Jesus will offer up his life for the salvation of mankind.

But the scribes taught that Elijah had to come first for a ministry of reconciliation (Mal 3:24). The tradition spoke of peace, but Jesus goes against this teaching, or rather he changes its premises. He is able to obtain peace for his disciples, but that is because he had previously consented to carry his cross. Was John the Baptist not like Elijah and, as the precursor whom no one ever confused with the prophet, did he not bear witness to Jesus at Machaerus?

■

The principle of imitation is possibly one of the only principles that distinguishes man from animals. Animals do not imitate; they copy or "ape" what they are shown. To become fully himself, man needs models and examples, and both psychologists and sociologists recognize that one of the greatest dramas of the modern age is caused by the lack of witnesses with whom we can identify ourselves. We cannot live without roots, and we can only fashion our own history by learning from others and from those who have gone before us about the values on which we can model our own development. We are always inheritors.

We are born into a home that is our cradle. We have learned from our fathers in faith the stories on which our commitment is founded, and also the actions which are the signs and the sacraments of the covenant into which we have entered. In that home, the Church, we have learned to speak the words and to perform the actions of our faith. And in exploring all its nooks and corners, we have let ourselves be introduced to its memories. And that is why we are able to live.

For the home where we were born is also a school and we have learned to grow up in it. The growth of our life as believers presupposes that we should find some nourishment for ourselves in that house and that we should also learn how to walk, to speak and to take up our place. Our home, the Church, is a place of education and advancement. It enables us to stand up.

The principle of imitation is an apprenticeship in freedom and innovation. We imitate in order to become ourselves. We choose models in order to exist. We learn about our past in order to set up our future. That is the distinctive aspect of man—he invents, discovers and goes towards what is to be. Imitation does not turn us back towards a past that is closed and completed for ever. On the contrary, it establishes a future that is to become a reality. And we recall our holy history and appeal to Noah, Abraham, Jesus and so many others with the aim of initiating ourselves into a history of the present that has, by the grace of God, become holy.

■

Lord our God:
Jesus transfigured—
  we see the beauty of your plan
  revealed for a moment.
The bread shared—
  it is the broken body of your Son,
  the pledge of our communion with you.
With our eyes still full of light, we ask you:
let us come down again to the plain.
It is there that our journey has to be made—
the journey that ends in eternity.

FROM MONDAY OF THE 7TH WEEK
TO SATURDAY OF THE 9TH WEEK

Taking on the Form of Christ

Jesus' and his disciples' journey takes them in the direction of Jerusalem, the city that kills the prophets. The drama is tightening. The kingdom is being brought about. Easter is already at work in this journey to Jerusalem.

"Follow me"—that is now, as it always will be, the disciples' vocation.

According to Paul, being a Christian was in one's mind "being the same as Christ Jesus," modelling oneself on him, imitating him and assuming his shape. It is possible to dissociate the doctrines of Plato from the philosopher's life, or the system of Karl Marx from his death, but, in the case of Jesus of Nazareth, his teaching forms such a close unity with his destiny, his life and death, that no system of general and abstract ideas can fully reproduce its content. Jesus' person, his teaching, and his life and work while he was on this earth coincide so completely that believing in the good news that he proclaimed is believing in him. This applies to Jesus even more after his entry into life and his being confirmed by God.

The "teaching" contained in the New Testament, then, cannot be dissociated from the person of Jesus himself. This means that believing in the Gospel is having the same attitude as Jesus Christ. For Christians, Jesus is undoubtedly the Master, but at the same time he is also much more than that. He is himself the personification of what he proclaims. We must therefore "in our minds be the same as Christ Jesus" because there is, in the strict sense of the word, only one Christian—Jesus himself.

The living Christ does not ask us to do no more than simply adore him, nor does he even call us to a mystical union with him or to a servile form of imitation. No, it is a question of taking on the form of Christ, of making our lives conform to his. What we have to do is to root our lives in an attitude, a pattern of behavior and an orientation, all of which are directed towards those of Jesus. We have to accept a completely new conception of life, a different scale of values. We do not simply have to carry out a program, a law or a "Christian" ideal. We have to place our trust in Christ Jesus and let the Spirit mold us into the form of our only Master. Jesus is not simply an example of a man living the life of the kingdom of God. He is that kingdom in its fulfilment.

Jesus went on the way to Jerusalem and took his disciples with him on his journey towards Easter, like a trainer leading his team towards a new life-style that conformed to the ideal that was his aim. He was, in other words, begetting Christians.

∎

In our search for your kingdom, Father,
it is good for us to contemplate your Son,
who, like you, is the richness of life.
All that is yours is also his
and all that he gives us of himself
brings us closer to you.
Father, when we call to mind that hour
when your Son was stripped of everything,
we proclaim that he became our inheritance
and that he fills us to overflowing with life.

Because you have chosen us to become your children,
we ask you to give us your Spirit to overflowing.
May that Spirit, the power that dispossesses us,
lead us away from our corrupted wealth
and, as the Spirit of youth that renews us,
destroy the old man still lying dormant in us,
clean our faces marked with the stains of our abilities.
Clothe us again in your mercy
and make us throw away our garments of sin.

May your Church be seized by the love of Christ
and live with its whole being stretched,
so that it may know the pearl of great value
that it has to reveal to all men.
May it, at the table of love,
discover your tenderness, Jesus our Lord.

Blessed are you, Father—
you restore us to our original beauty
and purify us of everything that disfigures your work.
Let us, we pray you, Lord,
always be astonished by your grace.

MONDAY OF THE 7TH WEEK

REMAKING MAN

Sirach 1:1–10. Jesus Ben Sirach, the author of this book, was not only a high-ranking official in Jerusalem, but also a man of letters and a teacher who lived in the second-century B.C. Aware of the developments that had taken place in ideas, he attempted to renew the long tradition formed by the masters of Hebrew wisdom (see the Introduction, 25th week of even years) that he had inherited.

In his introduction, he tries to define wisdom in his own very characteristic way. Rather than limit himself to a precise concept of wisdom, he juxtaposes a number of statements to delineate the totality of the phenomenon insofar as it can be experienced by man. In the first place, he says, wisdom is something that remains close to God. In other words, it is divine wisdom itself and is absolutely impenetrable (vv. 1–3). From verse 10 onwards, however, he deals only with human wisdom, as a kind of charism that is given by God to those whom he loves.

What, then, is the wisdom of which he speaks in verses 4–9? In these verses, Ben Sirach is describing a reality which has already been considered by his predecessors. The wise men of Israel had always regarded the world with good will, believing that a kind of complicity existed between it and man. As a result, they thought that the discovery of rules governing the world or of a relationship existing between man and creation enabled man to find his position in it. These rules and this harmonious relationship were, in their opinion and in that of Ben Sirach, the work of God and they constituted the wisdom that Yahweh had judiciously distributed among his creatures. This wisdom of which the author speaks in verses 4–9 contributes towards the primordial order of the world and "inheriting her is sweeter than the honeycomb" (Sir 24:20).

Allied to the canticles of Zion, *Psalm 93* was first used for the enthronement ceremonies of Yahweh in the sanctuary at Shiloh at the time of the occupation of the Promised Land and later in Jerusalem, after David had made himself master of the country.

Mark 9:14–29. The first prophecy of the passion ends with the story of the healing of the epileptic child. Several changes have been made in the text, but these have neither succeeded in suppressing the description of the boy's illness, nor have they destroyed the unity of the pericope, which is centered on the final action of Jesus—his taking the boy's hand to help him to stand up (literally to "wake him up"). This act obviously calls to mind both the healing of Simon's mother-in-law and the resurrection of Jairus' daughter, and draws attention to the power that Jesus has to bring dead people to life. Mark was aware of this and therefore stresses the corpse-like aspect of the child during the exorcism: "most of them said 'He is dead.' "

It is, then, indisputably resurrection that is at the center of this incident and, what is more, Jesus' own resurrection. This is borne out by the context. Not only has Jesus just announced his own suffering, death and resurrection, he has also been "transfigured" in the presence of three of his disciples. Mark even notes that, when they saw Jesus coming down from Mount Tabor, the people were "struck with amazement," using the same word that he uses to describe the reaction of the women on the morning of Easter.

This crowd plays an important part in this story. Unlike the resurrection of Jairus' daughter, the healing of the epileptic takes place in public. It is therefore for the crowd like a proclamation of the future resurrection. So, just as Jesus proclaims publicly to the crowd that it is necessary to carry one's cross, immediately after announcing his passion to the disciples alone, he also tells the people about the certainty of his triumph over sickness and death after having confined his transfiguration to a handful of witnesses chosen in advance.

Another theme, which is more catechetical in character, is also present in this passage. It has to do with the need for prayer. After the exorcism, the disciples ask Jesus why they failed to heal the boy. Jesus tells them that demons of a kind that could only be driven out by prayer and fasting were involved. In other words, this exorcism called for complete abandonment to divine providence. Finally, emphasis is also placed on the part played by faith. The unbelieving generation consists not only of the crowd and the disciples, but also of the father of the epileptic child, with the result that Jesus only carries out the healing after his profession of faith. The father also asks Jesus to strengthen his faith. "Everything is possible," Jesus insists, "for anyone who has faith."

■

Man is sick. Possessed by powers that empty him of his true self, he no longer belongs to himself. He is no longer in possession of himself. He is a slave whose freedom is in fetters, a wretched being avoided by those like him, an idiot at the mercy of forces more powerful than himself. He is no longer a man. "How long has he been sick?" Jesus asks the father, who replies: "Since childhood."

Yes, from the first days of the world, we have been sick. Almost since the beginning of our history, we have not really belonged to ourselves. Our freedom is held captive by so many constraints that cause us to fail and so many base characteristics that rob us of our honor. Our will is harmed by so much despair that causes us to suffer, and our hearts are so blemished by shameful faults that it is difficult for us to find love in them. We are sick and no longer truly in possession of ourselves.

Jesus questioned the unclean spirit closely, we are told. The word that is God's challenge! God puts back into man his own spirit by breathing his grace into him. Man becomes a new creation. He is given back to himself and to those to whom he belongs. He is at peace, reconciled and saved.

Jesus questions closely. The only task that the Church has is to proclaim in season and out of season the good news of man's restoration to his original dignity. Today, a new wise man such as Bernard-Henri Levy can write, for example: "No, we do not bear men's dreams in our arms because we know they are empty and we know how lacking in strength we are. But the demand is still made and we shall make it our task to take up the most senseless and insane of wagers—to change man into something much deeper." Today, in Mark's story, God gives us a sign that this change into something much deeper—and is that not what we call salvation?—is not "the most senseless and insane of wagers." And God himself takes up that wager! And we are that sign when, under the guidance of the Holy Spirit, we form the Church of Jesus Christ.

Like all men and women, we are alienated and subject to the law of the "unclean spirit." But we can take the risk and dare to stand up and question closely the power that is holding us captive. And it is in that wager which we dare to take up when we confess that God is our Savior, and it is in that risk which we dare to take when we work for true liberation, that we will bear witness to God's readiness to hold men's dreams in his arms and to make those dreams reality.

■

Our freedom is in fetters
and we do what we do not want to do—
speak your word of life over us
set us free and have mercy on us.

Our will is shackled
by our passions and desires—
speak your word of life over us,
set us free and have mercy on us.

Our lives no longer belong to us—
speak your word of life over us,
set us free and have mercy on us.

■

God, our Savior,
you created us for freedom and life
and not for us to be enslaved
by forces that destroy us.

Show us the power of your breath!
May the Holy Spirit reshape our earth
and your will be made manifest:
that we should stand upright
in the truth of our being
now and every day of our lives.

TUESDAY OF THE 7TH WEEK

THE TIME OF THE CHILD KINGS

Sirach 2:1–11. Is suffering in any way meaningful? What is its origin? Such questions were bound to arise in the writings of the masters of wisdom. Their knowledge had, after all, an empirical foundation and the experiences that they had which pointed in different ways troubled their minds.

The function that they attributed to suffering was the result of their own special status as wise men. Were they not above all teachers? This led them quite naturally to think that suffering had an educative effect on man, making him grow. They believed that it was often caused by an inner disorder in man, but that persistence in it put an end to that disorder and restored man to communion with God.

Above all, however, man had to continue to trust in God, because that would turn him towards the future, take him out of himself and enable him to see the finality of things rather than their appearances. Trust in God was in this way also able set free great powers of perseverance.

The alphabetical structure of *Psalm 37* expresses the intention of the psalmist, which is to praise the righteous man for having obeyed every one of the Lord's commandments—for having obeyed them, in other words, from A to Z.

Mark 9:30–37. Galilee, Caperrnaum and house—all these words have a special resonance in Mark's Gospel. After the transfiguration, Jesus went through Galilee, just as he was to do after his resurrection, stopping at Capernaum, as he did during the first days of his ministry, and entering a house—the place, in other words, reserved for his teaching of his disciples. There, for the second time, he proclaimed his passion. According to the mysterious plan of the Father, the Son of Man, whose glory the disciples have now seen, is to be "delivered into the hands of men," who will do what they want to him.

The disciples did not dare to question Jesus—they were too preoccupied with an argument about precedences! "If anyone wants to be the first," Jesus tells the Twelve, the men who have been called to found the Church, "he must make himself last of all and servant of all." Then he calls a child to him and says: "Anyone who welcomes one of these little children in my name, welcomes me." Today, then, is the day of the child king but, in the ancient world, this did not arouse much interest. Jesus—and with him God—identifies himself with all those who are rejected by society. He identifies himself with children, the poor and sinners. In this way, he overturns generally accepted values, causing a peaceful but very deep revolution. The last will be the first!

■

Jesus is already on the way of the cross. He takes his disciples through Galilee, but secretly. The time is past when he went through the towns and villages scattering the word of God to the winds. The time for sowing seed is also past and the harvest will take place elsewhere. The enthusiastic welcome by the crowds and the exuberant happiness caused by the rather insane proclamations—these also lie behind him. Everything seems to be lost now and the Master makes somber suggestions: "The Son of Man will be delivered into the hands of men."

The disciples are dumbfounded. They had, after all, hoped that he was the one who would deliver Israel! If he is not, then an urgent decision has to be made. Who is to be the leader of the movement? Prognostications begin to circulate. If Peter had been rejected, then surely one of the others could try his luck! "Which one of us will be the first?" is the question in everyone's mind. But they have a great deal to learn. They have still to experience the complete newness of Jesus' word: "If anyone wants to be first, he must make himself last of all."

At Capernaum, Jesus, who has experienced the fervor of the crowds and the enthusiasm of initial success, once again speaks, but this time not in public, but "in the house" and, as usual, in parables. He takes a child and sets him on his feet in the midst of his disciples. Here is, he suggests, the prince of the kingdom. The mustard seed is the smallest of the seeds in the garden, but it will become a great tree where the birds will make their nests. The kingdom is not revealed to "the learned and the clever," but to "mere children," to those who can discover the secrets of growth. Adults, and those who claim to be grown up, are concerned with everything and with nothing. Their hair becomes grey with the urgent attempts they make to calculate the why and wherefore of things, their use and their profit. Children, on the other hand, love the flowers that open today and are withered by the wind tomorrow. The kingdom, whose prince is a child, can never be founded on calculation and cleverness. It can only be founded on grace and astonishment. What Jesus is saying is: When you have done everything, tell yourselves that you have been useless servants.

Only the child is grown up and this is because someone else has set him on his feet. Adults always claim to be able to manage their affairs on their own. The kingdom, whose prince is a child, belongs to those who are like children. The only ones who will enter that kingdom are those who are audacious and whose behavior is not affected. How happy are those whose hearts are simple! They shall become God's friends. The only ones who will have a place in the kingdom of God are those who, like children, will never cease knocking on the door that has not yet been opened to them. How happy are those who are as persistent as children! God will not be able to resist them. How happy are those who, like children, are bold enough to take hold of the hand of the one whom they trust to lead them! They will become citizens of the kingdom of God. And how happy are those who abandon themselves totally to God's mercy! They will be taken far beyond the point that they hoped to reach.

The child is there, as a sign of the life that is beginning now, in the midst of the disciples, who are reasoning like adults and arguing about shreds of power. The grown man, who claims to occupy the first place, has no future ahead of him, but the child has a great future and has to welcome it. The fabric of the kingdom is made of such hope and life.

"If anyone wants to be first, he must make himself last of all and servant of all." Adults build their shoddy little kingdoms on power and misuse, violence and exploitation. The Gospel founds the kingdom of which it speaks on powerless and defenceless children. Jesus upsets the order of walking. We have to walk behind him like children following their leader. Being last is not being lower in command. It is the sign of the person who relies on the one who seeks out the way. It is a way of walking.

"Anyone who welcomes one of these little children," Jesus says, "welcomes me." So do not let the child in you be suffocated by the adult who is always threatening your life! Let him rise up in you! Jesus will always be such a child and his kingdom is only open to those who are like children.

■

God our Father,
  let us express the longing
  that draws us towards you.
  Let us praise the power of your Word!
It penetrates our silence
  and we can give you, Father,
  the response that your Son inspires in us.

Let us be permeated by your will!
We shall then recognize the authority of your Word
  and bless you for the life that he manifests.
He is in the midst of us
  as the one whom you have sent—
  as the face that is always new with your love
  and the mystery that we have glimpsed for a moment.

Blessed is the man
  who is at one with the good news!
Blessed is the man
  who is steeped in the grace of your revelation!
God, who makes you close to him,
  strengthen your Church—
  let it proclaim the Gospel today
  and make the grace of your presence incarnate.

Blessed are you, Lord God,
for the power of your Christ
    who dwells in us
    each time we become open to your word
and let your Spirit create in us
a people of children.

With all those
    who rely on your tenderness,
    we praise you, God our Father.

WEDNESDAY OF THE 7TH WEEK

A KINGDOM WITHOUT FRONTIERS

Sirach 4:11–19. According to Ben Sirach, the search for wisdom should be man's main preoccupation. Consequently, he exhorts his readers again and again to engage in this search. At the same time, however, wisdom is not exclusively the result of human effort, and Ben Sirach points out repeatedly that wisdom goes ahead of man on the way of life. She in fact takes the initiative and goes out to meet man on that way.

The masters of wisdom had frequently used the language of love to describe the relationship between man and wisdom. The Old Testament scholar G. von Rad has expressed this relationship very well. Something quite remarkable had happened, he claims, to the rational human mind that was open to a knowledge of the world. It had encountered an opposite and had even been overtaken by the voice of primordial order, wisdom, since that voice had already addressed itself to mankind. It had already set out to meet man and was already speaking of the good that human reason was looking for, but had never found. And because that mystery of the world had gone out to encounter man, that wisdom could and had to be loved by man. In its search, then, human reason finds the primordial order and that order, wisdom, speaks to man of the sovereign good. According to the book of Proverbs (8:35), "the man who finds me (= wisdom) . . . will win favor from Yahweh."

Psalm 119 expresses the psalmist's joy in obeying the law of the Lord. And is that law not true wisdom?

Mark 9:38–40. Jesus has just spoken about welcoming little children "in his name" and Mark takes advantage of this to report another episode in which demons are expelled in Jesus' name. This is a case, so common in the Bible, of using one word as a hook on which to hang two actions or two discourses which are otherwise not related to each other.

John believed that he had acted correctly in turning a strange exorcist away from the group of disciples, but Jesus, who did not want to confine his activity to any special group, even that of his own disciples, explicitly disagrees with John. He rejects all sectarianism and wants to widen the group to include all men of good will. "Anyone who is not against us is for us," he declares. Whatever believers may think, God's acts go far beyond the visible frontiers of the Church.

To judge by the number of statements Jesus made stressing the great value of service, the first disciples must have been sorely tempted to dominate others. But his disciples were and are called not to rule over others, but to serve them. Every disciple of Jesus is required to welcome all "little ones" as brothers, and in the same way he is also a little one who must allow himself to be welcomed by others, because he belongs to Christ.

■

All of us must at some time or other have heard the proud slogans proclaimed by those who claim to possess the truth. Some are good and others are bad. Some really do have the truth or an aspect of it, but others are enslaved to error. Some have a right to speak, while others should remain silent.

Those of you who are on the side of the pure must avoid contagion with the impure. You may purify and cauterize, but you must not listen to lying voices. Try to convince others, but know that you can learn nothing from those who have nothing to give you. If you tolerate error you are already accepting it and in league with it.

Throughout history, those who claim to possess the truth have always lived in an enclosed space and their ghettos always smell of mildew. They lock their doors and even board up their windows, because they can no longer endure the fresh air and sunlight.

There is pure truth and pure error, they claim. It is tempting to place these two irreconcilable opposites over and against each other and insist that there is an insuperable barrier separating them. But the reality is quite different. Men and women are made of flesh and heart, weakness and life, stiffness and flexibility. They look passionately for the truth of their lives and are at the same time also tolerant of lies and pretence. They go in search of a more human earth, but also like compromises that make no demands on them.

We do not live strictly in one country or in another. We live in a vaguely defined no-man's-land that separates two frontiers. With the disciple John, we also say: "We saw a man who was not one of us casting out devils in your name and because he was not one of us we tried to stop him." But Jesus' reply is: "Let both the weed and the wheat grow until the harvest. If you pull out the weed, you might pull up the wheat with it."

No one can claim to possess the Spirit. He blows wherever he pleases and you cannot tell where he comes from or where he is going. Those who are moved by this uncontrollable wind to act—the prophets and those who perform miracles—are not necessarily men who have been appointed as disciples. Thanks to God, the Spirit is not enclosed within the registers of our dusty sacristies. Saint Augustine wrote: "Non-Catholics are found inside the Catholic Church and Catholics can also be found outside the Catholic Church. Many of those who seem to be outside are inside and many of those who seem to be inside are outside."

No one can claim to possess the truth of God. The frontiers of the kingdom are not marked with signs and no one can be sure of being a citizen. Nor is there any way of becoming a naturalized citizen of that country, however seriously one respects and observes its customs and laws. No, the kingdom belongs to those who do violence to it, to those who, whether they know it or not, let themselves be possessed by some part of the Spirit of the Gospel. "No one who works a miracle in my name is likely to speak evil of me," Jesus said.

No one has ever really entered the kingdom apart from the Son, the only real believer. Until the day when he will be "all things to all men," we shall always be travellers in search of the land of our inheritance. Both the history of mankind and that of each individual will always be a risky adventure of coming close to a truth that will not be fully revealed to all of us until that day. We have always wanted to erect barriers and mark frontiers and territories. We have always needed clearly defined evidence and certainties. But in the case of the kingdom, we have to follow risky and unknown paths that have to be sought out and discovered. The only grace that we are given as believers is this: We can be sure that the kingdom exists where it is being built. And that knowledge is a very great gift! And we can also be sure of our task: To bear witness to the kingdom.

■

May the Lord make his Gospel reverberate in us
and may the newness of its message
make us pray according to the Spirit.

Let us pray for the whole Church and its leaders,
for the members of all other churches,
for all those who are looking for God.

Let us pray that the Spirit of cooperation will increase
between men and nations.

Let us pray that our community may be welcoming
and open to all those who join it.

May our prayer, God, the Father of all the living,
*   be made truly in the name of Jesus*
and may it be open to every man
*   who holds out his hand to us.*
We ask this of you
*   through the one who will one day*
*   be "all things to all men."*

■

Lord Jesus,
*   send your Spirit to us.*
May he gather us together in your peace
*   to sing your praises*
*   and to welcome every day*
*   the first-fruits of your glory.*
May the peace that we share together
*   proclaim that grace*
*   now and for ever.*

THURSDAY OF THE 7TH WEEK

A TASTE FOR EXCESSIVE LANGUAGE
Sirach 5:1–8. Presumptuous people who put their trust in riches and blindly follow their passions, calmly following the way of sin while counting on God's mercy—they should watch out! In relying on God's goodness, they are forgetting his justice.

The wisdom to which the masters devoted their lives cannot be reduced to mere intellectual knowledge. It is a commitment to serve truth and ultimately life. The masters believed that, when a reality impressed itself on man, he should no longer be free to choose. This means that their statements are often value judgments to which men's lives should conform. Much of what the masters of wisdom say is therefore expressed in the form of exhortation and this is because they were afraid that their disciples would be neglectful. The wise man is confronted by the senseless, stupid man. Such a man is not unintelligent. He is simply unable to submit to the rules defined by wisdom.

The first reading for today recalls *Psalm 1,* in which the senseless man is contrasted with the wise man, who is congratulated.

Mark 9:41–50. This is a difficult text and has therefore to be approached systematically. The only logic that can be found here is, as in the preceding Marcan text, in the "hook" words used by the author to hang together apparently unrelated concepts.

After having spoken about welcoming little children, Jesus puts his disciples on their guard against possible scandals. The word "scandalize" is unfortunately translated as "cause to sin" in many versions, but it really means "cause to stumble." In the Bible, scandal does not point to a bad example or an outrageous fact, but a trap which causes people to trip and fall. Jesus was himself called an object of scandal, a stumbling-block, by his adversaries because he questioned them at the deepest level of their being and disturbed them.

The text speaks of the scandal caused to "these little ones who have faith." "These little ones" are the disciples, and more especially those who, in the community, are less well instructed or neglected. Causing them to fall is so serious that it "would be better to be thrown into the sea with a millstone round one's neck." Jesus' words are in no sense an appeal to conservatism. He is not forbidding innovations because it might be wrong to offend Christians entrenched in their habits. The opposite is also true—it is also wrong to scandalize those who would be upset by the absence of reforms.

This allusion to scandal makes it easier to compare these words of Jesus with his other statements about the source of scandals. That source is to be found in man's heart, and scandal only lays bare his inner attitudes and tendencies. When Jesus speaks of man's "hand" or his "foot," he is referring to man's temptation to dominate his brothers. When he speaks of man's "eye," he is alluding to the object of his desires. Jesus is therefore inviting his disciples to look honestly at certain aspects of their behavior. They are called to serve their fellow-men, but they more often dominate them. If they do not cut out the cause of scandal, they may find themselves in Gehenna—the public sewer of Jerusalem.

■

It is useless to sugarcoat the pill or to try to turn away the difficulty. It is no easy task, trying to reach the kingdom. It will only be entered by

those who can endure the violent language of the Word which cuts off and converts.

Cut off! Prune the vine! We have to learn the language of the vine-dresser who prunes his plant until the day that it bears fruit. The only way of converting an old plant is by this unreasonable love. If we cut off our hand or tear out our eye, it is not because we love mutilating ourselves, just as the vine-dresser does not love mutilating his vine. He knows that he has to sacrifice part of it so that the sap will be concentrated in the juice of the grape. If we prune, it is so that we shall bear better fruit. If we cut into our living flesh, it is to change our aging features into a new face. If we agree to pay the high price of the kingdom, it is because we know that it is worth selling everything that we have for the one pearl of great value. If, then, we mutilate ourselves in the eyes of the world, it is because we believe that God has already made a number of grafts in our aging bodies that will ensure that we shall live. And the Spirit bears witness to the fact that these grafts will take. They are the result of a love that is always young—the love of God —and every day they are new.

We have to stress the radical and mutilating nature of the Word of God today. At the same time, we also have to point to its aim; we have to pay the price if we are to enter the kingdom and thus enter life.

■

God, you fill the hungry with good things
and send the rich empty away.
Do not let us put our trust
in illusory riches.
Grant us your forgiveness
despite our attachment
to good things that pass away.
Tear us away from everything that diminishes us
and let us one day enter your kingdom.

■

There is no tearing away without pain,
but it is the pain of childbirth.
Purified from our false riches,
we are filled with the bread of your tenderness.
May thanks be given to you, Father,
for the word that recreates us—

that treasure is our happiness,
today and every day until eternity.

FRIDAY OF THE 7TH WEEK

THE RULE OF LOVE

Sirach 6:5-17. Ben Sirach prefers to deal with general themes. He writes, for example, about the attitudes his reader should have towards the poor, women and friends. Like his masters, he lays great stress on the virtue of prudence. The wise, in fact, preferred to play for time rather than to engage in ceaseless activity. They were well aware how difficult it was to form a true judgment of the reality. They knew not only that we can easily be deceived by appearances, but also that the reality itself is often ambiguous. Friendship may be a positive good, but it can also be disappointing. It is all a question of caution. Some circumstances are favorable, but others are less so. We therefore have to know when to speak and when to remain silent. This also applies to friendship. Only time can tell whether it will endure.

Psalm 119 is a long meditation on the law, expressing the joy experienced by the one whose friend at all times is the Lord.

Mark 10:1-12. Jesus leaves Galilee and goes up to Jerusalem. This change of place is extremely significant. From now on, all his teaching has to be understood in the light of his passion and resurrection.

The first teaching is the indissolubility of marriage. The Pharisees have approached Jesus to ask him whether a man is permitted, on the basis of Deuteronomy 24:1-4, to repudiate his wife. In his reply to this question, Jesus shows that the Deuteronomic text is only a concession and that the first law has not been abolished.

But it is important to note the reason given by Jesus: "It was because you were so unteachable." In the Old Testament, this "hardness of heart" pointed to Israel's unfaithfulness to Yahweh. What Jesus is stressing here, then, is that the Israelite has been unfaithful, both in his private life and in his socio-religious life. The individual has been unfaithful in respect to the marriage bond, just as the whole people has been unfaithful to Yahweh. Jesus is therefore forming a link between marriage and God's covenant with his people, and is in this way placing himself in the tradition of the prophets, who again and again pointed to the conjugal nature of the covenant. When he is engaged, then, in the task of inaugurating the kingdom and restoring the

127

covenant in its integrity, he recalls the indissoluble character of marriage, which therefore appears as an incarnation of that covenant.

Man is called to love, then, as only God can love. The law of marriage can only be understood in the perspective revealed by the kingdom; in other words, as a testimony given by God's faithfulness. If it calls on man to be heroic, this is because it is included within the perspective of the cross. But now man can be sure that the risen Christ is able to overcome the hardness of his heart.

■

Jesus is caught in a trap! "Is it against the law for a man to divorce his wife?" He will be accused either of betraying the demands made by the law or of contradicting his own preaching and his acts of mercy.

The Pharisees are anxious to discredit Jesus and to restrict him to a choice between what is permitted and what is forbidden. So he goes back to the origins of man. In the beginning, he points out, when God created man, he made them man and woman and he concludes: "What God has united, man must not divide."

Jesus does not argue. He is and wants to remain quite simple. If we keep to the law or to a regulation, then we shall lose the real thrust of our life. If we are to identify ourselves with God's aim for our lives, we have to recognize that love is more demanding than any law. If we are to know God's mind again, we have to go back to the beginning, when God in his tenderness drew man and woman out of the earth so that they would respond to his love.

For God, loving is in the first place speaking our language. For him, loving is keeping the only word that we are able to understand, the language of our flesh. Going back to our origins to find the rule of our life again is learning again that we have to speak the other's language.

For God, loving is making oneself vulnerable. It is also asking for favors. God has not remained in the heaven of his indifference. He does not simply give. He also needs to receive. Going back to our origins to find the rule of our life again means that we too must become vulnerable. If we are to love, we must long for, expect, ask and suffer.

For God, loving is also believing and hoping. God has not programed us. He has set us on our feet, made us free and creative. Finding the rule of our life again is learning again what hope is. Love is fertile. It rouses, resurrects, raises up, gives life and forgives. Love hopes and expects and looks forward to the other.

For God, loving is forgiving. Forgiving is much more than forgetting. It is continuing to love the other, even when he rejects us. It is continuing to hope in him, even when he disappoints us. Learning again the rule of our life is loving without ceasing to hope in the other, however much the facts seem to go contrary to our expectation.

For God, loving is finally giving one's life. God died of loving. The language of his love is forged in flesh and blood. Identifying ourselves with God's aim for our lives means recognizing that we cannot set a limit to how far we may have to go on our way and listening constantly to the voice that is always calling us out.

"Is it against the law?" The Gospel only knows one law—the law of boundlessness. God has always been a bit mad! On the first morning, after all, what could have been more mad than the idea of fashioning man out of the soil and loving him?

■

God, Creator of all things,
  your love goes beyond all bounds:
you gave up your Son
  as a sign of your faithfulness.
Save us from our narrowness,
  open wide our hearts:
let us love with the love
  that you will give us
  as our inheritance.

SATURDAY OF THE 7TH WEEK

THE FIRST

Sirach 17:1–15. What is man's real status? The priestly narrative of creation tried to find an explanation for man's domination of the world. Ben Sirach takes up this story here, but reinterprets it in his own way, that is, as a wise man who is astonished by man's great physical, intellectual and spiritual ability.

God has, for example, given men "a heart to think with." He has also "filled them with knowledge and understanding and revealed to them good and evil."

Ben Sirach's meditation reads in some respects like a hymn, but the themes dear to the wise men of Israel can still be heard clearly within his poetic framework. Like that of his predecessors, his work is marked by a certain determinism (see especially verse 2) and he regards the Torah as a simple means by which wisdom can be attained.

Psalm 103 is in the form of a hymn and expresses both the precarious nature of human life and the power of God's love.

Mark 10:13–16. The evangelist's intention in this pericope can only be understood if it is seen against the background of Jesus' proclamations of his passion. Jesus is going up to Jerusalem, where his adversaries are waiting for him, but even now he only wants to do God's will. He has never claimed the kingdom for himself; he will receive it from his Father's hands, "like a little child."

Serving the poor, the indissolubility of marriage and detachment from riches —these are the ethics of the kingdom. They are so demanding that they are impossible for man to fulfil, especially if he forgets that they are included within the perspective of the good news. There are certainly many obstacles on the way leading to the kingdom, but the disciple has to remember that, by his availability, Jesus has conquered the world. He has to receive the grace of salvation from God. He has to receive the Spirit, whose breath enables man to breathe with the rhythm of God himself.

In themselves, children are nothing. They have to receive everything from others if they are to live. This is why Jesus makes them living symbols of welcome. He lays his hands on them and in this way gives them the kingdom. In the same way, he also gives the kingdom to those who are like them.

■

Jesus is still in Galilee, walking along the roads between fields green with the signs of spring, walking resolutely at the head of the little group of disciples. They are not within three thousand miles of understanding what is really happening!

He is walking resolutely in the direction of Jerusalem. The loneliness of the righteous man! He stops only to teach his disciples. "The Son of Man will be delivered into the hands of men. . . . The prophecy of the Servant must be fulfilled. . . ." The disciples understand nothing of this. They rebuke the children and try to send them away. The Master has to be kept for adults. The good news is too serious to be given to children.

But Jesus takes a child and sets him in their midst. He is no longer in the corner to which he has been sent to play until he has grown up and can work and be paid for it. No, Jesus places the child in the midst of the Church and puts his arms round him. He, the Son of God who will soon be betrayed by a kiss, the kiss given by one of the twelve disciples, kisses the child.

But, before handing himself over to the fire of love, as an unreflecting child might do, Jesus hands over to us the words that proclaim an eternal revolution: "Anyone who welcomes a little child in my name is welcoming me and the Father."

Jesus, the eternal Son, is eternally in the midst of the Church, but he makes the little child the center of gravity of his kingdom. That kingdom can be entered by those who can love and let themselves be loved, by those who are poor and can receive their reason for living from others and by those who can only perform acts of love in order to grow up.

Surely you know that all that a little child needs to begin living again is a kiss—a sign of love. And do you not know that, thanks to children, everything can be grace and thanks? Jesus put the little child in the midst of the Church, and I have the impression that the disciples' hearts were suddenly filled with an overwhelming desire—they longed to run to him. To the little child or to Jesus—I do not know which one—to learn from him the way to grace, where the last will be the first.

■

Your Son, God our Father,
  has given himself up
  into your hands—
  may he be blessed!
In the midst of the Church
  he is the one
  who does your will perfectly.
Because he has put his spirit into us,
  let us be molded into his image
  and may the will to belong to your family
  and to welcome what you have promised us
  grow in us for ever and ever.

MONDAY OF THE 8TH WEEK

WITHOUT ANY LUGGAGE
Sirach 17:24–29. Ben Sirach praises man for his greatness, but he is also aware of his limitations. Man is weak and sinful. He is constantly in need of

conversion. The man who fears God will be obedient and loyal to the commandments, but he will also recognize that God is merciful.

Is the God-fearing man rewarded after death? There are passages in the book of Sirach, including our present text, which seem to indicate that Ben Sirach believed not in God's judgment of man after death, but in the idea commonly held in the ancient world of a survival without any true existence in Sheol, where there are no more living to give glory to God.

Psalm 32 describes how the converted sinner will be welcomed like a pilgrim coming to the temple to celebrate the good gifts of Yahweh.

Mark 10:17–27. The Pharisees wanted to set a trap for Jesus (see 10:2), but there is, on the contrary, something religious in the rich man's approach to Jesus in this passage. He kneels in front of Jesus and addresses him as "good master." But, Jesus replies, who is good but God alone? In coming to question Jesus, this man kneels in front of the one God—the God of the covenant.

Jesus reminds him of the principal articles of the Mosaic Law. This man assures him that he has observed them "from his earliest days." But he is available to go further. He is available for the kingdom. That is why Jesus loves him and calls him. He has scrupulously kept all the commandments and he is invited to become one of Jesus' disciples. The concrete action that Jesus asks him to take is to remove the "scandal" that prevents him from going forward: his riches.

But the man "went away sad." What precisely is his position, then? He has heard Jesus' call and has at the same time recognized his own present inability to follow him. Jesus has told him: "There is one thing you lack." That one thing is an awareness that God can bring about for him what he cannot do himself now. Welcoming the kingdom like a little child is in fact also recognizing one's own impotence and letting the Spirit of God act.

■

Jesus is going up to Jerusalem, the city that kills the prophets. He has left everything to be faithful to the word that has consecrated him. God's passion for mankind is his only treasure and he has sold everything for the pearl of great value. The Son goes off without looking back, not knowing where he will rest his head. The poor man of God will go to the extremity of stripping away and will let himself be laid to rest on the wood of the cross.

"Go and sell everything you own and . . . follow me." Leave everything! One feels like saying: That is simply not possible. It is not human. But God is never inhuman. When he asks a man for everything, he gives man to himself. Money, knowledge and power are so many idols that can imprison man in their dictatorship. God reveals that man is everything for him. We do not need anything outside ourselves to make us rich. Man is everything for man! "Go and sell everything you own. . . . You are worth more than the birds in the sky or the flowers growing in the fields."

"Leave everything." Jesus did not come to make man lose hope by demanding something from him that he could not give. If he has to liberate himself, it is so that he can walk, free of all shackles, on the way that leads to life. Jesus came to call us to grow in love.

"Leave everything." This is something that takes the whole of one's life, because growth is the task of a lifetime. "Go and sell everything you own." In the order of law, you might imagine that you have done your duty but, in the order of love, you are never free of the one you love. Love lives in the faithfulness that discovers itself every day anew and is always finding new horizons.

"Leave everything" is a call not to accept being trodden underfoot by the mediocre, the satisfaction of the self-satisfied or the false certainty of those who think they have arrived. "Go and sell everything you own" means: Tear yourself away! Do not let yourself be trapped by the evidence that the world provides or by the easy option offered by a legalistic religion. Flies let themselves be trapped by an attractive sticky surface. Do not trust appearances. The Gospel does not like such surfaces or the bad luck that they bring. "Leave everything"—tear yourself away from that part of yourself that is keeping you and holding you back.

"Go and sell everything you own." God drives us back into our last entrenchments. For him, renouncing is not the same as losing. If we sell what we would like to go on holding tightly in our hands, it is not to have empty hands, but to find our hands filled beyond our expectations. We are invited to experience renouncing everything we have as the Spirit's wanting to live in us; and renunciation is discarding everything that prevents us from living the fullness of life. If we sell everything that has cost us so much to acquire, it is not because we want to set off on an adventure, but because there is, ahead of us, a dwelling-place where everything will be given to us. In the meantime, we have to walk free and without any luggage.

■

Blessed are you, Lord,
  who fill beyond all expectation
  those who have aimed their lives at you.

Blessed are you for the table where you welcome
  those who, believing in your word,
  have left everything.
Keep us in the happiness
  of those you make rich with your love.

TUESDAY OF THE 8TH WEEK

NOTHING IS IMPOSSIBLE FOR GOD

Sirach 35:1–12. The Law plays a much more important part in the writing of Ben Sirach than in the work of his predecessors in the Wisdom literature. It is, however, difficult to precisely define that role. We know too that the masters of wisdom regarded the idea of the "fear of God" as very important. This notion is generally defined as obedience to God's will, but it goes further than a strictly moral point of view and includes the whole of man's relationships with God.

Ben Sirach had to reinterpret this idea of the "fear of God" for his own times, because it was widely accepted then that God's will was expressed in the written Law. He tried to show, therefore, the extent to which the Torah was the source of wisdom, above all because it illuminated the order that God wanted to prevail in the universe.

On the other hand, however, the wise men of Israel did more than simply formulate doctrines. They also aimed to make their wisdom a rule of life that was embodied in everyday experience. The high regard that Ben Sirach had for the cult of Israel therefore led him to struggle for an authentic form of religion. For him, God had to be worshipped "in spirit and in truth." The Law, then, has something to say about man's relationships with God, but external rites of worship cannot be separated from moral integrity. Only the offerings of the righteous man are acceptable to God.

Psalm 50 is an indictment of the hypocritical worship of the impious.

Mark 10:28–31. The disciples believed that they had to turn away the exorcist who was driving out demons in Jesus' name, but was not a member of their group, but Jesus had prevented them. So "many who are last will be first." There is a way of being first that guarantees that one will be last. True greatness is to be found in service.

But has the question not been answered already for the disciples? They have, after all, left everything to follow Jesus. He replies that their action has

---

effectively made them worthy of the kingdom. Because they are the body of Christ, from now on they will receive "a hundred times over" what they have left. With, in addition, the persecution that is inherent in their condition as followers of Christ. But, in the light of the whole event of Easter, that is also a gain.

■

There is no Christian way without the way of the cross. There is no way of living according to the Gospel without dying oneself. The resurrection is also an integral part of the cross, the life from which God has to tear away our lives in order to lead us towards his life.

Renunciation—that is a word that we would prefer to forget nowadays. But there can never be good wine if the vine-dresser does not prune the vine. And he does that because he loves the plant and wants it to bear fruit. The person who renounces is not mutilated. As Jean-Claude Barrault has said in his book on memories for tomorrow (*Souvenirs pour demain*), he is a man who is passionately dedicated to everything and clings to nothing. Renouncing is not failing in life. The kingdom, which is true riches, can only fill to overflowing those who are in love with life, because they are conscious of what is essential—their own poverty and their need to be saved.

Today's Gospel only seems to be "moral" in the wrong sense. It would be a mistake to think that Jesus is inviting us to go further and further in our respect for a law that is more and more demanding. No, what is at the heart of this reading is the question: "Who can be saved?" and the answer given by Jesus: "For men it is impossible, but not for God, because everything is possible for God."

Christianity may preach a certain way of living, but it can never be reduced simply to a form of morality. We have to recognize ourselves as poor in God's presence before we can rediscover what we were in the beginning, when we came naked and vulnerable from his hands. Salvation is like creation—it is always grace.

■

Father of men,
  you offer the riches of your kingdom
  to those who are poor in heart.
Make us ready to listen to your word
  and to put it into practice.

We stand in your presence,
God of life, with open hands
and give you thanks.
Your love has enriched us
with the only good things
that do not pass away.
Blessed are you for the infinite gift
that you have bestowed on us
in Jesus Christ, your Son,
our inheritance and eternal joy!
In him, you have set us free
from every useless burden
and the gate of heaven is open
to welcome the poor and humble.
Borne up in this hope
by your looking at us with love,
we bless you,
the God who calls on us to live.

■

Lord Jesus,
who can be saved
if you do not take him away
from the good things of this world?
Do not look at our doubts and hesitations,
but at the faith and poverty of your Church.
Bring us together in true peace
now and for ever.

READING AND UNDERSTANDING MARK (10:32–12:44)

On the way to Jerusalem! The third prophecy of the passion leaves us in no doubt about this fact: It is to the city that kills the prophets that Jesus is going, ahead of his disorientated disciples.

He is going there for a judgment. He drives the dealers out of the temple and curses the barren fig tree. There can be no doubt that this curse represents a condemnation of those who do not bear good fruit (11:11–25). Nonetheless, this whole scene is dominated by the temple: "My house will be called a house of prayer for all the peoples. But you have turned it into a robbers' den."

Are these words aimed exclusively at the dealers in the temple? Or is he not, through them, really addressing the Jewish leaders? What is the object of the debate? Surely it is the gulf that exists between worship and life? To those who ask him whether it is necessary to pay taxes, he replies that God calls for total obedience (12:13–17). That is something that the prophets had stressed again and again: that God is a jealous God who wants man's whole life, because he too loves man with a love that is absolute.

Worship "in spirit and in truth," then, calls for man's whole life and Jesus gives the whole of his life, while the scribes and Pharisees continue to measure out the portion that belongs to Caesar and the portion that is God's. What counts for Jesus, however, is simply the primacy of love (12:28–34). God, then, will side with him against authority. He will give him life and make him, the stone rejected by the builders, the keystone itself (12:1–12). God is not, in other words, "God of the dead, but of the living" (12:18–27).

Finally, the trial of the Son of man is a trial conducted by men who reject the light. To the Jews who ask him on what or whose authority he drove the money-changers and dealers out of the temple, Jesus replies by accusing them of lack of faith (11:27–33). If they had examined the scriptures more closely or if they had welcomed him impartially, they would not have asked this question, but would have recognized him as the Messiah, as the blind beggar Bartimaeus had when he was leaving Jericho (10:46–52; cf. 12:35–37).

Jesus' adversaries may have been thrown into disorder by the debate, but the wheel of history was not prevented by it from turning. Jesus continued on his way to suffering and death but, because he had given everything, no one was in a better position than he to appreciate everyone's offering (12:38–44). And, in spite of everything, there was still hope. One of the scribes was also clearly conscious of the primacy of love and Jesus assured him: "You are not far from the Kingdom of God" (12:34).

WEDNESDAY OF THE 8TH WEEK

WITH JESUS THE SERVANT
Sirach 36:1, 4–5a, 10–17. After a passage on religious duties, Ben Sirach provides us with a model of prayer. His aim is not confined to the formation of a merely "decent" man. He goes further and wants to form a truly pious man. He believes that faith is really formative and that the man whom God loves is the one who will give his heart to God.

The prayer contained in chapter 36 is probably an addition to the work of Ben Sirach. It has been compared to the psalm that follows 51:12 and the Jewish prayer known as the Eighteen Blessings. This may explain both the series of petitions in favor of Israel and the harshness of some of those against Israel's enemies (which are not included in the lectionary). The latter are in sharp contrast with the author's usually serene style. God is asked to show his greatness to the pagan nations, just as he has shown them his holiness by punishing Israel for its sins.

Psalm 79 is a national lament. The petitionary prayer, directed against the enemy, and the promise of a celebration of thanksgiving are retained in today's liturgy.

Mark 10:32–45. This passage is not only a final lesson on serving others, but also the constitutive charter for all ministry carried out in the name of the Lord. If it is not serving the community, the ministry is not genuine. "Anyone who wants to become great among you must be your servant and anyone who wants to be first among you must be slave to all." Mark reminds his readers of the Lord's will in the absolute sense, but he also has in mind practice in the communities of those to whom his Gospel is addressed and whose integrity has been eroded by the demon of personal ambition and authoritarianism.

A misunderstanding with regard to the person of Jesus has, however, first to be resolved. Like all Jews, his disciples looked forward to a glorious Messiah. Rather than disabuse them, Jesus defines the conditions to be fulfilled to attain glory. The way that he is following will be the way of his passion. That way is so close that Mark is able to reveal all the details by rereading his own account of the passion.

To attain the glory of the kingdom, it is necessary to "drink the cup" and "be baptized with the baptism with which Jesus must be baptized." These are very eloquent images. In the Old Testament, the "cup" symbolized both the bitterness of God's punishment and at the same time the test that purified the sinner. The image of baptism is more mysterious, but it is almost certainly a reference to the baptism of Jesus himself, who accepted it to the point of death on a way of humility and service. As the Suffering Servant, Jesus was in fact to become identified with sin in setting men free: "For our sake, God made the sinless one into sin" (2 Cor 5:21).

■

"We want you to do us a favor." In the Gospel, it is James and John who ask this, but who would not speak in this way to God? Burdened with cares, the believer turns to God for help and strength. Committed to serving the kingdom, he asks his Lord to let his plans succeed. Urged on by the spirit of the Gospel, the disciple longs for the kingdom of peace and justice to be established. Why, then, does Jesus' reply make us doubt the legitimacy of this request?

Does it mean that we too, on the way of impossibility, should renounce ourselves like Jesus? Yes, that is what it means. This is clear from the fact that Jesus teaches this lesson as he is going up to Jerusalem, where he will give his life for the salvation of all men. As the Servant who has already made his life a perfect offering, he invites all his disciples at all times to follow this impossible way of service. Today, he is inviting the Church once again to follow not a way of honor, but one of service.

What, then, should be the effect of these words on us, hearing them today? It seems to me that we can interpret this reading as a call to solidarity with the needs of our fellow-men, a solidarity that should be experienced as humble service and not in a boastful spirit or in a search for personal advancement or reward. Jesus replies in a very disconcerting way to James and John, who claimed a place on his right and left hand! And on the cross, there were two thieves on his right and his left. Honor or reward, then, are not involved here. It is a question of solidarity with human suffering to the point of humiliation and death. This is a hard lesson to hear and the Church has often preferred honor to service.

Why does the word "charity" so often have unacceptable connotations nowadays? Acts of charity—these are fundamentally admirable, but what do they call to mind for us today? We associate them with being committed to the point of compromise, unwanted clothing or other articles and the poor, without possessions, qualities or virtues. But that is surely our vocation—we should identify ourselves with the fate of those who have no name, no power and no morals. It is easier to obey the law of the world than to respond to this rough call that is almost impossible to understand. But we have to ask ourselves what place they have in our Church, our community and our personal reactions, those who are excluded and condemned by human justice or by human morals —the divorced, the isolated and those who are outside our accepted rules or norms. How much we would like to sit at the right and the left hand of the Lord, but he tells us: "I was crucified between two thieves and they are on my right and left hand."

Jesus' reply to those who asked him for this honor was: "You do not know what you are asking." And we too do not understand the way that Christ went, the way that he wants us to follow. But it is certain that this is the way which leads through the cross to the dawn of Easter. "Today," he said, "you will be with me in paradise."

THE WORD THAT SAVES

Sirach 42:15–25. Israel's wise men look at the world with serenity. They see man living in complete harmony with creation, because Yahweh has only created good things, all of which work for the good of those who love him (see Rom 8:28). Creation, then, is able to reveal God's goodness to man. At the same time, however, it is also important to remember the ambiguity of all reality. This warning occurs again and again in the book of Sirach: that we should never allow ourselves to be deceived by appearances.

But, if there is nothing in creation that is harmful to man, how do the wise men explain the world's disorder? They rely on God who, in his wisdom, does everything well. Did he not, after all, determine everything in advance? He has arranged a time for all things and knows where he is taking man and the world (vv. 18f.). It is worth noting here that this intuition in the Wisdom literature contains the seeds of the apocalyptic vision.

Psalm 33 is a hymn which echoes Ben Sirach's thoughts.

Mark 10:46–52. "Son of David!" The blind man's call is addressed to one of the main messianic figures in Israel's history and proclaims the final confrontation between Jesus and Jerusalem, the city of David.

The story of Bartimaeus is deeply symbolic. It is, as it were, a reply to the disciples' request to be allowed to sit on Jesus' right and left hand. These disciples have now to go through Jericho, the city which, in the biblical tradition, opened the way into the Promised Land. Coming out of the city, they pass a blind beggar sitting at the side of the road. Like the child whom the disciples wanted to send away, this blind man is rebuked by many people in the crowd who want to silence him. But Jesus addresses this same crowd to teach the people in it about the greatness of service and to ask them to bring the sick man to the light. The crowd literally "raises" the blind man, who throws away his cloak, jumps up and runs to Jesus. This action expresses in a very significant way the break that the man is making with his past, a past of power, because the cloak is a symbol of human power (E. Haulotte). The blind man also symbolizes the true disciple, who strips himself of the cloak that has up till now blinded him and who from now onwards places himself in Jesus' hands and follows him on the way to Jerusalem.

■

He was sitting at the side of the road. He was blind and his only future was to remain enclosed for ever within his own darkness.

We are overwhelmed and we lack the strength to raise ourselves up and react. We do not know where life is leading us and we cannot see what our future may be. Events are taking place before us and we do not know where to go or what road to take. We see the economic war that is being waged between the powerful countries in the world and we are caught up in crises and conflicts over which we have no control. We have for years heard of the ever-increasing burden of suffering of the poor nations, but our good-will is not enough to relieve it. We know that the world is marked by evil and we are conscious of our own hidden complicity in it.

We too are blind and we are also sitting powerless at the side of the road.

But, like Bartimaeus, we can hear and that is where our healing begins. The word of God reaches us and we hear it as a call to salvation: "Lord, let me see!" That cry of faith that rises up in us encounters the movement of love from Jesus' heart and his word becomes a word of salvation.

A word of power that makes light appear. Through the grace of that word which raises us up, we are able to see the end and fulfilment of our time of testing and follow Jesus on the road.

All those who have followed the way before us—the whole Church—say: "Courage! Get up! He is calling you!" All those who have been looking for a new world carry within themselves that invitation to the whole of mankind: "Courage! Get up!"

Every page in the Gospel assures us that this way of the blind and the lame is the road to Jerusalem. It is going up with the Son of God and passing with him through the cross to life, because on this road we place ourselves totally in the hands of the Father. And in each one of us this way points in a more precise direction: courage to confront opposition, to make decisions and to become reconciled; love, which is stronger than all hatred and lying, truth and justice shining out clearly; renunciation of everything that holds us back.

"Courage! Get up!" This way takes us forward through the conversion of the cross, but it also leads to Easter. We can therefore say with Simeon: "Now you can let your servant go in peace, because my eyes have seen the salvation which you have prepared for all the nations!"

■

Blessed are you, God our hope,
  for the salvation we receive
  in this bread which gives us life.

Blessed are you for the light
  that shines on our ways!
May the fire of your love
  shine in our eyes,
  now and for ever.

FRUITFULNESS

Sirach 44:1, 9–13. Ben Sirach closes his book with a eulogy of Israel's Fathers, from Enoch to the high-priest Simon. Several ideas underlie this passage. There is an obvious desire to provide models to be imitated, but, as wisdom and piety appear as characteristics that are common to all these ancestors, one is tempted to think that what the author is really celebrating through them is divine wisdom.

The nationalist dimension should also not be overlooked. The personalities praised in this long eulogy were all faithful and pious men of God who were dedicated to their people. The author in fact presents us with a history of Israel which is one of an ideal order that God wants and which has been only gradually built up and has often been endangered, but which will in the end be fully established. To reach this end, Israel still needs liberators, prophets and above all priests. We should not be surprised by the importance that Ben Sirach attaches to the institution of the priesthood. The time when he was writing was one of its best periods.

Psalm 149 invites us to join with our ancestors in faith in praising God.

Mark 11:11–25. "On that day, his feet will rest on the Mount of Olives, which faces Jerusalem from the east" (Zech 14:4). "Rejoice heart and soul, daughter of Zion! Shout with gladness, daughter of Jerusalem! See now, your king comes to you; he is victorious, he is triumphant, humble and riding on a donkey, on a colt, the foal of a donkey" (Zech 9:9). "There will be no more traders in the temple of Yahweh Sabaoth, when that day comes" (Zech 14:21).

Let us be guided by the words of the prophet, not only because they inspired the author of our Gospel, but also because Jesus' symbolic acts, reported in this passage, are in the manner of the prophets. The lesson is clear: Jesus is going up to Jerusalem for a judgment; he is going to cancel out the religious institutions of Israel. On the day of the Feast of Tabernacles, he enters Jerusalem as a king and looks at everything that he sees as a judge.

142

The prophets had again and again protested against the secularizing worship of the temple, which relieved good practicing Israelites of the need to examine the depth of their own life and faith (see, for example, Jer 7:1–15). Israel had forgotten that Yahweh preferred mercy to sacrifices and had made the temple, which was "a house of prayer for all the peoples," into a "robbers' den." Israel itself had become like a fig tree that had ceased to bear fruit.

When he cursed the dead tree and drove the money-changers and dealers out of the temple, Jesus was tearing down the barriers preventing pagans from entering the sacred enclosure. From then on, the whole of the earth was made sacred to God. From then onwards, it was no longer to be on Mount Gerizim or in Jerusalem that men would worship God. They would offer themselves as a living sacrifice, holy and acceptable to God.

■

In the music of Wolfgang Amadeus Mozart, it is possible to distinguish the roots of his own style and the elements that he took from his father, Leopold, and from Johann Christian Bach, Sammartini, Haydn and many other composers. But this still does not explain the phenomenon of Mozart! In him, intensely interested as he was in the whole musical tradition that was available to him, it is possible to find all the genres and styles of the period in an astonishing universality and a harmonious balance. Analysis of his work can distinguish between what is German and what is Italian in his style, and between what is homophonic and what is polyphonic. It can also reveal the learned and the lively elements and the sober and the contrasting aspects. But, for all this, it is still not possible to define precisely what is new, specific and unique in Mozart's music.

I would suggest that it is the sublime unity of his work—a totality rooted in a great freedom of spirit, Mozart himself living in his music— which makes the phenomenon of Mozart new, specific and unique.

We can try to discover the "difference" of Christianity. We can look for all the possible parallels with Christian faith and emphasize all its motivations. We can bring out the specific qualities of Jesus' statements and their effect on those who heard them and explore the depths of spirituality present in his disciples. But, whatever course we follow, something new, specific and unique in the life of the Christian will be left that eludes clear understanding. I would call that something the fruitfulness of faith.

"Have faith in God," Jesus tells his disciple Peter. "Love makes life sing," said the poet. Faith brings about an inner revolution in our lives. Why is the life of the Christian new, different and unique? It is made unique by the attraction, the allure of Jesus. What makes Mozart is Mozart himself. What makes the Christian is the bond with his Master.

"Have faith in God!" Our foundation is Jesus and reference to his name is for us quite different from an empty formula. The source of our fruitfulness is our attachment to Jesus Christ. Our faith has no other content.

Our lives as Christians have no other fruit to bear but a stronger and stronger attachment to Jesus. That is why we are unique; we are in love with Christ. The rest is a question of personal life, collective options, fitting into our cultural environment, and so on. The Christian model is Jesus himself. And our attachment to him is the fruit of our faith.

■

God, you reveal yourself in the life of your Son
—be yourself the cause of our faith!
Let us taste the words that reveal your name
and let us be attached to the actions
that make your love incarnate.
May our faith bear in us
the fruit of eternity
and may it be our joy for ever.

SATURDAY OF THE 8TH WEEK

HE WAS KNOWN
Sirach 51:12–20. Chapter 51, which consists of two psalms, forms an appendix to Ben Sirach's book. The first (vv. 1–12) is a psalm of thanksgiving, whereas the second describes the author's search for wisdom. Biographical passages occur frequently in the Wisdom literature. This does not mean, however, that the events contained in them really happened.

It is worth noting that vv. 13–20 appear in a scroll discovered at Qumran. This version stresses more emphatically than the traditional Greek text the passionate nature of the search for wisdom. The psalm makes graphic use of the language and sentiments of human love: the relationships of a child with his nurse, and of a young man with his beloved. The use of this imagery can be explained in the light of Ben Sirach's definition of wisdom as the primordial order of the world: creation, which has something to say to man, is trying to make him listen to her and is going out to meet him. The wise man's efforts, his progress and his prayer are, from then onwards, dominated by a thirst for knowledge. His search is a real attempt to overcome reality.

In *Psalm 19b*, the psalmist professes that he will be faithful to God's law. It is presented as a hymn consisting of statements that are at the same time praises formulated by the psalmist.

Mark 11:27–33. The Sanhedrin has been thrown into disarray. On what or whose authority did Jesus expel the money-changers and dealers from the temple? How did this misuse of power arise, when the captain of the temple was responsible for order there? Jesus' trial had already commenced.

Jesus, however, reveals his adversaries' real motives. What will really be called into question in the trial is the absence of faith of the Jewish leaders. They do not believe in Jesus. They do not recognize him as the one sent by God, just as they did not believe in John the Baptist. What is at stake here is Jesus' divine origin. In throwing his adversaries into confusion with regard to John's baptism, he is in fact reaffirming his own origin, discreetly but firmly. Yes, his trial has already begun.

∎

However great a man may be, he will not be great for those who know him intimately. No one is a prophet in his own country! "What authority have you for acting like this? Or who gave you authority to do these things?" How could these good people have given their faith and their lives to this man Jesus, whose human, in many ways far too human, origin was known to them? How could they have believed this prophet whose accent, whose past, whose very flesh and blood was known to them because they were their own? They would gladly have welcomed a strange, unknown, solemn, eternal and omnipotent god, these good people, but a prophet, a so-called man of God, a man exactly like themselves—how could they have recognized God in him?

Listening to Jesus, the teachers of the law asked each other: "Where does his wisdom come from?" To be able to be astonished and to give thanks to the God who speaks through little children, the poor and the humble, they would have to have been little children, poor and humble themselves, instead of being saturated with their own knowledge and power. They reasoned as all good people reason, and accepted as a matter of course that a carpenter worked with timber and a scribe repeated the lessons of antiquity. For a man to do and speak differently in an attempt to draw attention to the claims of religion and to explain God's intentions—that was a scandal and one had to be on one's guard against it, seeking shelter behind firmly established principles and decisive statements. It goes without saying that, if God has something new to say and wants us to behave differently, he will present himself to us with all the prestige of a God.

"What authority have you for acting—or speaking—like this?" In another context, when all those present were only thinking of saving themselves and condemning others, Jesus said: "Woman, I do not condemn you." He chose to associate with insignificant people, when everyone else was only wondering: "What will others think?" He declared that the poor were happy, when others were all using their hearts to increase their possessions. That is the wisdom of God and that is where Jesus' authority came from. God is very disconcerting and a witness who is refuted.

No one is a prophet in his own country! There are men and women who, in their attempt to live the Gospel, keep a distance from the accepted models of behavior. They try to be faithful to a Word that is different from what most of us naturally believe about God. Should we then be surprised if such people are outlawed from respectable religious society and if they are ostracized by decent people? All the more so if they are too well-known—they and their shortcomings which weaken them, their unfaithfulness of which they are ashamed, and their hesitations which make them suffer.

"What authority have you . . . ? Miracles are necessary if the Gospel is to bear fruit! But even miracles may have no impact, and they call for faith. Who was Jesus claiming to be? The real miracle may perhaps be to listen, to be astonished by the Gospel that is always new and challenging and to be converted to the style of life of a disciple who follows such a Master.

■

He comes to his own,
  but is he known to them?
The Lord is in our midst,
  but do we hear his voice?

The cattle know their herdsman
  and the creature knows its creator,
  but we do not know you!
God of mercy and tenderness,
  keep our hearts watchful
  and change our habits,

so that we may be astonished
by your unexpected presence.

IN THE WINE-PRESS OF THE COVENANT

Tobit 1:1a, 2; 2:1-9. In the year 733 B.C., the king of Assyria, Tiglath-pileser III (not Shalmaneser, as in the text) occupied the territory of the tribes of the extreme north of Palestine and deported the Jewish population. These events formed the background to the "novel" of Tobit. It is certainly a novel and not a history. The historical details given are deceptive, but the errors and improbable statements contained in the book are soon exposed by a critical reading.

The author tries to provide religious teaching through the medium of the vicissitudes of two families, one deported to Nineveh (in modern Iraq) and the other to Ecbatana (in Iran). Certain situations take us back, for instance, to the period of the patriarchs, the intention being, it would seem, to show that God's promise will remain unchanged if the wandering of Israel's ancestors is continued by those who have been deported. Another example is that the destiny of the people is interpreted in the light of the prophets: did Amos not foretell Israel's present misfortunes (2:6)? What Yahweh expects of the Jewish families is that they should hand on faithfulness to his person and his commandments. Faithfulness to the Law takes on a new dimension in a country of exile and good works and burying the dead foreshadow the Pharisaical communities of the post-exilic period.

Another alphabetical psalm! *Psalm 112* was employed as a song to welcome pilgrims to Jerusalem.

Mark 12:1-12. "A man planted a vineyard. . . ." The canticle at the beginning of Isaiah 5 was in everyone's mind in Israel at the time of Jesus. Scandalized by the ingratitude of the people of Judah and their leaders, the prophet had transformed a love song into a harsh parable. In the Gospel, it is used by Jesus to pronounce a verdict on his adversaries. The vine will be taken away from them and entrusted to others, because they have failed in the mission entrusted to them by Yahweh.

In letting the members of the Sanhedrin know that he has understood their plot against him, Jesus provides evidence of his own perspicacity and deliberately takes his place among Israel's many prophets and martyrs, his immediate predecessor being John the Baptist. But God has not yet said the

---

147

last word. That is the impending death of his Son: "the stone rejected by the builders" (the scribes) will be the "keystone."

■

The hillsides of Palestine bathed in the light of the East, were covered with vines and for centuries men inspired by God compared the Jewish nation to a vineyard. The prophet Isaiah, for example, celebrated the grace of the Lord and his care for his people in these words: "Let me sing to my friend the song of his love for his vineyard. . . ."

"A man planted a vineyard. . . . When the time came for the harvest . . . ." Following Isaiah, Jesus takes up the same familiar secular image. To those who are watching him in order to accuse him, he reveals in this parable the meaning that he gives to his death. What he says to them in other words is: "You are planning to kill me because you believe that you own God and you refuse to recognize the one he has sent, his Son. But you are the ones who will be rejected and the great wonder is that the new building will be built up on me!"

This is a dramatic challenge. Jesus' gaze is intense as he looks at the men who are going to decide to put him to death. He has just made a breathtaking pronouncement that an Israel without frontiers is going to enter the blood-stained vineyard. He has just given a sharp warning to all those who have been tempted to usurp in one way or another the power of God. The only Son will be killed, but the vineyard will continue to belong to God. The blood of the beloved Son will be shed, but God will restore it as a life-giving force. The new covenant will be sealed in the blood that is shed. The pressed grape will become the wine drunk at the feast to which all men of good-will will be invited.

Jesus takes up the Old Testament image to proclaim that God is faithful to his covenant. And the same story continues throughout history: the suffering of God's servant, the only Son, continues in every century. From the first martyrs to those who suffer persecution for the sake of justice today, how many people have been the victims of violence, while their brothers have remained ignorant or indifferent! But from Abel to Martin Luther King and the young unknown worker tortured in a Latin American prison, and from Father Popielusko, the innocent man who is persecuted, to the unnamed prisoner in a Gulag in Eastern Europe—they are all following Jesus, a light for the world and the finest harvest of all, because the wine from God's vineyard is the blood of Christ.[4]

■

Faithful God, fill us with a longing
  to enter into your covenant.
Make us a people made holy by your love,
  the vineyard that you have planted with tenderness,
  the vine that you take care of.
Then we shall bear the fruit you expect,
  the fruitfulness of the Spirit of Jesus.

What a wonder this Eucharist is, Lord our God:
  your Son, rejected by men,
  made of his death the power that saves them!
Let us grow in faithfulness
  and let our lives conform to the life of Jesus,
  who was obedient to death on the cross,
so that, thanks to him,
  we shall enter into eternal glory.

TUESDAY OF THE 9TH WEEK

HE REMAINED FIRM

Tobit 2:10–23. Tobit becomes blind, but it is for the glory of God. Despite his misfortune, he continues to trust in Yahweh, like the blessed Job before him. (Saint Jerome made this comparison between the two wise men in his translation of the Bible, the so-called Vulgate.) Like his model, Tobit also has to endure the sarcasm of those near to him, including his wife. What value is there in being faithful, when his blindness shows clearly that Yahweh has punished him? This episode ends with a last call to observe the Law. The kid has to be given back to its owners, as it may have been stolen from them.

Psalm 112. See Monday of the ninth week.

Mark 12:13–17. The Gospel began with a set of five controversies (2:1–3:6), which concluded with the decision taken by the Pharisees and the Herodians together to destroy Jesus. Here too, the Gospel ends with a series of discussions leading to Jesus' arrest and condemnation.

His adversaries present him with a dilemma: "Is it permissible to pay taxes to Caesar or not?" This is a very crude trap, because payment of the emperor's tax was regarded as a sign of submission to Roman rule. The Zealots refused to pay it. The Pharisees were opposed to it in principle, but agreed to pay it in practice. Finally, the Herodians tried to please those who were in power. This meant that, however people reacted to this imperial tax, Jesus was bound to encounter difficulties and his enemies had a good excuse either for bringing him into discredit with the population, or for accusing him of rebellion against the occupying forces.

But you need a diamond to cut a diamond! Jesus first asks his opponents to show him a denarius, a coin bearing an image of the emperor's head. This was proof that they used this coin themselves and that they were willing to take material advantage of a certain political order. Then he questions them about the effigy on the coin: "Whose head is this? Whose name?" If it is placed within the context of man as created in the image of God, this is in no sense a harmless question! Two powers are contrasted with each other here, religious power and civil power. Ultimately, in whose image is man? He is in the image of God! Political power is only a human reality and, as such, it has only a relative value. What goes back to God is the whole of life itself. Jesus will bear witness to that reality on the cross.

■

Tobit became blind. God allowed him to be put to the test in this way so that he could give an example of patience to posterity. He remained firm in the fear of God. Living far from Palestine, mixing with strange people whose language, customs and gods were quite different, the Jews were bound to suffer.

Written to strengthen the people of Israel in their exile, the book of Tobit is full of memories and canticles and is primarily concerned with Israel's faith. This was a new situation for the Jews living in such great cities as Alexandria, Athens and Rome. Their faith received much less support from the traditional sources. It was more exposed to different cultures and to religions that were opposed to the Law of the eternal God. The challenge had to be accepted and the exiled people had to be helped to remain faithful to their religion. This new situation called for new and always hesitant responses. It also meant that risks had to be taken.

Christians today are citizens in a secularized world. Our communities are often very reduced in numbers and widely scattered. The memory of the Church's earlier image of an indestructible city, based on the existence of powerful Christian states and great gatherings, has faded and we are living in a twentieth-century diaspora. We can no longer rely on a solid framework of institutions regulating morals, practices, civil

laws, traditions, public opinion and human instincts. We are confronted as believers with one vital demand. We have to reappropriate our faith. We have to make it our own again.

Some Christians try to build up ghettos, but these have to cling very closely to each other if they are to survive. The icepack has broken, but each small fragment hopes to re-form a mini-icepack around itself. The strategy of withdrawal is in itself a sign of death. Faith is the situation of a people in exodus, a people on the way. Risk is the normal condition of that faith.

We have to take a risk, even a radical risk. We may have to risk everything without any assurance apart from the adventure itself. In taking such a risk, we are saying that we have our "reasons" for acting as we do and are attracted by the adventure. Our faith is a risk because it lives by trying, finding out, making mistakes and exposing itself to the enemy's fire. But it can only expose itself in that condition of risk. It dares to take a risk because the uncertainty that forms part of its hesitant search and many failures, which are the flesh and blood of its longing to seize hold of reality, point to an even more tenacious passion. The faith that is ready to take a risk is a faith that will last.

Some people see taking a risk as the manifestation of a sick faith that no longer knows "which saint to have a devotion to." Others see it as the condition of a faith existing at the same level as unbelief, wavering between the two equal values of certainty and uncertainty. I regard taking a risk as a patient search for the truth that gradually acquires its form as it becomes more conscious of the object of its own tension, as the laborious incarnation of an ideal that is slowly given an outline with growing awareness of the demands that define it. Taking a risk is not something that is not known and not experienced. The fulfilment of faith is our ultimate assurance. The last word is our "yes," given in trust.

Tobit remained firm in the fear of God!

■

God our Father,
you let the earth be born every day
and let us make it a place fit to live in.
May your Spirit fill our hearts,
because only he can teach us
    how to be men and women
    with a new heart
    on a new earth

that will be born
now and for ever.

FROM FAILURE TO HOPE

Tobit 3:1–11, 24–25. Prayer also plays a very important part in the book of Tobit. When they went into exile, the Jews lost their temple, which the glory of Yahweh had left to accompany the people in their exile (Ez 11:22–25). Good works, almsgiving and prayer took over from the national sanctuary. Almsgiving strengthened the bond between the members of the exiled community and prayer was increasingly regarded as the ideal way of welcoming God. Despite his misfortune, Tobit gives thanks for God's justice and at the same time confesses the nation's sins. Tobit's confession foreshadows the national confessions of the post-exilic period.

After Tobit's prayer, the action of the novel becomes more complex, but tighter. The author introduces the story of Sarah, the young woman whose seven bridegrooms had been strangled one after another by a demon, in parallel with the story of the old man Tobit. Sarah also prays for Yahweh to help her and this leads to intervention on the part of the angel Gabriel.

Psalm 25 is alphabetical in form, but it is an individual lament. The antagonism that separates the righteous man from the ungodly is one of its themes.

Mark 12:18–27. The Pharisees believed in the existence of angels and in the resurrection of the dead, but the Sadducees rejected these doctrines, which they regarded as innovations. They only accepted the books of the Pentateuch on the question of revelation. They also believed that the Pharisees went too far, because they based their teachings on the hereafter on terrestrial realities and claimed that, at the resurrection, men would be given new powers (especially in respect of fertility).

In this Marcan text, Jesus opposes the Sadducees and proclaims his faith in the resurrection, while at the same time rejecting the altogether too simplistic imagery of the Pharisees. Jesus' faith presupposes God's faithfulness. Yahweh, he insists, is "the God of Abraham, the God of Isaac and the God of Jacob." For the Jew, "someone's God" was "the God who was someone's protector." This means that God is presented as the protector of the patriarchs, their shield and their rock. But what kind of divine protection would it be if it were interrupted by death and if man were reduced to the condition of a shadow without true existence after death? Jesus bases his argument on the hope that runs through the whole of the Bible and claims that God's faithfulness goes beyond the frontiers of death. "He is God," he insists, "of the living."

Jesus also rejects the too familiar images of the rabbis. "When they rise from the dead," he says, "men and women do not marry; no, they are like the angels in heaven." He takes this parallel from the apocalyptic view of the universe. It does not in any way devalue human sexuality, but rather expresses what it is the sign of. As J. Rademakers has pointed out, "Procreation linked to the terrestrial condition of man is the manifestation of the perennial nature of the victory that man, who has been promised immortality, must continue to achieve over physical death. At the resurrection, he will no longer need to beget. . . . Being raised from the dead is living in God in a state of interpersonal communion of which the relationship in the flesh between man and wife is the figure."

■

Tobit "sighed and wept and began his prayer of lamentation. . . ." We too are in exile. We are living far from a country that is truly human, a country in which justice reigns and true peace prevails, a country where all people share the same destiny. We are in exile in a world that has been made inhuman by man's eternal search for his own self-interest and his eternally repeated acts of hostility to his fellow-men. In that situation of exile, we "sigh and weep" with Tobit and pray, lamenting our own sinfulness and the many times we have failed in our responsibilities.

"On the same day . . . ." It is only those who reflect regularly and deeply about the lessons of the past and the painful events of the present who will ever be alert to the grace of a new dawn. It is only those who are so deeply hurt by the failure of man and by the absence of God that they "sigh and weep" like Tobit, who will ever receive the grace to be able to bear witness to a new presence of God in our own times and to work with him for a new future for man.

Such men and women will perhaps only ever be a small remnant in a country of exile. But then, is it not true that it is always such small remnants of the people of God who have crossed the difficult passes? Those who have formed part of these small remnants have never feared what so many people fear. They have never been troubled by the hesitant attempts to make necessary changes or by the futile arguments which so many people seem to enjoy so much.

No, they are only concerned with the essential questions at the root of modern man's lack of faith. They recognize that God's silence today is

his silence, and not the silence of the void. They know that the language
that men use to speak about and to approach God is inadequate and that
this is not simply a problem of vocabulary. This inadequacy is for them
as painful an experience as the birth of a new poem in which the living
God and living man communicate with each other in human words. They
know they are near to God in the darkness, but they cannot take
pleasure in that nearness, nor can they show others the way to achieve it
with a single act. They wait in hope and expectation and in humility.

■

Lord, our God,
   your will is justice
   and all your ways are mercy and truth.
Remember us
   and do not call our weakness to mind,
   but think of your covenant and your faithfulness.
Lead us forward in your Spirit
   and be the power that enables us
   to bring about in this world
   the kingdom that will fulfil your promise.

THURSDAY OF THE 9TH WEEK

MY FIRST IS . . . , MY SECOND IS . . .
Tobit 6:10–11a; 7:1, 9–17; 8:4–10. A marriage after God's heart! In exile the
family assumed an even greater importance. It was the cell in which the
spiritual inheritance of the nation was transmitted. There was also an ever-
present danger that the exiled people would become assimilated with the
pagans among whom they lived through contracting mixed marriages. The
wedding of the young man Tobias and his bride Sarah therefore served as a
model for marriage. In the first place, it was God's will that they should
marry. Yahweh had sent his angel with this one happy conclusion in mind. In
the second place, their marriage conformed in every way to the Law. Finally,
the young man's prayer established a link between the institution of marriage
and Genesis 2:18.

The story also contains numerous allusions to the history of the patriarchs.
Like her namesake in the book of Genesis, Sarah seems to be dedicated to not

having a child. The conclusion of the marriage is a literal copy of the wedding of Isaac and Rebekah. The healing angel is, of course, the incarnation of divine providence in the life of the believer and reminds us vividly of the one who led Abraham's servant to the young woman Rebekah (see Gen 24).

Psalm 128 is included among the songs of ascents and served to remind the priests responsible for welcoming pilgrims of their duty.

Mark 12:228b–34. It has been estimated that the Torah contains no fewer than six hundred and thirteen commandments. This explains why the scribes were anxious to single out a few fundamental principles. What, then, was the one commandment that could serve as the basis for all the others? That is the question that is put to Jesus by a scribe, whose sincerity is clearly stressed by the author of the Gospel.

Jesus bases his reply on the confession of faith recited morning and evening by every pious Jew. The first commandment is to love God. Because God is one, he is able to call for deep and total commitment of the whole person. But there is also a second commandment: to love one's neighbor. This commandment also calls for total commitment. This is how Jesus experienced the first and second commandments on the cross, when he went further than all the sacrifices made in the temple.

After Jesus had driven the money-changers and dealers out of the temple, the scribes and the elders had contested his authority. Here we are told of a rabbi who recognized that love was more important than holocausts, and it is on this note of hope that the third of the three Jerusalem controversies ends. The adversaries withdraw at this stage and the public debate is concluded.

■

You may remember the guessing games that you used to play as a child: "My first is . . . . My second is . . . . My whole is . . . ." The Gospel gives us one of these today.

This is my first: "Listen, Israel . . . (or "Listen, today's Church . . ." or "Listen all people on earth"): the Lord our God is the one Lord." We are brought back again and again to our God, the one God. He is not only the answer to all our needs. He is the one God, the only God, the God who is completely different, the God who goes far beyond anything that we can say about him. We have to use words to speak about him and he has himself assumed our way of speaking. We have also to call on him when we suffer and he has himself shared our sufferings. We have tried to express the mystery and he has himself come close to us to reveal it. But, at the same time, we also must remember that he is the completely different one and that the Bible tells us: "You will fear the Lord." This fear does not mean being frightened, but is an attitude of reverence, adoration and wonderment in the presence of the mystery. God has made himself known to us and has enabled us through his grace to enter into his covenant: "Listen, Israel: God, who is unknowable, tells you his name. He is the one God."

How can we do anything else but love him with our whole being? This is not obeying a commandment. It is a response that rises up from an astonished heart. It is a call, an offer and a way lying open before us— the way of happiness and fruitfulness. Proclaiming that God is the one God, the only God—surely this is ceasing to claim him for ourselves and to think of him according to our own measure in order to welcome a Love that will give us great joy.

That, then, is my first. And this is my second: "Listen, people of God . . . Listen, all men of good will. Your brother is the one Son, the only Son. You must welcome him, listen to him, respect him, do him justice and let him develop and expand in his oneness. This, too, is not obeying a commandment. It is also a response that rises up from an astonished heart. We are all brothers, born of the same tenderness. We are one in the same blood, and one spirit is the breath of our life.

These, then, are my first and my second. What is my whole? It is that the first is my second. The love that we have for God should overflow from our hearts into the whole of his work. Everything is, after all, part of the same whole. We are held together by only one love, which makes us seek communion with all things. We are led to God and to each other by one and the same impulse.

We can look for and find that impulse in Jesus, the one who offered himself once and for all time, the one with whom we enter into communion in the power of the Spirit. Because the Son told us this when he was about to offer himself, we are able to understand that it is a true love that enables us to give ourselves totally to each other. How difficult that love is! How often it is thwarted, weakened or mocked! But we receive it as a grace that enables us to live.

My first, then, and my second and my whole are that love which is a gift and will become our vocation.

■

With all our hearts
and urged on by the Spirit of Jesus,

we give thanks to you, Lord our God,
because you are the one God, the only God,
from whom all love comes.

    Blessed are you, Lord,
    God of tenderness and love!

Through Jesus Christ,
who offered himself for many,
you have gathered together your scattered children
to make them one in the same faith
and to lead them to your Kingdom.

    Blessed are you, Lord,
    God of tenderness and love!

Through your Spirit
you enable us to love you
and to open ourselves to each other
in the power of that same love.
We bless you
for having filled us to overflowing in this way.

    Blessed are you, Lord,
    God of tenderness and love!

FRIDAY OF THE 9TH WEEK

THE CROWDS HEARD HIM GLADLY

Tobit 11:5–17. All's well that ends well! The young man Tobias comes home safe and sound. He spreads the fish's gall over his father's eyes. The white skins fall away from them and the old man is able to see again. This therapy was well-known in the ancient world, but in this case it is a good angel (Raphael means "God heals") who teaches men how to apply it. This detail is quite important. It legitimates the art of healing in the eyes of people who, on one hand, attributed sickness to demons (Sarah's healing was an exorcism) and, on the other, believed that only Yahweh had the privilege of healing. But all's well that ends well and all those present, even the dog, express joy and thanksgiving.

157

Psalm 146 can be regarded as a hymn, but it is composed of widely differing elements. Its core, however, is a psalm of congratulation addressed to the believer who seeks Yahweh's help.

Mark 12:35–37. According to the Jewish tradition that was based on the oracle of Nathan (2 Sam 7), the Messiah would be a descendant of David. Jesus, however, always refused to accept this title, because he was convinced that it did not adequately cover the full reality of his person.

But, assuming that the Messiah had to be David's heir, what explanation can be given for the fact that he is called "my Lord," as in Psalm 110? What is more, according to this psalm, this descendant of David will be seated at God's right hand. Does that not indicate that the messianic king is much more than an ordinary monarch? If the scribes had examined scripture more closely and had welcomed Jesus without prejudice, they would not have needed to call his authority into question after the incident in the Temple.

■

The crowds heard Jesus gladly. And we too are there—among those people who are astonished to see a face reveal God, to hear a voice speak of God and to find that they are loved.

We too have come to Jesus. And whom do we see? A man dedicated to his mission. At the end of the Gospel, the cross will reveal his true face, as it has been shaped by the choices and decisions made throughout his life. His birth—poor and abandoned in Bethlehem. The choice that he made again and again in favor of the poor and the abandoned—a choice that earned him the hostility of those who wanted to seize hold of God and reduce man to insignificance.

The crowds heard Jesus gladly. Soon they will see a man with fettered feet, unable to take a step towards his fellow-men, unable to join those with whom he had been so close throughout the whole of his life. They will see a man with his hands nailed to the wood, unable to stretch them out to those to whom he had so often extended them as a sign of tenderness, to heal their sickness and to overcome their fears. They will see a man whose eyes are closed by the pain he is suffering and who can no longer let them rest on those whose faces he has always looked at so lovingly. They will see a man made silent by suffering. They will see a man who is the image of our human condition, the son of David and of the human race.

We too are fettered, but by our selfishness. That is what prevents us from moving towards our fellow-men. Our hands, too, are nailed, but by the fear that prevents us from stretching them out in a gesture offering peace and consolation. Our eyes too are closed, but by fear—we are afraid to see on the faces of those we look at a hope that we cannot fulfil. We too remain silent, because our hearts are hardened and we cannot find words of tenderness and solace. It is also because we are so disappointed by repeated failures that we dare not risk any more words of love in case they are rejected.

But the Jesus whom we hear, together with the crowds in the temple, is certainly a son of our earth. Shortly after leaving the temple, his feet were fettered, his hands were nailed, his eyes were closed and he was silent. But he had told us who he was: "I am the light": a light of the kind that could bring out the clarity that illuminates every human existence, however obscured it might be. "I am the way": a way that helps us to find others and with them to create a true human community. "I am the Word": a Word filled with meaning and able to reveal to us the meaning of all life, however mean or unhappy it might be. He also said of himself: "I am the Life": a life that is triumphant over death and is the promise and pledge of a victorious and full life. The Jesus we hear is a son of our own lineage. He is also the Lord and Master who sits at the right hand of the Father.

That is why I know that through him an indissoluble unity has been established between our human life and God's will for us, between the men and women that we are and God himself.

How can we ever understand that union? There is only one way. It is by joining Christ where we are able to join him—in our human condition. If we are to enter the kingdom which he invites us to enter and which he bears within himself, all that we have to do is to present ourselves to him in the fabric of our poor and simple human life. If we do that, a resurrection will be brought about in us. Our words—those poor words that cannot express what is in the heart—will become the vehicles of God's truth. Our deeds—those poor deeds that have never even succeeded in building up our world—will build the kingdom. And our lives, always threatened by death, will be filled with the fullness of God's life.

Jesus said: "David said that I am his son and that I am Lord." The crowds heard him gladly and, with them, we too look at him as Pilate did and, with him, we too say: "Here is the man." But in faith we also look at him as the Apostle Thomas looked at him and we too say: "My Lord and my God."

■

Jesus, son of David
and son of our own lineage,
take the whole of our life,
its poverty and its hope,
to your Father!
Son of the living God,
Lord, sitting at God's right hand,
save our life
and be the resurrection of our future.

■

Let us pray for our preachers and pastors,
that they may hear in the silence
the Word that is their mission to proclaim;
that they may live in the tenderness
that is their vocation to arouse.

Let us pray for our teachers,
that they may serve the truth
and let us pray for all poets and thinkers,
that they may show new ways to men.

Let us pray for all the churches,
that they may, in poverty and without pretention,
continue the mission of the Word
and that they may reflect the Gospel
and inspire faith in men and women.

God, who is worthy of faith,
we bless you because of Jesus.
In our world he has kept the one word
that expresses our prayer
and the certainty that it is heard.
May what you have revealed in him
be accomplished today.

Hear our prayer,
because we are listening today
to the promise that will be kept
for ever and ever.

WE MUST CHOOSE

Tobit 12:1, 5–15, 20. The last act: The angel Raphael abandons his anonymity and invites his hosts to turn to God. It is God who has been providence for the two families and who has, from the first day, watched over history and has heard the prayers of Tobit and Sarah and made their houses happy.

It is clear, then, that the book of Tobit takes into account the Jewish belief in angels, a belief that developed above all during the exile in Babylonia. As X. Leon-Dufour has said: "The discourse on the angels is rooted in the representations of Eastern mythologies, according to which God was surrounded by a court of 'sons of God' destined to heighten his glory and place him at a height that was inaccessible to human beings." Under the Persian influence, these angels tended to increase in number and were even given names. No attempt was made, however, to throw light on their nature.

Echoing Raphael's invitation, the old man Tobit sings in praise of God's providence (chapter 13).

Mark 12:38–44. We must choose! Jesus exhorts us to serve others and not to be like the scribes and Pharisees, who cling to places of honor, but oppress the poor. The mark of the true disciple is his welcome of the poor! Faith and reconciliation must be at the heart of all authentic prayer (11:24–25). Jesus' enemies, however, pray in order to be seen by others.

Yes, we must choose! The crowd is above all invited to make a choice—those people who will shortly let themselves be led astray by the very men whom Jesus is criticizing now. But who better than Jesus could judge what the poor widow had given? A couple of small coins, everything that she possessed. Who could assess her gift better than the one who would, on the cross, give not what he "had over," but his own life?

■

"I am going to reveal the truth to you," the angel told Tobias. And indeed he discloses to him the hidden meaning of his life and the secret and unexpected significance of his actions. Almost inevitably one is reminded here of Jesus' words in Matthew's Gospel: "As you did this to the least of these brothers of mine, you did it to me," and later in Mark: "I tell you solemnly, this poor widow has put more in than all who have contributed to the treasury."

We go on living as well as we can. Very often we lead our life at a very low level, without any stimulus or breath of hope to raise it up. We have so many unhappy experiences and disappointed dreams that we soon learn the wisdom of not getting too involved. It is not that we will probably fail—failure is often most likely! And it is always deeply wounding. This leads the strongest among us to develop an impassive attitude, while those of us who are weaker only dream of doing what is possible. We all make our hopes tame and manageable.

"I am going to reveal the truth to you," the angel Raphael told Tobit and his family. "When you were at prayer and weeping, it was I who offered your supplications to the Lord." This is the grace we receive from the liturgy—it reveals to us the real significance of our lives and discloses their other aspects.

"I am going to reveal the truth to you." By the grace of the liturgy, the deepest part of our being has already been taken into the kingdom of God. A little piece of broken bread becomes the pledge that every offer of love and every attempt to share has the value of eternity. A gesture of peace becomes the sacrament that every effort to bring about reconciliation builds up a people who are brothers.

Everyday words become the prayer of sons who are loved by the one Father. At the center of our existence, which is often unhappy, our celebration bears witness to the fact that tomorrow is always possible and that it has indeed already arrived. Our hopes are not foolish. Made holy by the Spirit of God, they become the fabric into which the promised future is woven. Our prayers are not in vain. Taken by Jesus to his Father, they become the humble certainty that God will fulfil his promise.

"I am going to reveal the truth to you." We are already living in that tomorrow and, despite our many mistakes and failures, our lives already have the value of eternity.

■

God, you are faithful to your promises.
Let your Spirit
open our minds to your plans,
*   so that the hidden taste of our present life*
*   may be revealed to us.*
God our Father, your love for us is sovereign.
Let your Spirit
enlarge our hearts to contain your tenderness,

so that the greatness of our calling
  may be revealed to us.
And may your grace be manifest
  for ever and ever.

God of our praise,
  you reveal to us the secret of our life.
A little piece of bread bears witness to your presence
  and our fellowship is the sacrament of the kingdom.

Let us see your love
  and let us receive your salvation!
So our lives will be illuminated by charity
  for ever and ever.

EVEN YEARS

ORDINARY TIME
WEEKS 1–9

Gospel According to Saint Mark
First Book of Samuel
Second Book of Samuel
First Book of Kings
Letter of Saint James
First Letter of Saint Peter
Letter of Jude
Second Letter of Saint Peter
Second Letter to Timothy

"Tell me a story, Mommy!" Children need to dream and to live in the company of their heroes. Stories are essential to teach them about life.

God is taught through stories. He only lives through these stories told by believers. That is why we read and reread the story of the children of Israel and the slow adjustments and readjustments that took place in their national life, the risks and dangers that existed during the monarchy and the messianic hopes aroused at that time. That is why we turn to the life of the first Christian communities and the responses that they had to make day after day, when the words of the Gospel were confronted with the realities of life. Above all, that is why we turn and return to the one Word, proclaimed in the life, activity and preaching of God's herald, Jesus of Nazareth.

This is the scandal of our faith: that God is only God-with-us where the believer discovers him as such. The covenant is only the covenant where believers are committed to it. This is because God has shown nothing but the faces of men and women who believe in him. Jesus' disciples saw nothing but a man who believed in God, a Son who believed in the Father.

God is taught through stories. The Bible tells us about God. And history, our story, as told and interpreted by men of a previous age then becomes the place, the only place, where our faith is born. We have nothing but a prayer—a humble petition expressed by children: "Tell me a story!" That is the grace of the liturgy—it preserves the memory of what has happened to us in order to give birth to us in the history of God.

From 1 Samuel to 2 Kings

If we look superficially at the books of Samuel and Kings, we shall probably see no more than a monotonous succession of reigns, some happy and others unhappy. But, assuming that David's ascent to the throne of Jerusalem, the temporary division of the kingdom, the fall of Samaria in 721 and that of Jerusalem in 587 B.C. and other events all form part of history, then surely the historian's task is to go further than the mere facts and try to find the thread that connects them. In this respect, the Deuteronomist historian was a supreme master.

The first question that we must ask, however, is: Who was that historian? But, in recent years, the work of several different hands has been discovered in the great fresco consisting of the books from *Joshua* to *2 Kings* and so we should rather ask: Who were those historians? Some of these historians assembled the oral or written traditions that existed before them, while others worked on editions following the shared work. All of them, however, worked in the spirit of *Deuteronomy*.

During the reign of Josiah, the "Book of the Law" was, we are told, accidentally discovered in the temple (2 Kgs 22:8–10). This was what is now known as the "Deuteronomic Code" (Deut 12–26). This Code seems to have been brought to the Sanctuary by refugees from the Kingdom of Israel. It was, however, very soon lost. The discovery of this collection of laws had a considerable influence on the Jewish people, both from the religious and from the literary points of view. From the religious point of view, because it played an important part in the reform carried out by King Josiah, in which his aim was to centralize worship and, from the literary point of view, because the Deuteronomist historians were inspired in their judgment of the events that had taken place from the entry into the Promised Land until the Babylonian exile by the Deuteronomic Code.

What, then, was that judgment? The Deuteronomic Code ends with a series of blessings and curses addressed to those who were either committed or not committed to living according to God's law. According to the ideology of the ancient world, such blessings and curses were, as we say nowadays, "performative." This means that they were effective words, which brought about what they affirmed. The Deuteronomist work was, moreover, begun before 587 B.C. and was finished during the exile. It was, then, quite natural that these historians should make a statement about the causes of this exile. In other words, what sin had been committed by the people, and above all by the king who was their incarnation, that should incur the curse that the law provided?

The work of the Deuteronomist historians, therefore, became in the end a great indictment of the kings of Israel and Judah. The question that they inevitably asked as a result of this was: To what extent had those kings been faithful to the demands made by *Deuteronomy* and ultimately to the covenant of Sinai? This was a very important question, and in asking it the historians combined two traditions which had until then been independent of each other: the Mosaic tradition and the royal ideology. In other words, they measured the legitimacy of the Davidic covenant against the background of the Sinaitic covenant.

The answer that they provided had also to be quite subtly shaded, because not everyone had been in favor of the institution of the monarchy. Two texts in particular are worth noting in this context. The first is the history of David's ascent to the throne and especially Nathan's prophecy (2 Sam 7). The second is the commentary on the exile of the penultimate king of Judah (2 Kgs 25:27). Recalling Nathan's prophecy was in fact asking whether the Babylonian exile had not rendered null and void the divine promises made to the house of David. On the other hand, the passage on the exiled king (2 Kgs 25) allowed a glimmer of hope to remain because the pardoned Jehoiachin took his place at the table of the Babylonian king. The Davidic covenant was therefore not nullified by the exile in Babylonia, despite the deplorable behavior of those who sat on the throne.

The same applies to other obstacles. The story of the successors to the throne of David both reveals, in a way that resembles the manner of the Abraham cycle, the difficulties that had accompanied the dynasty and at the same time bears witness to the perennial nature of the divine promise. There were countless misfortunes. For example, Queen Michal, Saul's daughter, bore no children (2 Sam 6:23). The aging king was guilty of weakness with regard to his sons and this gave rise to serious troubles. Bathsheba went to great lengths to ensure that Solomon, the fruit of sin, should be enthroned. The Deuteronomist history is above all a human history and we should be grateful to its authors that they did not try to conceal anything.

They did more than this, however—they also succeeded in revealing the presence of the hand of God in that history. Despite the many obstacles, Yahweh kept his promises and showed the people that he was the master of their history. One of the great merits of the Deuteronomist historians is that they again and again stressed that God did not behave as the master of history in the manner of a *deus ex machina*. He was not alongside events, but within them. The framework within which the Deuteronomist history takes place is totally profane and men act quite autonomously. Yahweh is the master of that history, yes, but, as G. von Rad has correctly pointed out, "the place selected for this conduct of history is the human heart and Yahweh made use of mens' impulses and decisions to achieve his historical plan."

But God can do again today, the Deuteronomist historians seem to be telling us, what he has done in the past. The work of these historians ends on a hopeful note partly because the thread of messianic hope also runs through it. The exile in Babylonia was not Yahweh's last word!

FROM MONDAY TO SATURDAY

OF THE 1ST WEEK

The Kingdom of God is Close at Hand

Confronted with Jesus

"The time has come!" It is with these words that the weeks of ordinary time begin and straightaway we are immersed in that experience. Mark is a man in a hurry. He is hastening towards what is essential. Jesus begins his ministry ("That is why I have come") and with him the kingdom is close at hand. He teaches and heals. He drives out evil spirits and purifies men. The powers of evil that enslave men feel threatened. And rightly so, because Jesus, simply by coming, inaugurated the time of deliverance. All the people of Capernaum gathered at the town's gate, which was open to receive a new day, and the street was transformed into a place of miracles. In the crowd, the question was asked: "What is happening?" The evangelist in a hurry gives us the answer: "The shock of Jesus' coming." That is the impression that Mark makes on us.

Our time of waiting is over. God's time is here and it is first of all this challenge. Are we going to leave the nets that are holding us back? The word of God is running like wildfire over the earth and it has already set fire to Galilee. An urgent decision has to be made! The new time has begun! Jesus moves forward and, where he passes, God's fruit is ripening. Samuel—"God is listening"! It is in this way, then, that the Gospel begins its victorious race.

The crowd quickly gathers. The people do not yet know that God's time will also be that of Calvary. They have still to penetrate the mystery of the one who has been sent and to spend a long time in prayer ("Speak . . . Your servant is listening") before coming to an understanding and knowledge of faith. But the deliverance that Jesus came to inaugurate is becoming a reality. Jesus declares war on everything that disfigures man, who has come from the hands of God.

"What is happening?" The evangelist takes us to Calvary, where our profession of faith will be made. In our name, the centurion will say: "In truth this man was the Son of God." But, in the meantime, a corner of the veil is already lifted while we are waiting. After the day at Capernaum, the controversial questions lead us even more deeply into the mystery. The "shock of Jesus" has already alerted us. Now it brings us to the point where we are ready to make a decision.

We are invited to belong! "All authority in heaven and on earth has been given to me." Jesus claims nothing less than that! The power that he exercises is that of the grace of God. What he has power to do is to manifest the irrational love of the Father. Yes, the kingdom is really close at hand. It is here, in the Man of God!

MONDAY OF THE 1ST WEEK

THE TIME OF WAITING IS OVER

1 Samuel 1:1-8. The books of Samuel (the division between the two books is quite artificial) incorporate oral traditions which go back fundamentally to the days of Saul and David. These traditions were probably written during Solomon's reign but, after the disappearance of the Davidic monarchy, the historians known as the Deuteronomists reconsidered the early work with the aim of including it in their own great historico-theological work consisting of the books of Joshua, Judges, Samuel and Kings.

The Deuteronomist historians were very severe in their judgment of the institution of the monarchy, principally because the majority of its representatives had failed to obey the Mosaic Law. They regarded David as the ideal king. For them, he was the only monarch whose "heart was wholly with Yahweh his God" (1 Kgs 11:4). This explains why belief in the guarantee of eternity given to the Judaean dynasty persisted until the eventual coming of a son of David who would be worthy of the promises made to the founder of the dynasty.

This makes it possible for us to understand why there is such insistence in the first chapters of the book of Samuel on the calling of the prophet. It was essential that the one who consecrated David should be recognized as Yahweh's spokesman. God's choice of Samuel was highlighted by the barrenness of Hannah, who later became the mother of the prophet Samuel.

The second half of *Psalm 116* which features in today's liturgy, is the conclusion of a psalm of thanksgiving, expressing the believer's longing to offer a thanksgiving sacrifice in the presence of all the people.

Mark 1:14-20. See p. 10.

■

Mark's Gospel is short, dense and incisive. Mark is a man in a hurry! We begin reading and are at once caught up in the adventure. John the Baptist is arrested, Jesus leaves the Jordan and goes into Galilee. There he puts into words the hope that no one had yet dared to express: "The time has come!"

"The time has come" means that God's history with men has reached a turning-point and the way ahead is clear. There is no going back. Jesus at once begins to recruit followers. Then he heals the sick and addresses the crowds and is greeted with amazement, enthusiasm and lack of understanding. He is also rejected.

An evangelist in a hurry! News that turns everything upside down! The shock of Jesus! "Follow me!" The Word calls for a response. It is impossible to be indifferent to it. Whoever hears it must make a decision because it confronts him with God's plan: "This is my Son, the Beloved; my favor rests on him. . . . Listen to him." You are called: "Follow me!"

God's time is above all a challenge. For you it means: Your time of waiting is over! The happy event that you have been looking forward to has become a reality. God is urging you forward. That is why the happy proclamation is at once followed by the call to believe in the good news: "Repent and believe!"

The time of waiting is over. God has entered your life for ever. He has turned you completely upside down! Will you leave all the nets that are holding you back and have the courage to respond to these words: "Do not wait! It is I! God's salvation has come to you!"?

■

Blessed are you, God our Father,
because your word has made our barren earth fertile.
We thought that we had been abandoned,
but your Spirit asked us:
  "Why are you weeping?
  Can you not see that you have risen
  and have been born again?"

Blessed are you, God:
you tear the fabric of our despair

and loosen the net that holds us back.
   May the time of your salvation come,
   may your rule be established on earth
   and may the bread broken
   be good news for us!

Today is fulfilled the word of grace
   left in our hands by the one
   who inaugurates your coming.
We proclaim his death
   and the Spirit gives life to his last words.
We celebrate his resurrection
   and the Spirit inaugurates a new age.

Be with us, Word of hope,
   come to those you make rise again
   to be born to your words,
   walk with those you send into the world
   and put your breath into the hearts of those
   who should be raised up by your grace.

Convert us!
   May Justice and Peace embrace each other,
   may Love and Truth increase
   and may your kingdom come!

Call us to follow your Son!
   May we abandon our false peace and tranquility
   and risk our lives on your word.
Let us set off in his footsteps.
He will take us to you, our Father.

TUESDAY OF THE 1ST WEEK

SHE WAS CALLED HANNAH

1 Samuel 1:9–20. Shiloh—in the highlands of Ephraim. There was a sanctuary of Yahweh at Shiloh, served by a levitical family, Eli and his two sons. Every year a man of the tribe of Ephraim came to this sanctuary to worship with his two wives. One of them, Hannah, was his favorite, but she had no child. This made her despair, because she was no longer young. She vowed that, if she had a son, she would dedicate him to God.

Hannah's prayer gave rise to an amusing incident. Because she was praying in a whisper, Eli thought that she was drunk. She, however, denied this and told the priest why she was troubled. He calmed her and reassured her that God would hear her prayer. Hannah, whose name means "God gives grace," expressed her happiness with the words: "Your servant has found grace in your presence." When the time came, she gave birth to a son, whom she called Samuel (which can mean "His name is El").

The *Canticle of Hannah* is the song that inspired the Canticle of Mary, the *Magnificat*. Hannah's song celebrates the change in the situation from which the prophet's mother has benefited: "The barren woman bears sevenfold, but the mother of many is desolate" (1 Sam 2:5).

Mark 1:21–28. See p. 13.

■

She was called Hannah, that is, "God is listening." She was barren and her life, which was made for giving birth, did not bear the fruit that she longed for. But the Word of God rests on her. She rises and her face is no longer the same. When God passes by, his word does not remain without result.

Jesus in a hurry—that is the aspect of the Lord presented by Mark. Jesus does not waste time. He arrives at Capernaum *and immediately* begins to teach. Mark does not enlarge on the subject matter of Jesus' sermon. All that he notes is the effect that it has on the listeners, because Jesus teaches as a man who has authority. He does not teach as the scribes taught. He does not restrict himself to the usual practice of preachers. He does not confine himself simply to providing explanations and arguments and to quoting authorities. He speaks as someone who has received his authority from God—full power and a mission to speak. Jesus comes and the world is already changed. At the same time, his coming also means the end of demonic power.

The man was possessed by demons. He was no longer master of his own life. But the Word of God appears and his face is no longer the same. His life, which was made to grow in freedom and peace, bore only the fruit of death. But God comes. He speaks and the powers binding this man know that their defeat is close at hand. "What do you want with us, Jesus of Nazareth?" The man who is dispossessed of himself finds himself again, free, set on his feet, given back to life. Barrenness gives way to life and the man, raised up, can utter "a loud cry" of rebirth. The woman had even forgotten her own name. Now she finds it again, in wonderment. She was called Hannah—"God gives grace."

Jesus is in a hurry because God cannot wait. "The kingdom is close at hand—the time has come." And the people in the crowd "asked each other what it all meant." "He gives orders even to unclean spirits," they say, "and they obey him."

■

With Hannah, in the presence of God, we pray:
"Listen to us, Lord,
if you do not take our cause to heart,
*   who will be our salvation?*
Overcome the powers
*   that threaten our lives.*
Give us freedom.
Raise us up
*   to receive the love*
*   of the one who has conquered death*
*   your Son Jesus,*
*   your Word of grace,*
*   raised up on our little faith.*

Call us together by the word of your Son.
Keep us outside ourselves, Lord,
*   set free from our fears and anxieties.*
Give us back to the freedom of our dreams
*   and the fascination of your light.*
May your mercy be our power
*   and your grace be our salvation.*

Then we shall be astonished
*   by what your Spirit can do in us.*
We shall be made new
*   —disciples of your Son*
*   and sons of your tenderness."*

WEDNESDAY OF THE 1ST WEEK

THE OPEN DOOR

1 Samuel 3:1–10, 19–21–4:1a. The story of Samuel's childhood ends with the account of his calling as a prophet. It is as a prophet that he will later anoint David as king, and in this way name the dynasty within which the Messiah will be born. Samuel is for the history of David what John the Baptist was later to be for Jesus.

The author stresses, in a very simple but delightful story, the divine choice and the availability of the boy Samuel. Yahweh's calling him followed a period in Israel's history when the Spirit had been very seldom manifested. The boy rises after the first call and the old priest confirms his vocation. From that time onwards, Samuel is accredited as a prophet in the whole of Israel.

In its present form, *Psalm 40* is in fact two psalms. Verses 14–18 form part of an individual lament, whereas vv. 2–13, which are included in today's liturgy, are a song of thanksgiving. The psalmist recalls his prayer to Yahweh in times of unhappiness and then goes up to the temple, where he is congratulated by the priest (v. 5) and explains his attitude. God has not in fact inspired him to offer sacrifice, but has persuaded him to come in person to the temple to express his gratitude. The words "Here I am! I am coming!" were at a very early date given a messianic significance.

Mark 1:29–39. See p. 15.

■

A great crowd of people were jostling one another at the door of Simon's house. Everyone wanted to see and hear what was going on. Were the stories true—that the fisherman's mother-in-law had just been raised up, healed of her fever?

A great crowd of people at the gate of the town. Everyone wanted to see and hear the man who, it was claimed, at last fulfilled their expectation. No empty words or long speeches of consolation—no, this man took on himself man's suffering.

Then, later, another great crowd of people—or perhaps they were the same people—at the gates of the city—the city that killed the prophets, all wanting to see the man who bore the sin of the world.

Today, however, he does not allow those who were face-to-face with him to speak about him. The fact that there were so many people gathered around him as a healer certainly points to his success with the crowds, but it also expresses the ambiguity of those face-to-face with him. He healed people, yes, but he did this to confront them with the decisive question: "Who is this man?"

On that day, later, but not so very distant now, when no one will be able to mistake his power and his greatness, a foreigner, a Roman centurion, will say: "In truth this man was the Son of God."

"It is for this hour that I have come." Even as Jesus begins to go through the whole of Galilee, this "hour" is already approaching. It is not the fame of the healer that is spreading, but God's call that is being thrown out in every direction. The good news of the Gospel is beginning its victorious journey.

A great crowd of people were jostling one another at the door of Simon's house in Capernaum. Good news was being proclaimed there. A great crowd of people is on the threshold of Peter's house—the Church. Good news has been proclaimed there throughout the centuries to all of you—people who are crippled and lame, a great crowd without hope. God is proclaiming the grace of his Kingdom to you!

■

Speak, Lord, your servant is listening!
  Rid us of our useless anxieties,
  our nagging cares
  and the protective shell of our habits.

Speak, Lord, your servant is listening!
  Open our doors to the one we do not know
  and open our hearts to your word that is always new.

Speak, Lord, your servant is listening!
  Tell us again those words of tenderness
  and show us your salvation.

Speak, Lord, your servant is listening!
  Let your Church welcome you
  and let all your promises be fulfilled for us
  as only you can fulfil them.

The words are not yet on our lips,
  but you know them already, Lord.
Keep us from empty chatter
  and let us have nothing else to express
  but your word and your love.

THURSDAY OF THE 1ST WEEK

WAR IS DECLARED

1 Samuel 4:1c–11. The background to the books of Samuel and Judges is the settlement of the tribes of Israel in Palestine. The conquest of the country was slow and difficult. The inhabitants were firmly established either in the highlands or behind the strong walls of their cities. Towards the end of the period of the Judges, moreover, the Philistines, who occupied the land along the Mediterranean coast, threatened Israel constantly.

Israel's struggles therefore soon assumed the character of a holy war. The people's enemies had to be entirely destroyed and their possessions had to be burnt in homage to the Lord. In battle, it was Yahweh—symbolized by the ark of the covenant—who was fighting for his people. It was not enough, however, simply to take shelter behind the ark. The people had to measure up to the demands made on them. Israel suffered the bitter experience of total defeat at the hands of the Philistine army at the battle of Aphek.

Psalm 44 is another composite canticle. Verses 2–9 are in the form of a hymn, while the remaining verses are a very good example of a national supplication. Psalms of this kind are very valuable for prayer. Without a trace of pious suffering, they let us hear the firm and confident voice of the supplicant.

Mark 1:40–45. See p. 17.

■

War is declared! The people rise up, refusing to be enslaved. War is declared because those who hear the word of God are not of this world.

We are sons of the light and we do not belong to the darkness that surrounds us. The world around us is always making us long to possess power and domination exclusively for our own use. Enslavement to money encloses us in a gilded prison. Individual egoism and collective selfishness have become a habit and we modestly draw a veil over them in the name of fortune.

Yes, there are many Philistines ready to attack us and they are often victorious in their fight against the people made holy by God. It is not enough just to cry out: "Lord, Lord, we are lost!" if we are to be victorious in the struggle for life. Nor is it enough simply to shelter behind the ark in order to be saved! No, it is those who have again and again taken up the struggle to make the Word of grace the light of their lives who will be victorious! "Let us give up the things we prefer to do under cover of the dark," Saint Paul admonished us, "Let us arm ourselves and appear in the light . . . and let that armor be the Lord Jesus Christ!"

War is declared! Jesus has risen and, as he goes forward, the darkness retreats in terror. Man was so disfigured by the leprosy of evil and sin that he became no more than a sick shadow of his original and beautiful self. But the holy one of God came close to him and purified him and he ceased to drag himself along under the weight of his crippling disease. He too rose, victorious.

War is declared! You may be certain that, every time you decide to fight for the reign of Love to be established in your own life and in the life of the world, the darkness will retreat in terror. You may lose the battle, but do not forget: The war has already been won for all time! Love rose victorious and left the tomb on Easter morning. The world is always marking you with its imprint of sin. Its sickness is, like leprosy, contagious. But you can be quite sure that Jesus has already refashioned your face. You are children of the light, so live as children of the light!

■

We are surrounded on all sides!
How difficult it is for us to love!
Disfigured by sin, we are, Lord,
pale reflections of your holiness.
Restore the work of your hands,
we beseech you.
Say again the saving words:
"Of course I want to! Be cured!"

■

How good it is to give thanks to you,
Lord our God!
You do not leave us alone
in tears and in darkness—
you open for us a way of light
and your Son leads us forward on it.
He came so that the lame would walk,
the deaf hear and the blind see.
We bless you,
God of the promise that never disappoints.
Your Son prepares the table of mercy
and we know how faithful he is.
Let us, then, sing
with all those who have been filled with your love
and let us praise you
with all those who share the happiness of the good news.

ALL AUTHORITY HAS BEEN GIVEN TO ME

1 Samuel 8:4-7, 10-22a. The inhabitants of Palestine offered fierce resistance to the Israelite invaders and several battles took place. At dawn, the army set off behind the ark of the covenant, which had been brought from Shiloh. This time, events were favorable to Israel and the ark was taken back to the sanctuary by the people crying: "Yahweh is king" (see Ps 94, 98 and 100).

So Yahweh ruled as king over Israel. But the time came when the people decided that they wanted to choose a king from a Jewish family. This need reflected a desire for stability among the tribes of Israel. Up till then, they had been nomadic, but now they wanted to become, as it were, settled, middle-class and respectable. Their aim was to reinforce the bonds between the clans so that, together, they could overcome the common enemy, the Philistines.

This wish, however, gave rise to a very serious theological problem. Would the choice of an earthly king not put an end to God's supremacy? When he decided to choose Saul, the prophet Samuel took care to seek divine approval for his choice. This was a way of safeguarding Yahweh's privileges. Samuel also put his compatriots on their guard against the practices of the monarchy. This passage is not seen nowadays as a condemnation in anticipation of the behavior of the Jewish kings, but rather as a memory of royal conduct that was widely known throughout the whole of the Near East from the second millennium onwards. However sacred he might be, the king could not, in the opinion of the Deuteronomist historians, offend the only true king of Israel, Yahweh.

Psalm 89 is another composite psalm; verses 2-5 and 20-38 constitute a dynastic poem, whereas the verses included in today's liturgy form part of a cosmic hymn (vv. 6-19) expressing the glory of God's power.

Mark 2:1-12. See p. 21.

■

The story of the healing of the leper concludes a section describing the very hopeful beginnings of Jesus' activity. The proclamation of the coming of the promised times, the calling of the first disciples, the driving out of the evil spirits and the healing of a number of sick people —these all take place without any open opposition. But Jesus did not in any way want to go through the country simply performing miracles and preaching edifying sermons. In the second section of the Gospel, neither his miracles nor their influence are very significant. In fact, the events narrated become less and less important, while the fundamental questions about man and God have an increasingly central position.

"Give us a king!" The people wanted a sovereign so that they could conquer their enemies. "Give us a king to rule over us like the other nations," they asked, believing that he would march at the head of their army and fight for them.

Then, for a people who despaired of winning battles against sin, a king arose. "All authority has been given to me." This king does not, like Israel's kings, make us plough and harvest for his profit or make us his slaves. On the contrary, he comes to us in humility, seated on an ass and says: "Shoulder my yoke and learn from me, for I am gentle and humble in heart."

"All authority has been given to me." We need a king to set us free. What is at the center of today's Gospel is not the healing of a man who cannot walk, but the forgiveness of a man's heart. Jesus' raising up of the bed-ridden man is the sign of a much more radical raising.

"Your sins are forgiven." Jesus does not simply express confidence or even a certainty with regard to the forgiveness of sins—he forgives sins himself. Who is this man? The Son of man was to manifest himself at the end of time and it is because he is this Son of man that Jesus is able here and now to exercise the right that is God's alone. The power that will come one day is present in him now. "All authority has been given to me."

■

Brothers, on your feet! Rise up with Christ!
Despite your weakness, you can walk!
Christ is going ahead of you on the way.
God will not turn his eyes away from you.
The kingdom has come to you
    and will heal you.

Lord, we fall and cannot get up.
We are paralysed and cannot go on.
Sustained by the faith of your Church,
    we come to you,
      for who can forgive our sins
      if not you alone?

Raise us up and heal us,
because of your great mercy
and because of Jesus our brother,
  for you have raised him from the dead
  and he lives close to you
  for this world
  and for all time.

SATURDAY OF THE 1ST WEEK

BEARING WITNESS TO LOVE

1 Samuel 9:1-4, 17-19a; 10:1. Both the Israelites and the Philistines living in the coastal district wanted to make sure of their supremacy over the whole of the country. The Israelites were at first defeated and the ark of the covenant had fallen into the hands of the enemy (1 Sam 4). Then Saul arose as a charismatic leader and succeeded, at least partly, in rectifying the situation. The tribes decided to raise the man who had proved his valor against the enemy to the dignity of the monarchy. In conformity with the republican traditions that persisted in the north of the country, the prophet Samuel was given the task of consecrating him as king.

Psalm 21 forms part of the ritual that established the procedure during the ceremonies that took place when Israel was victorious over its enemies. Victory was attributed to Yahweh and part of the liturgy consisted of a procession around the sanctuary and a dramatic presentation of the flight of the enemy. After the choice of Jerusalem as the capital, the liturgy took place in the temple within the framework of the Feast of Tabernacles.

Mark 2:13-17. See p. 23.

■

Taking the tax-collector on board to make a disciple of him—that is a bit much! Taking a man of evil reputation into your intimate circle—that is going too far! Surely Jesus knew very well how proverbially greedy and ruthless the agents of the power of Rome were. Why, then, did he pretend to forget the scorn in which the collaborators were held?

It was risky, taking such a man on board! A man who extorts money from the tax-payers and takes his own ten-percent might leave his desk and no one would complain. But welcoming a great number of tax-collectors and sharing a banquet with them—men of very doubtful character, regarded as impure—no, that was not acceptable! The scribes and Pharisees were only expressing the disapproval felt by everyone when they asked: "Why does he eat with tax-collectors and sinners?"

Who, then, is this man? "The Spirit of the Lord has been given to me, for he has anointed me as the Messiah. He has sent me to bring the good news to the poor, to bind up hearts that are broken, to proclaim liberty to captives, freedom to those in prison, to proclaim a year of favor from the Lord." The message of Jesus is credible because of his person. We can believe in it because his personal attitude reveals God's will to save all men. In welcoming sinners to his table, Jesus showed God's mercy and his longing to make the life-blood of Love circulate among men.

Jesus reconciled men to each other, even if that was only during a meal, when there were no longer righteous men and sinners, pure men and impure men, but only men who were equal in the presence of the poverty and tenderness of the Father who had made them all. Jesus' proclamation was this: God is not as a tax-collector sitting behind a desk, dealing with us as though we were accounts. What we are aware of here is something of the crazy love of the God of the old covenant, who never forsook his people, but again and again, with a patience that defies human understanding, drew them back to him.

"Why does he eat with tax-collectors and sinners?" Sharing a meal with such people is enough to cause deep scandal, but Jesus knows that he is the consecrated man of God. He takes the tax-collector away from his office and his aim is to take everyone on board to change their lives. He is marked with God's seal and this means that a new age can be inaugurated—the age of the new covenant. Jesus came to call not the righteous, but the sinners.

■

Blessed are you, God our Father,
your mercy is boundless
  and your goodness is infinite.
In Jesus, your beloved Son,
you have revealed yourself to us
  as a God of love
  who forgives us again and again.
Yes, Father, we give you thanks
  for your favor and your loving-kindness.

With all those who, today and yesterday,
  have been drawn by your tenderness,
and with all those who, fascinated by your mercy,
  have begun to hope again,
we acclaim you and praise you, God.

FROM MONDAY TO SATURDAY

OF THE 2ND WEEK

THE HEIR CAME

Discovering Jesus

With Jesus, through him and in him, the kingdom of God is close at hand and the time has come. God is present among his people and the old covenant has been superseded. This is the essence of the debate that begins with this week's section of the Gospel. What does the breaking in of this new element mean for our lives and the life of mankind? Who is this man who claims for himself the lordship of this new creation? After the brief and decisive proclamation of the coming of the kingdom, we are at once led to discover Jesus.

■

The bridegroom is here. God's wedding with mankind takes place today. God's blessing of humanity begins with Jesus' mission. The bridegroom is here, inviting us to the feast, and we have to decide whether or not to enter the bridal chamber. He is the heir of the promise, the king who has been blessed by God. The Son of man, whose coming was proclaimed by the prophets, exercises his authority over the sabbath, because, with his coming, the universe was once again immersed in the time of the beginning, when God established a day of rest.

Why should we be surprised that the shadows have been dispersed? They cannot endure the light that overcomes them. There is constant war between the powers of life and those of death, and what is at stake is man's happiness. But "God's foolishness is wiser than human wisdom"! A child brings down the giant. A cross puts an end to the reign of death! But why can we not be clear about it? We cannot decide—our

---

181

hearts prevent us and, confronted with the mystery of Jesus, we are torn between belonging and not understanding.

Discovering Jesus is always ultimately an affair of the heart. It is only if we are intimate with him that we shall ever learn to recognize his true face. It is only if we come to know him closely as a friend that we shall ever learn the secret of his person and enter with him into the mystery of God. And that will always be a gradual process. Discovering Jesus will always mean being confronted with the boundlessness that God is proclaiming through his Son and bringing about in him.

MONDAY OF THE 2ND WEEK

THE BRIDEGROOM IS HERE

1 Samuel 15:16–23. The Deuteronomist historian begins here to prepare the reader gradually for the removal of Saul. He describes the king's victories, especially those over Israel's traditional enemies, but he also emphasizes the king's faults. He includes, for example, Samuel's criticism of Saul's having given way to the people's wishes. As it was God who chose Saul as king, Saul owed obedience to God alone.

After the reign of Saul, the account is influenced by the traditions of the Northern Kingdom. The throne of Jerusalem was characterized by great stability. The southern provinces, on the other hand, had the privilege of allowing the prophets to intervene in the matter of choosing and rejecting sovereigns. The interdict was also a practice of the holy war to which the prophets of Samaria were very attached. It consisted of giving to Yahweh all the gains made from a victory.

Psalm 50 reflects the traditions of the sanctuary at Shechem and is also an indictment. In it, Yahweh himself denounces the sinfulness of the people, who are putting their trust in an external cult and are not listening to the words of their God.

Mark 2:18–22. See p. 26.

■

When God falls in love with his people, it is a time for them to dance for joy, not a time of mourning and sadness. For as long as the bridegroom is with them, his wedding guests cannot fast. Jesus interprets his presence, then, as a time of salvation, during which God's promise is fulfilled. His coming inaugurates God's wedding with his people. How, then, is it possible to go on fasting when God is introducing us to something quite new?

When they speak about the new things that are to come, the prophets are describing the new creation, the new order that God will establish at the end of time. Jeremiah proclaimed that God wanted to enter into a covenant with his people and that he would, on that day, write his law in their hearts. Later, Ezekiel announced that God would give them a new heart, removing the heart of stone from their bodies and giving them a heart of flesh. And Isaiah prophesied the creation of a new heaven and a new earth.

The bridegroom is here and the wedding is about to take place. God's new thing, his blessing and salvation, begin with the bridegroom's mission. If it is possible to fast in anticipation of the Day of God, why should we not take part in the wedding feast when the bridegroom is here? But we should not be satisfied with half-measures. Does anyone mend an old garment with a piece of unprepared cloth that will shrink when it becomes wet? Of course not, because that would lead to another tear alongside the first. Also no one would go to a wedding feast in old patched clothes—we would put on the wedding garment that God offers us. Who would put new wine in old skins? Fermenting wine would burst them! For a new proclamation, we need a new heart!

It is time to throw away the flowers that are fading in our hands. The bridegroom is here, the wedding has begun and the time of salvation will not come again.

So, brothers, give yourself over to God. Let yourselves be carried away by his tenderness. In marriage, not to give oneself entirely is already failing to be faithful. Saul wanted to make sure of his future and did not abandon himself to the risk of the covenant with God. This meant that he had already broken that covenant. God does not enter into a trial marriage with us. He gives everything that he has and everything that he is. Including his only Son. And in return, he calls for a heart that gives itself totally to him. The bridegroom is here and he is calling you. Will you decide to enter the bridal chamber where God will keep you for ever? Or do you prefer a short-stay room and superficial love affairs?

■

Your Son, the beloved,
  is standing at our door and knocking.

We hear a cry in our night:
  "The bridegroom is here!"
God our Father, we beseech you,
  let him make his dwelling-place with us;
  let him take us and show us his tenderness.
Your grace will then be our salvation
  for ever and ever.

■

The bridegroom is here—
  a little bread tells us he is present.
Why do we not join the feast
  inaugurated by his Passover?
The bridegroom has disappeared from our sight—
  we wanted to hold him,
  but he was taken from our grasp
  and a little bread tells us he is absent.
God of the covenant,
  let us enter more deeply
  into the mystery of the wedding of your Son,
  the Eucharist of today and of eternity.

■

The bridegroom has awakened us to the secrets of your love.
We bless you, God our Father!
Your Spirit has been poured out—
  foolish wine that lets us be born
  to the joy of your Kingdom!
Tear our patched garments
and clothe us in the cloak of holiness
and let us celebrate this feast for ever.

TUESDAY OF THE 2ND WEEK

THE HEIR

1 Samuel 16:1–13. Yahweh has rejected Saul and has instructed Samuel to choose a successor. Eliab will not be elected, however, nor will his brothers Abinadab and Shammah, because neither an impressive presence nor titles carry weight with God. David, the beloved, is the one who is to be anointed king. The divine favor that is attached to the throne of Jerusalem can already be discerned in him.

This account is a late addition to the story of David's ascent to the throne and it is completely subordinated to the religious ideas surrounding the Davidic dynasty, conceived as the nursery-bed of the messianic ideology. The naming of the future king by the prophet therefore anticipates his later adoption by God (see 2 Sam 7).

Today we have the other part of the *Psalm 89* (see Friday of the 1st week), that is, the dynastic poem. This psalm has only one theme, namely God's promises concerning the irrevocable election of the Davidic line to the throne of Judah. Verse 33 suggests that the poem was written at the court of Jerusalem to accredit the dynastic idea among the people.

Mark 2:23–28. See p. 28.

■

"Of fresh complexion, with fine eyes and pleasant bearing"—he was the youngest boy and he spent his days looking after the sheep. That was the heir to the Promise. God made the weakest of all king! "If I should decide to boast," Paul wrote, "I am glad to make my weakness my special boast." So God looks at David and, because of his "fine eyes," he cannot forget Jerusalem, his city. So God looks at David and, throughout its long history, a nation continued to turn back and look at the king who danced in front of the ark of the covenant.

He was just an ordinary man, like any other. His father and mother were well-known. He had worked for a long time in Nazareth. He had set off to go through Galilee, in search, he said, of the lost sheep of the house of Israel. But he was also the heir to the Promise. He was the king who was blessed by God. He was to call all men together at the place where God manifested himself. His arms, stretched out between heaven and earth, were to be a rallying sign. He was to build a temple that was not made by the hands of men, so that thanksgiving would echo from age to age as the song of the Church that is his living body.

He is here—the son of David. His disciples have gone ahead of him, their master, and they have broken off ears of corn to clear a path, a royal way for the one who announces the coming of salvation. He is here —the real fulfilment of the sabbath, which is the day of God himself. You have not received the spirit of slaves. You have not been begotten in order to be afraid. You have received the Spirit who turns to God to tell him: "Abba, Father." The whole of our life will not be sufficient to discover the wealth of our inheritance, because the heir has given us everything that he has himself received: the life of God himself.

■

Eternal Father,
*   you have placed everything that you possess*
*   in the hands of your Son,*
*   relying on his word and on his life.*
He who was born of you has given everything.
He gave himself over to death
*   so that the treasure of your promise*
*   might bear fruit.*

We pray you:
*   since he has consecrated us through his Spirit,*
*   let us be the heirs of your covenant,*
*   today and every day.*

God, you said:
*   "Let light shine in the darkness."*
You are yourself that light shining in our hearts
*   to make them reflect the glory that spreads*
*   over the face of your risen Christ.*
You know that we carry that treasure in us
*   like stoneware of no value.*
Do not let us become again the slaves that we were
*   but make the freedom of your Spirit*
*   break out again in our rigid bodies,*
*   so that we can sing, with our hearts rejoicing,*
*   of the life of Jesus who is our joy.*

WEDNESDAY OF THE 2ND WEEK

THE CHILD AND THE GIANT

1 Samuel 17:32–33, 37, 40–51. David and Goliath! Israel's position had been greatly improved by Saul's victories, which were not, however, in any way definitive. Each of Israel's adversaries was still trying to regain lost ground until that final and definitive battle took place. In the meantime, there were skirmishes and smaller encounters, like the mutual challenge between David and the giant.

The child and the giant! On the one hand, a professional soldier, armed from hand to foot and, on the other, a boy with his sling and a handful of stones. But that, surely, was Israel's position with regard to the other nations. Israel's cause, however, was sacred and Yahweh was fighting on the people's side. The future king was going to perform a brilliant action, which would enable him to take his place in the legendary company of charismatic liberators.

Psalm 144 is something of a mixed bag. It contains a thanksgiving, a theophany and a number of beatitudes. The verses chosen for today are thanksgivings; they bless Yahweh for the protection with which he surrounds the king.

Mark 3:1–6. See p. 30.

■

Up till now, there have been skirmishes and each side has been aware that the other has been trying to regain lost ground. Saul's victories have certainly improved the situation for Israel, but none of them has been definitive. The Philistines have been on the look-out for any weakness in the enemy of which they could take advantage in order to achieve a clear-cut victory.

Up till now, there have been skirmishes. Jesus proclaimed a new era and he was not contradicted. The facts would speak for themselves and would dispel the people's illusions. They were, of course, looking for something new. His healing of the paralyzed man had been followed by silence. His eating with people of ill-repute had been greeted with scandalized cries. But his claim to be the bridegroom whose coming would bring about a revolution was insufferable. He had, after all, been warned not to touch the traditional teaching. Up till now, the controversies that surrounded him had not lasted very long. This time, however, he was going too far and it would lead to open warfare.

Jesus heals a man with a withered hand and, at the same moment, the scribes consult together to kill him.

Evil encloses us on all sides and deprives us of our freedom. Handed over to the power of death, our hands and feet are tied and we feel defenceless. We fight, but it is futile, because evil is always on the look-out for any weakness of which it can take advantage in order to achieve a definitive victory. The Philistines will, it would seem, always have the last word. We are condemned to be crushed under their heavy boot. Our victories are no more than temporary respites in the endless struggle and, if we are for a time liberated, this just helps to preserve the illusion of freedom.

But the child rises up to confront the giant. His weapons are ludicrous. Can the world be transformed by letting oneself be hung from a gallows? A few days before, Jesus had proclaimed the total liberation of the paralyzed man by forgiving his sins. Today, the scribes plot together to silence him.

Up till now, there have been skirmishes in the fierce struggle that was taking place between life and the shadows. Each side was holding itself in reserve for the final battle. Then the child came and the Philistine fell to the ground, brought down by a little stone—a derisory cross. That was God's response—to throw himself into the battle in which man's happiness was at stake.

■

A boy's sling—
  and a people's history is transformed.
A cross raised on a hilltop—
  and the face of the world is changed.
God, you dumbfound us
  and we bless you.
You reveal your salvation to the poor and the humble
  and hide it from the wise and the powerful.
Let us discover the signs of your grace
  in our everday existence—
  the place where the eternity of your salvation is born.

■

You laugh at all restraints.
Your Spirit goes in search of a forgotten boy.
Your Son heals the sabbath day.
God of freedom,
  break our habits
  and tell us again
  that your salvation is unconditional.
Nothing can shackle the life
that you have promised us in abundance.

BETWEEN BELONGING AND REJECTION, CONFLICT AND FRIENDSHIP

1 Samuel 18:6-9; 19:1-7. Saul's kingship, which had originated because of the Philistine threat, lacked roots in the tradition of Israel. David's success, combined with the prophet's dismissal of the king, dealt that kingship a blow which in the long run proved fatal. From then onwards, Saul's distrust of the young David was only equalled by his resentment towards him.

Jealousy, distrust and plotting—the Deuteronomist author does not cast a veil over the intrigues in the royal palace. The contrast is made even more striking by the friendship between David and Jonathan, which is as generous as the summer sun. In his movement towards the throne, the newly elected king's most sincere friend is Saul's son.

Psalm 56 is a good example of a lamentation. In it can be found, in turn, accusations directed against the adversary of the person at prayer, an expression of his trust in Yahweh and his promise to offer a sacrifice of thanksgiving. Even a reprimand can be discerned in verse 9. "Is all that not written in your book?" sounds like a discreet criticism addressed to Yahweh and motivated by the delay in hearing the believer's prayer.

Mark 3:7-12. See p. 33.

■

The decision has been taken to get rid of Jesus, but, at the same time, the evangelist shows us the crowd following him. The people come from every quarter—from far and near, from the holy city and from pagan countries. His teaching bears fruit, despite all the obvious opposition. The force of his message of salvation and the power that emanates from him are proof that he comes on behalf of God. His presence alone is enough to make evil leave its victims. The cry of the possessed people breaks out above the crowd, revealing the mystery of Jesus.

But let us make no mistake! The opposition to Jesus is increasing and the evangelist ends the passage that begins today's reading with words describing his rejection by the inhabitants of Nazareth. The people are torn between belonging and rejection, enthusiasm and condemnation and agreement and lack of understanding! They will always be divided, and the frontier between conflict and friendship is not something outside us—it passes through our hearts.

The crowds celebrated David's glory in song and dance, they were so delighted with his achievements. He had beaten the Philistine and saved the nation. But their enthusiasm for the young man made Saul think of ways of getting rid of this embarrassing rival. Jonathan, on the other hand, tried to protect him. Father and son were divided! One took sides with the chosen ruler, while the other rejected him. "If a kingdom is divided against itself, that kingdom cannot last."

We were in that crowd. We were enchanted by that man, who spoke about us and our life as no one before him had ever done. We acclaimed him with the words: "Blessed is he who comes in the name of the Lord!"

We should be on our guard, then, in case we are also in that crowd of people who shouted: "Crucify him!" We are, after all, people who are always torn between acceptance and rejection.

■

The crowds ran to Jesus,
because they had heard what he had done.

  Let your Spirit draw us to you, Lord,
  and have mercy on us!

Jesus was attacked because he healed every infirmity.

  Look at our sin, purify our hearts
  and have mercy on us!

And the people said: "The Son of God is here!"

  Show us your face
  and we shall be able to recognize you.
  Have mercy on us!

■

However far away a man is when he complains,
  you are there and your Passion continues.
The suffering of the least of your brothers
  becomes the pain of your own body.
Because we are members of your body,
  let us also feel the anguish that crushes our brothers,
  so that we may also be there, where light is reborn
  if we are able to see with your eyes.
Let us share your passion to such a degree

that men and women find in us
that peace for which you surrendered your life.

TWELVE—A NATION FOR THE WORLD

1 Samuel 24:3–21. The first book of Samuel ends with a scene that does credit to David. Saul has learned that his young rival has sought refuge in a cave on the banks of the Dead Sea and follows him there. In order to satisfy a natural need, the king has to squat down in the depths of a dark cave. He does not know that David is nearby. He is therefore in a very vulnerable position, but David does not take advantage of this and kill him. He does no more than secretly cut off the border of Saul's cloak and then make it clear to the king and his followers that he is innocent.

This story has been amplified by tradition so that David's loyalty and his sense of the sacred nature of the kingship are stressed. Although the Lord has put Saul within his grasp, he refuses to touch the one who has been anointed with oil and therefore consecrated. This decision could only be to David's advantage, since he too has also been anointed.

Psalm 57 is another psalm of supplication. May God "rise high above the heavens" like a bird and fly to the aid of the one who is praying!

Mark 3:13–19. See p. 36.

■

Jesus withdraws from the crowd and goes up a mountain, where he will be near to God. He also takes "those he wanted," in other words, the Twelve whom he calls to be with him, into this intimacy with God.

Twelve—representing the twelve tribes of the holy people of Israel, whom God called together at the beginning of the history of salvation. In a prophetic act, Jesus claims this people of God for himself. At a time when the enthusiasm of the crowds is very ambiguous and the authorities are opposed to him, Jesus gathers around him a few men whom he wants to initiate into his mystery.

These are the people God chooses for himself: men and women who arise throughout the ages and are ready to follow the prophet, the Church whose members are prepared to enter, day after day, more deeply into the mystery of the beloved Son. These are the people who go up the mountain with Jesus. The Church is always called to be a community sharing Jesus' destiny. It is a community founded on a call and it has come from the freedom and the grace of God.

Twelve—Jesus called them for a mission, these people whose task is to proclaim the good news. The Church was set up to be a sign of God in the world. At a time when men become immersed in their own false certainties and are set on fire by ludicrous dreams, men and women are called to look in the direction of God's future, to look further and higher, with the aim of building up man as God wants him to be.

Twelve—for the world. One of them was called Judas, "the man who was to betray him." The Church, built on the foundation of these Twelve, will continue to be, like the world, under the sign of the mystery of evil. It is, after all, not made of anything other than human flesh. It is only different in that it proclaims to the world the grace that God has given to it.

■

We give you thanks, Lord Jesus,
for the Church that you have established
in the unity of one faith and one baptism,
for the glory of the one God and Father.

  People chosen for the unity of all your brothers,
  open your arms and recognize the Father's gifts.

We give you thanks for your holy Church,
for the firmness of its hope
and the tenderness of its love for the poor.

  People chosen to proclaim a hope,
  show your Christ—he has filled you with his presence.

We give you thanks for the Church,
which you have set up as a house of prayer for all nations.

  People chosen to exist in prayer,
  take in your hands the whole world and its misery.

We give you thanks, God who calls us
for your apostolic Church,
rooted in the faith of the apostles
and built on the foundation of the prophets.

People chosen to be one day his glorious body,
keep your gaze fixed on the course of his history.

SATURDAY OF THE 2ND WEEK

FACE TO FACE
2 Samuel 1:1–4, 11–12, 19, 23–27. Pursued by Saul, David sought refuge in the caves on the banks of the Dead Sea. There, he gathered around him a band of adventurers and with them went to serve the Philistines. He lived by raiding and made friends among the southern tribes. He did not, however, fight the Israelite tribes. At this time, he was distrusted by the Philistine princes, who for a time avoided fighting against Israel.

The Philistines did, however, begin once more to harass Israel. Saul was totally defeated in the battle of Gilboa and killed, together with his son Jonathan. When he learned of Saul's death, David ordered that a day of mourning should be kept. Tradition has also attributed to him an elegant elegy, in which his friendship for Saul's son is expressed.

Psalm 80 is used especially during the time of Advent. It expresses Israel's bitterness in defeat. It may perhaps also refer to the invasion of the southern provinces by the Assyrians. What is certainly the most characteristic note is the barely concealed criticism of Yahweh: "You have fed us on the bread of tears; you have made us drink them in such measure."

Mark 3:20–21. See p. 38.

■

Jesus comes down from the mountain and returns home. He has no illusions. He knows that, from now on, only his disciples will have access to his true personality. He comes down into the world of men, where a deceptive popularity prevails. His exhausting activity and his extraordinary enthusiasm for anything to do with his mission make his relatives think he is "out of his mind." They feel it is their task to bring the gentle dreamer, the exalted spirit who is oblivious to everything, back to reason. They will let him preach if he wants to, but he must keep within reasonable limits. He can even proclaim a time of blessing, so long as it can be reached. And he ought to give more thought to what people are saying about him. He should try not to offend people. That is very wrong. And it is dangerous to denounce publicly the privileges of those who speak in the name of God.

He ought to be more moderate! He disturbs people too deeply. He disturbs them because he speaks of God in a different way from that of the scribes or the Pharisees. "Be reasonable and we will believe in you." One can almost hear the words: "Come down from the cross and we will believe in you."

But no one can know Jesus if the Spirit does not reveal his mystery to him. And no one can claim to be one of his own, one of his family, if he has not received the light. Jesus is not cut to human size. Our understanding and our heart may succeed in raising a corner of the veil covering his secret, but only the Spirit can enable us to enter and be face to face with it.

Just be reasonable! It was probably out of friendship for him that his own wanted to bring Jesus back to reason. That has, after all, always been the Church's temptation throughout history and probably always will be: to bring the mystery of Jesus back to the reasonable limits of human hopes. Believers have always been and will always be scandalized, because what God demands always goes beyond what is possible; what God suggests always goes beyond what is foreseeable and what God establishes always goes beyond what is desirable. Jesus, they thought, was "out of his mind." Yes, he was, in a sense, because God is only conscious of the boundlessness of love and that mystery is a scandal.

■

God, what is your name?
  Your mystery transcends our understanding
  and your way of acting dumbfounds us.
Put your breath into us!
May it invite us to share your secret
  and make your foolishness acceptable.
Your mystery will never be exhausted,
  not even in the endless ages to come.

■

You came to your own, Lord,
  and they did not know you.
Give us enough discernment
  to be able to recognize you today—
  you, the unexpected one—
  wherever you are at work.

The Harvest is Already Beginning

Entering into the Dynamism of Salvation

The kingdom is close at hand and everyone is driven now to make a decision, to be converted. The person who hears the good news has to enter into the movement that it brings about. If he listens to it, he is already saved, because the Word works in his heart like seed. The farmer has, after all, to do nothing to make the seed germinate!

God cannot reach the person who refuses to open his heart and listen, but prefers to remain imprisoned within himself. Such a person is a sin that cannot be forgiven. He is deliberately setting himself outside the sphere of God's influence. But those who take their place near to the one who is himself the Word of salvation and listen to him already belong to the Savior's family. The Word makes progress in them and sets hope free—the hope that others condemn as an illusion.

The Word comes from the Father and is sown like seed in men's hearts. What dangers threaten the life of the seed, but what a promise it contains! Seed sown on the ground germinates and the tree grows until it is big enough for birds to nest in it.

Our today will also bring eternity about. Light has appeared in the darkness and is raised up like a beacon guiding human history. It is the responsibility of every Christian to see that it is not hidden under the bed, but set up on a lamp-stand for all to see.

"The secret of the kingdom of God is given to you." The kingdom will never be a truism. It is always something that speaks to the heart. The parable of the kingdom only enlightens the one who is already open to what it proclaims. Some see more clearly into it, whereas others remain firmly enclosed within their own blindness. But be careful! The kingdom is very much like love. To paraphrase Guy de Maupassant, you only have put your little finger into the web of such circumstances to be drawn into it completely. The Word functions like seed and you will be swept along with the dynamism of salvation.

■

God of our praise,
    you reveal to us the secret of our life.
    A little bread tells us you are present
    and our communion as brothers
    is the sacrament of the kingdom to come.

Let us see your love
and give us your salvation!
Then our life will be illuminated
    by the charity of eternity.

MONDAY OF THE 3RD WEEK

SINNING AGAINST THE SPIRIT

2 Samuel 5:1–7, 10. All that David has to do now is to gather the first fruits of his skilful policy. The tribes of Judah have already raised him to the dignity of kingship at Hebron (see 2 Sam 2) and now the northern tribes, those of Israel, want to offer him the crown. They come to Hebron and conclude a treaty with David, who is then anointed king of Israel. It should be noted that each of the two kingdoms preserves its independence. Judah and Israel are united only by the person of the king.

The sovereign now has to choose his capital. He does not want Hebron, centrally situated in Judah, nor does he want any town in Israel, despite their letters patent of nobility. Instead, he chooses a city in neutral territory on the periphery of both Judah and Israel, one which the tribes have not yet conquered. His next step is to set siege to that city, Jerusalem, and subjugate it with the help of his mercenaries. He then makes it the seat of his personal residence. Jerusalem is henceforth known for ever as the "city of David."

Psalm 89—this is the psalm that one would expect for today's reading. With its irrevocable promises, there is no better one in the psalter to celebrate the enthronement of the king and the establishment of the whole house of David in Jerusalem.

Mark 3:22–30. See p. 40.

■

Jesus' family found his attitude unacceptable and his behavior dangerous. As responsible relatives, they saw it as their main task to bring the black sheep back into the fold.

The most serious danger threatening faith is the desire to cut God down to the size of man. But there is also another danger, darker and more deeply hidden—that of being satisfied with our own idea of what is right. We do not then reduce God to our human level—we force him rather to enter our own system. If God tries to shake us, he will not succeed—we will call him a false god, because he is not playing the part we have forced him to play. "It is through the prince of devils that he casts devils out." The Gospel marks the end of the power exerted by evil spirits, but Jesus' opponents continued to insist that he derived his power from the very forces that he was annihilating! Because God astonishes and shakes us, we say that he is lying.

Whenever men and women arise to work for justice and peace, they are always accused of collaborating with those who want to destroy Christianity and of trying to overthrow "traditional Christian values." If a priest lives among young delinquents to keep them from total despair, people comment about his long hair and his leather jacket. Those who do not confine their faith to the limits that are defined for it by certain people are always criticized.

"All men's sins will be forgiven and all their blasphemies; but let anyone blaspheme against the Holy Spirit and he will never have forgiveness." God can do nothing about a person whose actions are contrary to his intention. He cannot open the door of a room if a person imprisons himself inside it. He cannot force a person to slide back the bolt. If a person is deliberately blind, God cannot set him free. If someone says: "I do not believe that I can ever be awakened by a light coming from elsewhere," God is powerless.

But, if there is a weakness in our defences, then the man who is stronger than our strength—our intelligent minds and our closed hearts—will be able to enter at that point. And then, in our dwelling-places from which our false riches have been removed, there will be a trace of the coming of Christ the Savior.

■

Are you not, Lord,
wiser than the intelligent

more prudent than the knowledgeable
and more far-seeing than the sons of darkness?
Remove the veil covering our eyes
and let us recognize you,
God who astonishes those who seek you.

Call us together by the words of your Son,
take us outside ourselves, Lord,
and set us free from our fears and our anxieties.
Give us back to the freedom of our dreams
  and to the fascination of your light.
May your mercy be our strength
  and your grace our salvation.
Then we shall be astonished
  by what your Spirit can achieve in us.
We shall be new men and women,
  your Son's disciples,
  children of your tenderness.

TUESDAY OF THE 3RD WEEK

BECOMING JESUS' FAMILY

2 Samuel 6:12b–15, 17–19. The raising of Jerusalem to the status of capital was a very clever action and the setting up of the ark was a stroke of genius, because it formed a link between the Canaanite city and the ancient sacral tradition of the tribes and enabled the "mountain of Zion" to enter into the religious history of the nations.

Since the time when it had been taken back from the Philistines, the ark had been kept at Kiriath-jearim. It was to that place that David went, together with a great number of troops, to fetch it. It was taken in triumph to Jerusalem, accompanied by singing and dancing. It should be noted that, after his consecration by anointing, David behaved like a religious leader, dressing in priestly garments, offering sacrifices and blessing the people.

The incident of the taking of the ark to Jerusalem is the underlying inspiration of the story of the visitation (Lk 1:39–45). Mary presents herself to her cousin Elizabeth as the bearer of the new ark of the covenant. Elizabeth's greeting is expressed in the liturgical language of festive acclamation by the people and David's dancing is represented by the movements of John the Baptist in Elizabeth's womb.

Psalm 24 is a liturgical listing of the conditions that have to be fulfilled before entry into the sanctuary. The final verses have no parallel elsewhere in the Bible and come from a processional liturgy accompanying the ark.

Mark 3:31–35. See p. 42.

∎

He had been living in Nazareth for thirty years and was a member of their family. Everyone there knew him. He had worked with his father Joseph, a man people trusted. His relatives were responsible people. The women talked to Mary every day at the well. They spoke about the sun drying the seedlings, the illness of Magdalene's baby and Sarah's betrothal. They were good but not very important people.

There must have been criticisms. Poor Joseph, for example—he had trained his son to follow a good trade only to see him become a preacher. The young men of today! And the people he associated with—some of them were pretty bad. Poor parents! Why should such respectable people have to suffer so much? Mary did not speak about it, but she had to bear a heavy cross, knowing that her only son had become a vagrant.

So Jesus' relatives came to try to settle matters with him. They would talk to him. He was a good man at heart. He just did not know how much suffering he had caused. But he would understand.

"Anyone who does the will of God, that person is my brother and sister and mother." Those who decide to experience in their hearts his reason for living will inevitably bear the name of Jesus. Being a member of his family means gathering with others around him in order to listen to him and to live with him. Those who are born of the love that they have listened to, received and practised will be members of his family. Family, after all, always has to do with the heart. It is always a communion that has been initiated and shared. Adopting someone's name is agreeing to look at the things of life as he does, opening oneself to his influence, bearing his reputation, sharing his fate and belonging to him. Being a member of his family is having a share in the same inheritance.

"Looking around at those sitting in a circle about him, he said: 'Here are my mother and my brothers'." You are Jesus' family—you who are gathered around him, listening to his words and making your lives conform to them. You are his family—you who have been baptized in his death and resurrection and have received his Spirit as an inheritance. You are his family when you take as the only point of reference in your life what Jesus has said and done and when you hand yourself over to God's forgiveness and tenderness. You are his family—you who assemble to celebrate the coming of the ark of the covenant and welcome its dwelling among you. You are his family when you share what the Lord has left you—his word and his bread.

Jesus went home. He went back to people. With him, closely tied to him until the end, were the disciples whom he was leading to a discovery of his secret. They were members of his family because they had been born of God. At the heart of the world, tied to him until the end, there are also those who bear his name—the Church of God.

■

We are members of your family, God,
*   and we bear your name.*
Breathe your Spirit into us
and let him express once more
the grace of your adoption as sons
today and every day.

■

We give you thanks, Lord our God.
You teach us your name
*   and make us your children.*
Blessed are you!
You let us share your family table
*   and our communion is sealed with the same blood.*
Let us have a share
*   in the inheritance that you promise us.*

WEDNESDAY OF THE 3RD WEEK

THE SEED IS SOWN—AND THEN?

2 Samuel 7:1-17. Nathan's prophecy occurs at the turning-point between the story of David's ascent to the throne and that of his succession. The king is at the summit of his power. He is the ruler of both Israel and Judah and he has given a capital city to his states, but he has no one to inherit his kingdoms, because his wife Michal is barren. This is a repetition of the story of Abraham!

Who is to inherit the divine favor attached to the throne of Jerusalem? After several repercussions, Solomon becomes David's heir to the throne, and in this way God's freedom with regard to the hereditary succession is once again affirmed.

Nathan's oracle was gradually developed and enlarged. The original promise ensured that the crown would remain within the Davidic lineage. It was based on a play on words of the two meanings of the word "house." It was not David who was to build a "house," in the sense of a temple, for Yahweh, but Yahweh who was to build a "house"—in the sense of offspring—for David (see 2 Sam 7:5-7, 11b-16). The oracle was consequently applied in turn first to Solomon (v. 13), then to all David's successors (vv. 10-11a) and finally to the whole of Israel (vv. 10-11a).

"I have founded your dynasty to last for ever." These words appear again and again in *Psalm 89*, showing that the prophet's oracle continued to sustain Israel's hope for centuries. When the two kingdoms were shaken by the two catastrophes of 732 and 587 B.C., the Deuteronomist historian took David as a model and painted a vivid portrait of him as the figure of the ideal king who will live before Yahweh "in faithfulness and justice and integrity of heart."

Mark 4:1-20. See p. 45.

■

The sower went out to sow. The beloved Son goes out from the Father to sow seed in the heart of the earth. Jesus speaks of God and his word is bound to bear fruit. When he speaks, it is God who makes what he says. He gives back to the paralyzed man the ability to walk. To the leper with a disfigured face, he gives back his original beauty.

The seed will, of course, always seem ludicrous—a handful of small grains lost in the immensity of the field. And yet the time will come when the ground itself will no longer be visible—the thick golden covering of the harvest will express the power of the life lying hidden today in the soil. And so Jesus' astonishing claim is affirmed once again. He goes out to sow seed and with him the time of salvation begins.

Later he withdraws with those he intends to initiate into his secret. On Peter's boat, he reveals to his Church the mystery of the kingdom. In the meantime, can the crowds not understand the difficult days of the seed that is exposed to the risk of sowing? The time of the kingdom, Jesus declares, is a time of slow germination. God's work is handed over to the vicissitudes of a Word that can be rejected like a humble seed.

But the seed is not enough. Neither the quality of the seed nor the quantity sown can guarantee a harvest if it is not sown in soil that is fit to receive it. The sower will succeed in the end, of course, even though he may have to begin sowing again the following spring. But, according to this parable, the kingdom is at the end of history and also there are times of failure. God can do nothing with a heart that is shallow, stony or dry. So open the door of salvation at once—the sowing has begun!

■

The sower passes by
and the seed falls.
It is hidden in the heart of the earth.
For months nothing will appear,
but the harvest will come.
God passes by
and his word falls.
It penetrates into the heart of man.
May it bear fruit a hundredfold.

You speak, Lord—
a Word that calls for a response,
a name that arouses love.
Open our hearts!
May the seed that you sow in us
bear fruit in abundance.

■

From the seed that dies,
   make a hundred new seeds come, Lord,
and may our hearts be swept along
   by the crazy hope of a harvest
   that will spread in the sun of your love.

THURSDAY OF THE 3RD WEEK

THE GOSPEL IN THE LIGHT
2 Samuel 7:18-19, 24-29. David prays in response to the prophetic oracle. Because Yahweh has committed himself to "building a house" for David and to consolidating his reign, David asks him to be mindful of his promise. This

prayer also bears witness to the piety of the king who was to remain, in the memory of the people of Israel, the model par excellence to be imitated.

Psalm 132 is another dynastic poem. God's promise made to the ruling dynasty corresponds to David's wish to build a temple for Yahweh.

Mark 4:21–25. See p. 49.

■

"The true light that enlightens all men has come into the world." Who would be able to, or want to enclose light so that all men were plunged into darkness? God "causes his sun to rise on bad men as well as good" and salvation is for all men. Yet Jesus proclaimed his message and the people continued to be without understanding and faith. Only a little group of disciples received his words in faith.

But the light was made to be seen by everyone. The Gospel has to be presented as it is to everyone. A self-enclosed community is like a man putting his lamp under the bed. The Church is not a secret community. It is called together to be a sign raised in the presence of the world. The light is not overcome by the darkness. The Word bears fruit in abundance. But it is the grace and the vocation of Christians to be watchful over the earth and to proclaim the dawn in its victory over the night. What would happen to this earth of ours if it did not bear witness to the meaning of history?

■

We bless you, God our Father.
You make us your people for ever
and you become our promise.
In the midst of the nations,
you bring us together
to praise your covenant
and we become your holy Temple,
your dwelling-place filled with your blessings.
That is why,
with all those who live in the light
and already reflect the glory of your sons,
we sing your praises without end.

THE SEED IS IN THE GROUND

2 Samuel 11:1–4a, 5–10a, 13–17. The theologian is never absent from the writings of the Deuteronomist, but the historian is also always at work, placing events in their profane historical framework. He is always conscious of God acting unseen in men's hearts. The Davidic succession is therefore presented as a long series of sins and intrigues. Despite the brilliance reflected by the throne of Jerusalem, it was never firmly established. On the one hand, there was the clan which remained faithful to the house of Saul and, on the other, the ambition of the king's sons and the fact that David showed too many weaknesses with regard to them.

When springtime came, David saw Bathsheba, who was very beautiful, and loved her. This new favorite soon became pregnant and, in a cowardly act, David had her legitimate husband killed. David's sin, we are told, displeased Yahweh.

Psalm 51 is a unique example of a psalm of supplication. It probably belonged to the ritual of an expiatory ceremony for the people and the king.

Mark 4:26–34. See p. 51.

■

The sower went out to sow. God has begun to cross the earth, sowing into the wind. However harsh the weather is, the seed hidden in the ground will grow. All that the farmer has to do is to wait patiently until harvest time comes. The earth bears its fruits of its own accord. There is no need for anyone outside to intervene. Harvest time will come and all we have to do is to gather and store the crop.

The Son of God has gone out to scatter the Word into the wind. The sowing has taken place, the earth receives the seed and God's power is at work. Everything is happening in secret. The kingdom has already come. This is because the seed has been entrusted to the blood-soaked ground of Golgotha. The seed is already germinating and the plant is growing and grasping the history of men in its roots. On the day of God himself, the harvest will reveal the power of the life that is now still hidden.

When men and women recognize today that God makes all things new and when they say, without fully understanding, that God begets them into his life, who cannot be aware of how ludicrous this confession is in the presence of the heart-breaking tragedies of the world, the scandal of human suffering and the tedious drama of man's mediocrity? And yet the very boldness of this confession is astonishing, and we can already hear the earth itself acclaiming its recognition that God is all things to all men.

When men and women stammer in the silence of their hearts the name of the unnamable God, who cannot be aware of how absurd this search is in the presence of our human questions and fears? And yet this tentative dialogue contains the beginnings of the prayer of God's thankful children.

The kingdom—it is like a mustard seed, sown in the ground and becoming the biggest plant of all. The seeds of the kingdom and the fruit borne by the Word of grace can never be of the same size. And nothing can ever prevent the Promise from being fulfilled.

■

You have opened our soil to your sowing.
Each one of us is the ground
*   in which you sow the good seed of your Eucharist.*
We give you thanks—
*   the corn of your harvest grows*
*   and your crop ripens.*
Your storehouses will be full in eternity.

■

Blessed are you, God our Father,
*   for the Gospel of your Son,*
*   the pledge of hope*
*   and the seed of renewal.*
Your Word never returns
*   without bearing fruit.*
Seed hidden in our soil—
*   it is the promise of an immense tree*
*   in which all men will dwell.*
Let us, then, praise you
*   with all those who welcome it.*
Let us acclaim you
*   with all those who share the joy of the good news.*

AGAINST FEAR AND LACK OF FAITH

2 Samuel 12:1–7a, 10–17. David has sinned against the Lord. Nathan is sent by him to speak to the king. The prophet, who has guaranteed God's promise in favor of the house of David, now has to announce to the sovereign the verdict of Yahweh.

The prophet expresses himself in the form of a parable that is one of the jewels of the Old Testament. A poor man had a lamb that he cherished like his own child and a rich man stole it. "You are that man!" the prophet says to King David, pronouncing God's judgment over him "in the face of all Israel and in the face of the sun." Not long after this prophetic judgment, one of David's sons openly took possession of the royal harem with the aim of making his claims to the crown.

But David repented of his sin. The Lord forgave him and let him live. The child born of David's illegitimate union, however, died. David "consoled his wife Bathsheba. He went to her and slept with her." This time, the Lord loved the child born of their union and the prophet gave him the name Jedidiah, the "Beloved of the Lord." He was to rule under the name of Solomon.

The few verses of *Psalm 51* included in today's liturgy are interesting because they seem to be an exposition of the psalmist's own wishes, but they are an expression in the form of a prayer of the promises made by the prophet Ezekiel of a purified heart and a spirit of holiness. A vision of a new world is revealed in these verses.

Mark 4:35–41. See p. 54.

■

The boat was shaken by the waves, but Jesus slept, like a child who thinks that no harm can come to him because his father is there. Shaken! It is a truism to say that we are threatened nowadays on all sides. Even the most generally accepted values are called into question and the world seems to have lost its soul. We produce for consumption and we consume for production—an infernal cycle of a world that is looking for reasons for living. What will tomorrow be made of? We have lost our illusions and our dreams which, we thought a few years ago, were close to reality, have now faded. There is talk of the end of a civilization. "Master, do you not care? We are going down!" Does God not care about our anxiety and our confusion?

Shaken! The twentieth-century Church is shaken to its foundations. Our religious feelings are threatened. We are less confident in the way we express our faith. The bark of Peter is constantly threatened and even within the Church people are saying that the Church itself is being swept away by the waves. Even the disciples themselves are experiencing temptation.

"Why are you so frightened?" Jesus rises up and orders the unleashed powers of the wind and the sea to be calm. Why are we afraid, like people without hope? Have we not taken the Master of life on board? Not as a passenger in transit! He has come on board definitively and has identified his fate with that of the boat. "I am with you always; yes, to the end of time." Yes, we have taken the Master of life on board and it is on him that we base our hope, despite all the dangers that threaten the boat.

Faith is never entirely resting. It lives in life itself and is confronted with every kind of vicissitude. We go forward tentatively with our fellow-men. We share everything with them, including their mistakes and their anxieties about the future. But we are certain that God is on board with us and that he is leading us to the right destination. In the morning, after all, he woke up! We might have believed that death had overcome him, but no, he rose up! With the sun of Easter.

■

Do not remain asleep, Lord,
when we do not know where to go.
Wake up and rescue our hope.
Have mercy on us!

When the wind is blowing against us
and the darkness is overwhelming us,
rise up, Lord, and strengthen us.
Have mercy on us!

When we lose our foothold
and have no more contact with life,
hear our cry, Lord,
and have mercy on us!

■

God, creator and master of all things,
do not let our hearts be invaded by fear,
    but increase our faith.

*May we bear witness bravely in the world
that is made to rise again by your Spirit.*

FROM MONDAY TO SATURDAY

OF THE 4TH WEEK

THE CONFLAGRATION HAS BROKEN OUT

Waking Up to the Mystery of Jesus

The first message has been offered and the first signs of the coming of the Messiah have appeared. The fire has been lighted. Now it has become a conflagration and is spreading in the dry grass. The Word of God is burning men's hearts and the Spirit is making the waiting land fertile.

Jesus is going through the land. Everywhere he encounters human infirmity. He is pursuing the enemy in his own territory. He enters land inhabited by pagans and evil is driven back. That evil is called "Legion." It uses everything it has at its disposal to enslave man. Jesus passes by and calls out: "Come out of the man!" And the man is cured and at peace.

The man really wanted to love. He wanted to be free. He wanted to develop all the potentials that he felt were in him. But "death" in all its forms was destroying his expectations and reducing him to a permanent state of mourning. Then Jesus came and with him something new: Do not be afraid! What you are longing for is not a lie and your mourning will be transformed into feasting!

The conflagration spreads and the question becomes more urgent: "Who is this man?" If he is to welcome this new reality, man must leave the territory that he knows too well. The prophet always invites man to let himself be surprised. On the one hand, sending the disciples out on their mission extends the scope and content of preaching. On the other hand, it also widens the gulf between Jesus and the people who do not understand. There is an increasingly obvious tension between what Jesus is proclaiming and what men think they want. What, then, should we do? We have to change the direction of the movement and cling to the Word alone as our only treasure.

The conflagration can help us in this by burning all our false images. The signs proclaim the secret of the one who is sent. John the Baptist's fate

---

anticipates and expresses the destiny of the Messiah. The fire of the Spirit should lead us to confess Christ crucified. The time has, in a sense, already come. God is already gathering together his new people from among all those who, injured by their poverty and that of the world, are greedy to hear the voice of the shepherd raised up by God to lead them to happiness. The conflagration has begun and nothing can extinguish it.

MONDAY OF THE 4TH WEEK

THEIR NAME IS LEGION

2 Samuel 15:13–14, 30; 16:5–13a. The end of David's reign was darkened by the ambition of the princes who were anxious to succeed him. Absalom, one of his sons, was in open revolt against him and seized hold of the royal harem. David had to flee. The throne seemed to be shaken to its foundations.

The fugitive king and his followers make a very sad impression. As a sign of mourning, the king goes bare-footed and with his head covered. But he is still the king and his flight is that of Yahweh's anointed. Through him and for the first time, the Deuteronomist historian outlines a portrait of a suffering messiah, almost exiled.

It is the portrait of a king who is cursed. In his flight, David meets a member of the house of Saul who heaps curses on him. The king does not protest and entrusts his cause to God. Later, when he gives his throne to Solomon, he advises him to get rid of this man, Shimei, since the curse cannot be attached to the throne of Jerusalem.

Psalm 3 expresses the protest of an innocent man. He testifies to the fact that, according to Israel, Yahweh is the last bulwark against injustice. In verse 6 especially, there is a reference to a kind of "divine judgment" that took place in the temple at dawn. The accused man has spent the night in the sanctuary and was able to go to sleep without anxiety, as the Lord had taken charge of his case.

Mark 5:1–20. See p. 56.

■

This must strike us today as a very strange story indeed if we do not read it within the framework of the ideas and beliefs of its period. In the context of the Gospel, however, it can be easily justified and its meaning is quite clear. It leads to a peak in Jesus' activity and consequently in the manifestation of God's power.

Jesus is in pagan territory. He is therefore in the very homeland of the evil one. A man lives there in a graveyard—one of the favorite dwelling-places of unclean spirits. He is possessed by evil. He has therefore lost both his freedom of movement and the use of his senses. He is fundamentally no longer a man. But Jesus heals him, sets him free and gives him back to his condition as a man. At the end of the story, we see him sitting down, dressed and in full possession of his senses. His healing has such an effect on the people of the district, who knew him as a demoniac, that they are afraid.

Their name was Legion and they kept the man in chains. We too want to be free and to share with others, but the demons of money and profit keep us in chains. We would like to sow joy, but disappointment always overshadows us. We would like our bodies to sing of love, but sensuality again and again enslaves us. We would like to make separated hands clasp each other again and build up broken hearts, but we are betrayed by our own evil tendencies. We are made to stand upright, to be free in our hearts and to live with and for others, but we are brought low by our own mediocrity and excluded from fellowship. Their name is Legion.

Jesus passes by and calls out: "Come out of the man, unclean spirits!" To detach us from the powers of death, he lets himself be attached by nails to the hard, dry wood of a gallows. To lift us up, he lets himself be stretched out and crushed. To give us back the freedom of love, he lets himself be wrapped in a shroud. To raise us to communion with others, he lets himself endure the icy loneliness of the tomb. Jesus passes by and the pitiless rule of the one whose name is Legion is ended.

■

Lord God,
could you see us in chains
*   and not set us free?*
Could you see us on the ground
*   and not lift us up?*
Do not leave us to our own confusion,
but send ahead of us
*   the one who comes in your name,*
*   Jesus, our Savior.*

■

We are only men and women
and we are languishing in the tombs
  of our own mediocrity.
But if your Son passes by
  we shall be delivered.
A little bread proclaims our liberation.
Blessed are you, holy God!
Your Spirit gives us back our dignity as sons.

TUESDAY OF THE 4TH WEEK

MOURNING WILL BE TURNED TO JOY

2 Samuel 18:9-10, 14b, 24-25a, 30-32; 19:1-4. It was a day of great distress! Absalom's armies and the king's mercenaries confront each other somewhere in the wooded highlands of Transjordania. The usurper loses the battle and takes flight. In spite of David's explicit order, he is killed by Joab, the commander of the regular army.

But it is also a day of great joy, because the sun continues to shine, despite the storm of intrigues in the palace. Despite Absalom's act of betrayal, David still loves his son. He did not join in the battle, and the news of the young prince's death is brought to him by messengers. He expresses his heartbreaking grief as a father in a unique way.

Psalm 86 is an individual lamentation in which the theme of putting one's trust in the Lord is fully exploited.

Mark 5:21-43. See p. 59.

■

"And the day's victory was turned into mourning." The enemies of the throne had been defeated and the king's authority had been restored. But all that could be heard in the palace, which should have been filled with the sound of drums and joyful music, were the sad words of David's lamentation: "Absalom, my son!" The king found himself alone on his throne. Can any victory console a father for the loss of his child?

Another father ran up to Jesus. "My little daughter is desperately sick." She was a girl of twelve and she was at the point of death. All death seems absurd and scandalizing, but that of a young person even more so. Is it not intolerable that a body should be without life just when it is becoming capable of giving life?

The girl's father runs up to Jesus. Did he know him? It hardly mattered. A father will do anything he can for his dying child. So long as he arrives before it is too late! "Do come and lay your hands on her!" Is it still possible to avert fate? But already people are running up to them, saying: "Your daughter is dead." Does the father now have to accept what is inevitable? But Jesus' response to this news is: "Do not be afraid; only have faith."

"Absalom, my son!"—"Do not be afraid." There is a secret connection between that cry and this encouragement. We have given life. We have tried to build up love, peace and justice. But we have to accept what is inevitable. Death in all its forms seems to have the last word. We can only cry out in the presence of our dead "children." Then God's response comes to us: "Do not be afraid; only have faith." God looks at our lives, takes them in his hands and, because he is the God of the living, says: "Talitha, kum!—Little girl, I tell you to get up." To all of us, he says: Rise up! You have been born for life! Love is not made to die! Peace and justice are not sought so that they will remain barren!

"Why all this commotion and crying?" There are certain encounters that make life break out. Believing in God, meeting Jesus—that is believing in life. Death is absurd when it does not lead to this immense appeal. "My little daughter is desperately sick." The girl, he is saying, is the whole of my life and she is dying. "Do come and lay your hands on her to make her better and save her life." And God laid his hands on her— those hands that fashioned the clay of our origins. A new life came out of this, radiant with youth. "The little girl got up at once and began to walk about, for she was twelve years old" and the future lay open before her. She was called: my life.

■

Truly it is right for us
  to praise your name
  and to bless you,
  the Master of life,
  God, who gives us birth
  for immortality.
We glorify you!

Our life was exhausted
and we could not hold on to it,
but you gather it up in your hands
and it is wakened to your youth.
We bless you!
Where, then, is death's victory
and where is its sting,
since your Son has broken away
from the powers that wanted to hold him
and has taken us with him in his victory.
Because he is the first-born of the new world,
we can praise you through him and in him.

■

" 'I tell you to get up'.
And she got up at once and began to walk about . . .
And Jesus told them to give her something to eat."

Rise up, brothers and sisters,
and walk towards God's promise.
And, to keep your hope alive,
eat the Bread of life.

Your Son, living God, is our life.
Whoever believes in him will live.
Because you have shared with us
his body handed over to death,
let us wake and rise on the day
that will be without end
because it is for ever and ever.

WEDNESDAY OF THE 4TH WEEK

WHO IS HE?

2 Samuel 24:2, 9–16a, 17. The last chapters of the books of Samuel skilfully combine a very ancient tradition with the theology of the Deuteronomist historian. In that tradition, an attempt was made to explain the presence of an altar dedicated to Yahweh in the middle of the ancient Canaanite city of the Jebusites (Jerusalem). The tradition linked the building of the altar to the story of a plague that was eventually averted from the people by expiatory sacrifices offered on the altar. In the same tradition the census of Israel ordered by David was also given as the reason for this scourge.

The king's use of his military leaders to take a census of the Jewish population was a clear breach of the traditional rules of the holy war, which consisted essentially of a divine action in favor of the people who put their trust in God. The census was consequently regarded as a profanation. Only God could, the people felt, keep a detailed account of the number of the living and the dead.

In disrupting the sacred order, David had committed a very grave sin. God was bound to be angry with the people since, according to the theology of the Deuteronomist, the life of the nation was determined by the behavior of the king. But David was at the same time able to choose his punishment and, by his own attitude, modify the course of events.

He chose three days' pestilence. This was regarded in antiquity as the worst scourge of all, because it had a divine origin. In making this choice, the king also showed that he was relying totally on God's mercy. He was put to the test and this proved beneficial, because it resulted in the building of the altar. Sin, distress, repentance and redemption—these are the four steps to salvation stressed by the Deuteronomist.

Psalm 32 is a fine penitential poem, containing all the elements characteristic of an individual expression of thanksgiving. It opens with words of welcome spoken to the pilgrims by the priest on duty. Then, in his thanksgiving, the psalmist lists the events that he has experienced, and in this way enumerates the various reasons that he has for putting his trust in Yahweh.

Mark 6:1–6. See p. 61.

■

"I knew him well. We were at school together. He is a skilled worker now. He is still the same man—he has hardly changed at all."

That is how people speak, of course, always defining themselves and others by their past, and enclosing themselves in stereotyped formulas. Identity cards without a soul—that is what we are!

It was the same for Jesus. In Nazareth, he could only be a carpenter, the son of a carpenter, a cousin, an already known identity card. Like everyone else imprisoned within a label, a reputation. Even we who are believers often restrict Jesus to a few formulas. He is, for example, "the only Son of God . . . begotten not made, of one being with the Father." And we think in good faith that we know all there is to know. So we enclose the Living One in carefully measured formulas and subtle combinations of definitions. Forgetting that Jesus forbade unclean spirits to say who he was! Forgetting too that Jesus' response to the first enthusiasm of the crowd was to take everyone into the desert (Mark 1:45)! So that everyone might search at a deeper level for the Messiah and no one might say too quickly who he was.

If, in fact, people were to recognize that Jesus was other than the village carpenter, the son of Mary and the cousin of Jude and Simon, they should have looked at him more closely and let themselves be astonished by him! Instead of being in such a hurry to enclose him within an orthodox definition, we should let ourselves be carried along into the surprising, unheard of, unaccustomed experience of the entirely new future that he offers us. We should, in other words, "believe" in him. "A prophet is only despised in his own country." Those who "know him well" cannot agree to give up their certainties about him. The prophet is always going on ahead of others on unfamiliar roads. And, like water running through the fingers of our grasping hands, life always eludes anyone who wants to seize and hold it.

■

We have imprisoned you in names without a soul.
  Lord, have mercy!

We have enclosed your love
within the narrow bounds of our desires.
  Christ, have mercy!

We do not let your newness seize us.
  Lord, have mercy!

The cattle know their herdsman
  and the creature knows its creator,
  but we do not know you!
God our Savior,
  waken our hearts to your mystery
  shake our security
  and take us by surprise!
  Change our habits,
  so that we may be astonished
  by the newness of your mercy.

THE TRUE TREASURE

1 Kings 2:1-4, 10-12. On his death-bed, David gave his spiritual testament to his successor, Solomon. This testament is clearly the work of the Deuteronomist historian. "Observe the injunctions of Yahweh your God, . . . as it stands written in the Law of Moses." Yahweh had made a covenant with his people Israel on Mount Sinai and had entrusted his Law to them. He had also made a covenant with David and had entrusted the throne of Jerusalem to him. The Deuteronomist author merges these two traditions together, the king becoming, in his writing, the guardian of the Mosaic Law who has to ensure that it is kept in the whole of his kingdom. This means that the salvation of the nation is dependent on the behavior of the sovereign and the same question is again and again asked in the books of Kings: Has the king been obedient to God's will or has he disobeyed? The fulfilment of the word of God depends on the reply to this question.

The canticle for today, which is taken from the first book of Chronicles (Chapter 29), develops the ideas of its author, in particular that Yahweh is the only king both in Jerusalem and in the whole universe.

Mark 6:7-13. See p. 65.

■

"Observe the injunctions of Yahweh your God, following his ways . . . , so that Yahweh may fulfil the promise he made to me." When he was dying, David entrusted his spiritual testament to his son. What he handed over to him was much more than the riches and the good organization of his kingdom. He gave him a true treasure—God's Promise. In the words of the psalmist: "The Law of Yahweh is perfect, new life for the soul; . . . the judgments of Yahweh are true, righteous, every one, more desirable than gold, even than the finest gold; his words are sweeter than honey, even than honey that drips from the comb."

Jesus gave his disciples the task of proclaiming the good news, in this way entrusting his inheritance to them. He gave to them what he had received from his Father. They were to do what he had done, proclaim the people's deliverance from slavery and raise them up. He told them to set off and challenge everyone they met to welcome the Word, the treasure that had remained hidden until now. Everyone should sell everything he owns and buy this pearl of great value!

These, then, are the heirs of the Promise—those who have nothing except the Word of God. "No bread, no haversack, no coppers for their purses." On their feet, only sandals. Not even two tunics—just one! Nothing but the breath of the Spirit. Dressed in pilgrims' clothes. They had to be free of all bonds with nothing to hold them back if they were to pass on the one essential thing: the Promise.

We have, of course, wrapped our treasure up in numerous coverings. We have hidden the light under the bed and our house is plunged into darkness. We have erected railings so that none of the pilgrims may lose their way. We have enclosed the Word in dry definitions and moral codes. We have broken down our pastoral care into such tactical details that the Word is no longer unexpected and surprising. If you try to keep a fire alight for too long, you risk its going out. So set off! Throw the seed into the wind. It will germinate! Set off! Throw God's fire. It will burn the dry grass and become a conflagration.

■

You have placed your treasure in our hands:
Jesus, your Son, has joined himself to our words
and your Promise will be born in our lives.
So we ask you:
may your Bread be our only certainty
as we wait for the day of your manifestation,
God, you who are blessed for ever and ever.

■

Lord Jesus,
you who urged your disciples
to be completely detached from possessions,
grant that we may go forward in life
with, as our only wealth,
your word to make heard
and your love to share.

FRIDAY OF THE 4TH WEEK

DEATH AT THE END OF THE ROAD

Sirach 47:2–11. Jesus ben Sirach was writing about 180 B.C. For twenty years Palestine, which was governed by the Seleucids, had been powerfully influenced by Hellenism. The very existence of Judaism was called into question. Ben Sirach was very open to new models, but he nonetheless saw it as his task to protect the religious and cultural inheritance of his people.

In particular, he takes his readers on a conducted tour of a portrait gallery, in which there is a flattering picture of almost every famous Jewish king, counsellor, prophet or wise man. Each picture is, however, above all an act of homage given to God, in that Ben Sirach outlines in every case what God has done for the man portrayed. David, for example, is praised as highly for his warlike virtues as for his religious activity.

Psalm 18 can also be found in 2 Samuel 22. It is a long poem consisting of several parts, the main one being an act of thanksgiving (vv. 3–7, 17–30). A few verses taken from a royal thanksgiving (vv. 32–51) for a victory feature in today's liturgy.

Mark 6:14–29. See p. 67.

■

Who, then, is this man? The question is repeated like a refrain, but the mystery is never really elucidated. Jesus' fame only serves to deepen the roots of the question. His acts of power are signs of his mission. His preaching bears witness to the fact that the Spirit, who has been silent since the death of the last prophet, is speaking again. Who is this man? The enthusiastic crowds see him as the messenger of the eschatological age. He is Elijah, coming again after centuries in the Messiah's vanguard. He is John the Baptist, resurrected with the task of preparing the way for the one who is sent by God.

Who is this man? It is misleading to go no further than appearances. It is not enough simply to report his treatment of early criteria. Everything is new with him! There are, however, certain signs that point to the secret of his life. John the Baptist, the bridegroom's friend, has just become the victim of the perverse and wicked behavior of Herodias. In the past, Elijah was pursued by Queen Jezebel, who hated and wanted to kill him. The powers of evil always seem to triumph over the holy and righteous man of God, who dies rejected and outside the city walls. Because no one has heeded his message of conversion. And because of the evil intentions of a woman and the weakness of a man. Because of the darkness that enslaves men's hearts.

A sign is given to enable the sensitive heart to reply to the question of faith. A day will come when the bridegroom will be arrested and dragged in front of the great men of the world. A day will come when he will taste death. In the middle of his activity in Galilee, an activity filled with hope, there is this signpost pointing the way for the believer, who will one day have to reply to the question: "Who is this man?" At the foot of the cross, he will know, like the centurion: "In truth this man was the Son of God."

But, when he reads that John's disciples came to fetch their master's body to bury it, the believer knows that the man of God will find rest. And the day will come when the crucified Christ, the Lamb without spot or stain, will also be buried in a tomb from which the joyful news of the resurrection will come. That is God's reply to the eternal question: "Who is this man?"

■

Lord our God,
you have revealed your name
through the life and death of Jesus.
In him, you have revealed our Father.
We beseech you:
let us listen to him
so that we may recognize you
before the day of judgement.

■

For anyone who shelters in you, Lord,
you are a sure stronghold.
Proclaiming the testimony of your Son,
John gave up his life
to the very end.
We beseech you:
let us be faithful to your word,
you, the living one, for ever.

SATURDAY OF THE 4TH WEEK

A NEW PEOPLE

1 Kings 3:4-13. "The king went to Gibeon to sacrifice there, since that was the greatest of the high places—Solomon offered a thousand holocausts on that altar." Certain things can only be said in veiled terms! The fact is that Gibeon was a sanctuary provided not only with an altar but also with a stele, which was a phallic symbol or a representation of the deity. Gibeon was, in other words, a place where the Canaanites came to celebrate their cult. As soon as the Hebrews settled in Canaan, they were deeply influenced by Canaanite practices and their faith was tinged with syncretism. It was not until the prophets appeared and the later kings introduced their religious reforms, that the ambiguity concerning the ancient sanctuaries was resolved and the whole of Israel's cult was centered in Jerusalem. Until that time, Solomon continued to offer his holocausts at Gibeon.

This does not in any way reduce the stature of David's successor. What the king, whose authority comes from God, asks for is not a personal favor, but only wisdom; in other words, the ability to carry out in a suitable way the duties attached to his royal function. He does not regard that function as a personal privilege, but as a ministry in favor of the people of God.

Psalm 119 is an alphabetical psalm. It is written to the glory of God's Word, which is expressed by a synonym in each of the strophes. The verses contained in today's liturgy consist of a series of maxims written to make it easier for young men to choose the "right way."

Mark 6:30–34. See p. 70.

■

Jesus' contemporaries were preoccupied with an intense longing to become a nation again. They looked back nostalgically to the time of Israel's origins. They idealized the past.

Each Passover they told stories about the great things God had done in favor of their ancestors; how, for example, he had protected the scattered children of Israel in the land of slavery and how he had made a people of what was not a people. Later, of course, they had become divided again into two kingdoms—two hostile brothers. And during the time of the Diaspora, Israel had once again been scattered in a foreign land.

And now a man arises in whom the people recognizes the fulfilment of their expectation—the sheep always recognize the voice of their shepherd. Once again, they are gathered together in the desert—"the Lord is my shepherd." Only God knows where to lead his people and he has placed everything in the hands of his Son. But only the shepherd who has become a lamb so that he can be one with his flock can claim to be the shepherd. Only the one who goes to the very end in giving up his life can take them to the source of life.

The prophets had foretold his coming. In the fullness of time, God would send the shepherd who would gather his flock together. Ezekiel prophesied: "I mean to raise up one shepherd and to put him in charge of them; he will pasture them and be their shepherd." That shepherd would have mercy on the scattered sheep. "I shall look for the lost sheep, bring back the stray, bandage the wounded and make the weak strong. I shall watch over the fat and healthy." Jesus was that shepherd of Israel and his word of total power was to bind the people together.

You who are waiting with great longing for the day of renewal, recognize the water that can quench your thirst! You who are blessed by your poverty and that of the world, abandon yourself to the love of the one who can heal you! You whose heart is full of humility and tenderness, know the voice of the one who is gentle and humble in heart! You who are longing to love passionately, hear the cry of the one who calls on you to follow him to the cross! He calls you out into the desert and makes a holy people of you! You need have no fear of mirages, because he is the way and the truth and the life. Can you not hear him inviting you to join him on God's way?

■

Yes, we give you thanks, holy Father,
through Jesus, your beloved Son, our paschal Lamb.
He came to give men peace
  and fullness of joy and love.
He gave his blood
  to renew your covenant
  and to make the source of eternal life
  flow abundantly.
In him we recognize you.
Through him we are led to you
  and can remain in your presence.
That is why,
with all our brothers and sisters
  who have been made holy in his blood
  and renewed by the Spirit
  who expresses our praise of you,
we too sing your praises, God, our life.

God Beyond All Frontiers

An "Open" Faith

The conflagration has broken out. Nothing and nobody can prevent the wind of the Spirit spreading. Jesus goes off into foreign territory. He does not preach—his mere presence there bears witness to God's salvation. Pagans are also welcomed in the kingdom. Like the Jews, they also benefit from what the prophet proclaimed. It is the time of God's grace and they too can take their place at the table of the covenant.

No one can reduce the mystery of God. God is greater than our hearts and his word is deeper than anything we can say about it. No one can enclose faith in a framework of habits and stereotyped ideas, because the believer's very existence is the covenant that God works out with him and for him day after day. Faith only exists in a freedom that spreads with the fire of the Spirit.

No one can imprison God. He is permeating like yeast and nothing that has to do with man is alien to him. It is he, God, who is always changing his abode. He is, for eternity, our Emmanuel. We believe in a God who is always getting in the way, because he has made himself our neighbor.

If God is always moving house, we have to recognize that he also takes us out of ourselves. He takes each one of us below his surface and to his heart. That is the risk that we run as believers—that God will reach us in our hearts and give us new birth in the freedom of the Spirit.

The land of faith cannot be enclosed within any frontiers. No one can codify the future without risk of contradiction. Experiencing the faithfulness of the Word and the Spirit is welcoming what God has said about our human existence. It is letting ourselves be burnt by the Fire that comes from elsewhere. It is also accepting that there is no Word that is not incarnate and not risky. The word of God only exists because it is both a revelation for all time and a proclamation for today.

The conflagration has broken out! Both the life of every individual and the history of mankind are marked for ever by the Word which wakes us today to new birth. God has had compassion on our earth. The good news is for everyone and no one is beyond the frontiers of the action of the Spirit. The whole of our earth is the realm of God's activity.

GOD MOVES HOUSE

1 Kings 8:1-7, 9-13. Solomon, who had inherited a fine legacy from his father, pursued a policy of prestige. He extended the northern boundaries of Jerusalem and built a huge and magnificent palace, containing the royal sanctuary.

The memory of a procession in September each year, within the framework of the Feast of Tabernacles, in which the ark was brought to the temple, is preserved in tradition. There, the kingship of Yahweh was celebrated; in other words, his permanent presence among his people. The building of this temple was contrary to the principle of the movable tent in which God manifested himself. The keeping of the ark in the temple, however, was a guarantee of his presence there, which was in turn indicated by the presence of the cloud and by the formula of consecration: "Yahweh has chosen to dwell in the thick cloud."

Psalm 132 was used for pilgrimages and is a dynastic psalm of composite structure. Verses 1-5 allude to David's concern to find a dwelling-place for Yahweh. The verses included in today's liturgy recall the keeping of the ark at Kiriath-jearim, after it had been brought back from the Philistines (1 Sam 7:2). It was from there that David brought it back with great ceremony to Jerusalem.

Mark 6:53-56. See p. 77.

■

According to the home furnishing magazines, our homes reflect our personalities. This is confirmed by psychologists. "Show me your home and I will tell you who you are!" It could also be said: "Tell me where your God dwells and I will tell you who he is!"

Men have almost automatically enclosed God within a heaven that seemed all the more beautiful the more remote it was. God became a potentate enthroned in a palace of a thousand and one nights and surrounded by a great number of busy courtiers. He was made to live in the heights from which he looked down impassively in judgment, the monarch of all he surveyed. But man had his dwelling-place—earth—and God had his heaven, so there was a kind of power sharing. Man and God were each in his own place for the good of everybody.

But, isolated in his gilded palace and his soulless gardens, a king can very soon become bored. A queen soon wants to have little homes built where she can play at being a shepherdess and have the illusion that she is living. We must try to understand what was happening to God imprisoned in his heaven! He was becoming desperate, living in exile in a paradise far from his family, far from men and women. He had begotten the whole of life and he too wanted to live! Not by proxy and not by what his unctuous representatives might tell him about life. No, he wanted to see for himself. He wanted to live like men, He wanted to share their hopes and anxieties. He just wanted to live.

So God moved house. He risked everything in order just to live. His reputation, his credit, his peace of mind. He moved from his heaven and rented a furnished apartment on earth. He took a risk on the paths of the covenant and began to walk along them at a man's pace. From camp to camp. He inhabited man's desert. If you have tasted life in the open air, you can never go back to the stuffy atmosphere of paradise. So God, having shared men's lives and made his dwelling-place among them, could never again live elsewhere.

A God who is imprisoned in a heaven (or a tabernacle) does not disturb us. We can get used to power. But can we ever endure a God who shares our humdrum daily life? Our neighbors often get in our way. We visit palaces that are like museums. Life has left them. But we do not visit homes in that way. We live in them.

So where is your God? Is he living in the ruins of an abandoned religion, a shadow that is remote from everything that constitutes life today? Or has he made his dwelling-place in a tent among men? What is God for you? Is he a museum piece or is he the leaven in the lump?

But be careful! If you let God move house and live among you, he will, like every neighbor, soon get in your way. He may even succeed in throwing you out of your own home, your own habits and your own securities. He is as permeating as yeast. If you accept him as your guest, there is a risk that he will become your master. You must decide!

■

You have made your dwelling-place among men.
In Jesus, you came forward to meet us.
May your word transform our hearts!
May your Spirit live in our lives
  and may we live in you
    now and for ever.

■

You take your place at our table
  and distribute the bread.
May your love live in us
  and may we be with you
  without anything to restrict our communion.

TUESDAY OF THE 5TH WEEK

YOUR HEARTS—NOT SACRIFICES

1 Kings 8:22–23, 27–30. Solomon's prayer once again bears witness to the priestly role played by the kings before the exile, especially on solemn occasions. The king's enthronement made it possible for his relationship with God to be that of a son with his father and to address himself legitimately to him.

In praising God, Solomon also extols his loving-kindness. The one whom heaven and earth cannot contain now lives in a palace built by human hands.

Psalm 84 consists mainly of a pilgrims' song. The believers tell the priests how happy they are to be in Jerusalem and especially in the temple, the center of the Yahwistic religion.

Mark 7:1–13. See p. 80.

■

The worship you offer is worthless. The doctrines you teach are false. Your piety is useless. It has not transformed your hearts. Your worship is worse than worthless—it is dangerous. It gives you the impression of being justified. Your doctrines are not only false, they set God up against men and relegate him to the side-passages of life, where he can no longer get in men's way or disturb them. You give him some formal honor in the temple and then, as soon as you leave the building, forget him. You take pleasure in doing acts of charity, but behave like wolves towards each other in everyday life. You are actors, disfiguring faith. Take off your masks and live in the logic of the covenant!

We could stop there and just preach the logic of an active faith. But then we would not be following Jesus' criticism of the Pharisees to its

---

conclusion. Let us make no mistake, the Pharisees were exceptional men. They were fervent, committed men who lived the logic of the Law at a fundamental level. Jesus attacked them fiercely, but we are bound to ask: Why should he accuse men who were the religious elite of their people?

His criticism of the Pharisees was: You are setting aside the word of God! The drama was: You are playing the wrong game! A tragic mistake that intimately and permanently had a direct bearing on God. They washed their arms before eating the offerings made to them, and therefore believed that they were a truly priestly people. They were virtuous and identified themselves with an Israel that was pure and holy. Jesus did not say to these men: You are liars! No, he said: You have missed what you have been looking for. Your cultic practices are valueless. You will never encounter God that way.

You are mistaken about God! Jesus' criticisms echo a very secular accusation. Certain traditions are really no more than a way of avoiding the living God. But when you erect a protective wall between yourself and God, how can he ever reach your heart?

You and I are both hypocrites. Not that we are liars or actors. No, we are hypocrites, because we stay on the surface of our existence. Jesus wanted to go further and deeper. He wanted to penetrate to the heart.

■

Prayer turns us towards you,
but we remain without a heart.
Have mercy on us!

We practise our faith,
but do not live in love.
Have mercy on us!

We are very orthodox in what we say,
but little is changed in our lives.
Have mercy on us!

■

God, you search out men's hearts—
set us free from our limitations
and show us your Spirit!
May your tenderness not remain hidden from us
as we wait for eternal communion with you.

OUR HEARTS ARE UNCLEAN

1 Kings 10:1-10. David's spirit and the qualities of his heart astonished his contemporaries. His successor, on the other hand, was remarkable for his administrative abilities. There were no wars during Solomon's reign, and both trade and the iron and the copper industries could therefore be developed. The story of the visit made by the Queen of Sheba has to be seen fundamentally as a fable, but it probably also reflects trading arrangements that Israel made with southern Arabia.

The reigns of both David and Solomon also provided a fertile ground in which Jewish literature could flourish. Both the ancient traditions of Israel, which had until then been handed down orally, and the major historical works were written during this period. A school of wisdom was also born at the beginning of the time of the kings. Like the sovereigns of Egypt and Mesopotamia, the kings of Israel were able to surround themselves with a team of counsellors who, in addition to playing an important part in politics, founded cultural centers and evolved a body of doctrine.

Psalm 37 has an alphabetical structure, and praises the harmony that exists between God and wise and righteous men.

Mark 7:14-23. See p. 83.

∎

We think we can imprison our sinfulness and we like to make an index of our sources of misery. We treat our life as though it were a set of labelled bottles, some containing medicines and others containing poisons. So one part of our life can be used to good effect, but another part is forbidden. A basically very simple life, because we know what has to be done to preserve our original purity and to give back to God what he has given us. "Lord, you gave me one talent. . . . I had heard you were a hard man, . . . so I went off and hid your talent in the ground. Here it is; it was yours, you have it back." No doubt life is less easy than it seems to be, with scribes of all kinds overburdening us with the weight of laws and prohibitions. But at least we know how to lead our life and, if we happen to go beyond the frontiers, our sin can be named and defined.

"Nothing that goes into a man from outside can make him unclean." Jesus shuffles the cards. Evil comes, not from outside, but from the heart. It is a question not of what is allowed and what is forbidden, but of the call of the Spirit. We cannot define frontiers here, because the breath of the Spirit carries us a long way. Life is not a set of bottles that we have to open or keep closed. It is the long journey made with a freedom that always calls us to go forward, never back. It is a great risk, but we have to run that risk if the Spirit is to bear fruit. "You knew I was a hard master. Why, then, did you hide my talent in the ground?"

It may be possible to satisfy the demands made by religion by following a set of laws and prohibitions, but faith cannot be enclosed within such rules. It calls for the open air, freedom and breath. The life of faith is an uncomfortable life because, in it, our sin is not the breaking of a code of law or being made unclean by some impurity. No, our real misery comes from the many times we stop and even turn back on our journey and the restraints we put on the dynamic movement forward of our freedom. Our real poverty stems from closing our doors to keep out the breath of the Spirit, and from our hesitating to follow an unknown road. Our sin is rooted in unsuspected depths.

It is what comes from the heart of man that is unclean. Holiness is not a state of virginity that has to be preserved. It is a communion that has to be made a reality every day. Perfection is not a form of purity that has to be maintained. It is a heart that is always learning about the love by which it is loved. Grace is not an error that has been wiped out. It is breath received, freedom awakened and man raised up.

■

God our Father, boundless love,
  touch our hearts
  and transform us by your Spirit.
May your word be the call
  that leads us forward on our way
and may your bread be the grace
  that gives us life.
Then we shall live from your word,
  which is the demand made by your promise
  and the joy of our life.

■

Truly it is right for us
  to give you thanks,
  God, the Father of all men.
In your goodness,

without taking anyone into account,
you sent your only Son
for the reconciliation of all nations.
In him, you have purified us of all uncleanness
and have revealed to us
the kind of worship that you like.
That is why we can join all the saints
in proclaiming the glory of your Name.

THURSDAY OF THE 5TH WEEK

OPENNESS AND FAITHFULNESS

1 Kings 11:4–13. Solomon "did what was displeasing to Yahweh and was not a wholehearted follower of Yahweh, as his father David had been." David gradually came to be seen as the only king who was perfect, and the figure of David therefore became the norm by which all Israel's kings were measured.

It cannot be denied that Solomon wasted his father's legacy. He deeply offended the northern tribes by forcing them to carry out tyrannical unpaid feudal labor. He also turned the members of Israel's religious circles against him by making a number of politically expedient marriages with foreign women and, as a result of these, introducing idolatrous forms of worship into the land that belonged to Yahweh. The whole of Israel prostituted itself because of its king. The judgment passed on Solomon was very severe and confirmed the decline that was threatening the country. The southern tribes seceded and this caused a schism in the kingdom of David.

Psalm 106 is a national confession, the present edited version of which probably goes back to after the exile. It is the result of Israel's gradually becoming aware of its unfaithfulness with regard to Yahweh.

Mark 7:24–30. See p. 85.

■

The connection made by the evangelist between Jesus' encounter with a pagan woman and his criticism in the preceding passage of Jewish legalism is obviously not simply fortuitous. Jesus has left God's country and has entered the land of the enemy. The district of Tyre and Sidon, to which he has come, was pagan and had the reputation of being hostile to the Jews. The time for confrontation had not yet come and Jesus at first refused to heal the woman's daughter. The hour had not yet come for the Son of man to manifest himself to the nations. But he was already asserting his power over evil. The time would come when he would overcome sin in his own territory.

Faith and the world, the Spirit and the spirit of the age! It has always been possible to enclose faith and the Church within special spheres. Christians have always wanted—and still want—to limit the activity of the Church to the "religious" sphere, that of worship and liturgy. The priest's place is the sacristy and the Christian's place is in church. The Church should not interfere in politics and the things of this world, but keep to its own affairs. It should hold itself aloof from the world. Any commitment to the world is a form of prostitution.

Jesus, then, goes into pagan territory. No country is alien to God. Nothing that concerns man and the world is alien to the Church. Yeast is not the same as dough, but the only reason for its existence is to be mixed into the dough to make it rise. So the Church is in the world and exists for the world. When men and women take their brothers' and sisters' questions into the realm of faith, that is already the beginning of God's reply to those questions. When they share the anxieties of the world, that is also the beginning of God's future. It is only by being mixed into the human dough that the Church can be the sign of God in the world and salt for our life. Since Bethlehem, there has no longer been any division between God's earth and the world of men.

Does this mean that the Church is merged into the world? Does being open to the world mean being diluted? Solomon was led astray by foreign women and his heart was no longer close to the Lord. But the word that the Church has to proclaim today will always be new and astonishing. It will always be a stumbling-block, but at the same time also a block for building. Christians will also always be new and astonishing, hoping against hope, trying to go beyond the substitutes for love that the world gives us and love authentically. We are being unfaithful to the Word that saves us if we imprison it in rules and practices or enclose it in a special shrine. We are also being unfaithful to the Word if we try to eliminate the conflict that it inevitably causes with the world or to strangle the oath that it grafts on to life.

■

Cardinal Marty once said that "the Church no longer has to question itself about whether it has to go to the world. It bears within itself the world's conflicts and questions. . . . Our mission today makes us question the Church's faithfulness, its own identity and the quality of the sign that it gives of itself. . . . The best service that the Church can give to the world is being itself in the world."

■

You have placed in our hands the treasure of your Word
and we carry it as though it were in a fragile vase.
We ask you, Lord,
to make us bold enough,
so that it may be a word for today,
life of our life
and the present reality of your eternal promise.

FRIDAY OF THE 5TH WEEK

TORN AND RESTORED

1 Kings 11:29–32; 12:19. David succeeded in unifying the twelve tribes around his person, but his kingdom was still very precarious. On the one hand, there were many in the north of the country who did not favor the idea of an inherited monarchy and were seeking independence. On the other hand, both the mistakes made by Solomon's successor and Jeroboam's political ambitions contributed to the political schism. But that was not part of the tribes' past history.

The Deuteronomist historian, however, continued to be convinced that the only master of history was Yahweh. There were countless examples of prophets in the chronicle of the Northern Kingdom who, whenever a political crisis occurred, rose up and influenced the course of events. Ahijah of Shiloh behaved in a prophetic manner when he tore his new cloak into twelve pieces in a significant symbolic act. Only one tribe was to remain faithful to the dynasty of David.

Psalm 81 is in the form of an indictment. It enumerates the obligations undertaken by the people when they entered into the covenant, and also Yahweh's complaints. It ends, however, on a note of hope: "If only my people would listen!"

Mark 7:31–37. See p. 87.

A new garment that is torn—a kingdom divided when it has only just emerged from the darkness of history. The drama of a nation exposed to the risks of time. A man torn when he has hardly emerged from the womb of the earth. A heart that cannot speak—even before it has ventured to express a few words of tenderness, its voice has been silenced by the harsh experience of life. A heart that cannot listen— even before it has heard life breathing, it has been made deaf by the sounds of distress and injustice. Man—a kingdom divided against itself.

Jesus is in the Decapolis—pagan country. A man is brought to him who is so overwhelmed by his own wretchedness that he cannot ever stand at a distance from it. Imprisoned in silence, he is himself his own wretchedness.

"Ephphata!—Be opened!" The word of God which does what it says is pronounced. It does not ask to be heard. It is pronounced and life is changed. The sick man can hear a different voice, not the one spoken by the distress that is eating him away. He can speak and he can also say the words that set him free and save him. "Be opened!" The sick man is healed. Yet he is healed not because he believes—the evangelist says nothing either about his expectation or about his asking to be cured— but because the one sent by God has come as a sign of final deliverance.

When Jesus appears, the man becomes a man again. Not just the believer, the whole man. He rediscovers his original beauty. The wretchedness that has affected creation is healed. The original splendor is rediscovered and made manifest to everybody. This is a sign for every man of the new creation that God will make rise up on that day, at the end of time. On the first day of creation, God said: "It is very good." On the day of fulfilment, he will say: "I am making the whole of creation new." And while we are waiting, we say, as those who witnessed Jesus' healing of the sick man said: "He has done all things well."

"Ephphata!—Be opened!" We should repeat those words, so that our brothers and sisters may hear something other than the cries of their own wretchedness. We should work so that the new world may come and so that our brothers and sisters may express something other than their own despair. We should love our earth passionately so that your word may become the cry of its new birth: "Be opened!" On that day, at the peak of admiration, we will then say: "He has done all things well. He makes the deaf hear and the dumb speak."

■

Give us, Lord, a sign of life.
Make your creative word renew our earth.
May the day come when, in thanksgiving,
all men will recognize
that you have always done all things well
and will always do them well.

"Be opened!"
Open our hearts, Lord,
    to your word of hope.
Open our eyes,
    so that we may see
    your acts of tenderness.
Open our hands,
    so that they may be offered in sharing.
Open our lips,
    so that we may praise you until the encounter
    that will fulfil our prayer and our longing.

SATURDAY OF THE 5TH WEEK

MERCY

1 Kings 12:26–32; 13:33–34. The political schism was followed by a religious schism. The Deuteronomist author totally condemns what he calls Jeroboam's "sin." He enumerates the many acts of disobedience committed by the first King of Israel. These include the building of high places, feasts celebrated at places other than Jerusalem, the carrying out of cultic functions by Jews who were not members of the tribe of Levi, and the use of a new calendar.

At the same time, however, he is guilty of an anachronism. He judges the kings in the light of their attitude towards the one sanctuary of Jerusalem, forgetting that the primacy of the temple only dated back to the end of the Judaean monarchy. Worship only became unified under Josiah, one of the last kings ruling from Jerusalem. In opening the sanctuaries of Dan and Bethel to cultic practice, Jeroboam was simply renewing a connection with the tradition of the ancient sacred towns. As for the golden calves, these were never images of the deity, but, like the cherubim of the ark of the covenant, simply the pedestal.

The prophet Hosea was the first to suggest a religious reform and to condemn the golden calves. Before him, all that was prohibited was firstly the presence of foreign gods in both official and private worship and secondly the making of images of Yahweh for private religious purposes (see Deut 5:7–8). The story of the golden calf (Ex 32) was used to support this stricter reinterpretation of the commandment forbidding images.

Psalm 106 is a national confession written after the exile, at a time when the people had sufficient time to become fully conscious of the many times they had been unfaithful to the covenant. The religious schism was clearly regarded as one of Israel's major acts of treachery.

Mark 8:1–10. See p. 91.

■

"I feel sorry for all these people." Our God is a God of mercy and compassion! Let us make no mistake about that. Love that consists of mercy and compassion has a source that is different from our often impotent human expressions of mercy and compassion, which are greeted by our contemporaries with sarcasm.

Love is defined not by mercy, but by admiration. When God says: "I feel sorry," there is no feeling of condescension and there is no affectation in his attitude. He is only making an astonishing revelation—that he is in love with us. "Does a woman forget her baby at the breast or fail to cherish the son of her womb?" the prophet Isaiah asked. "Yet, even if these forget, I will never forget you." God is passionate. He is crazy! Like a lover, he lets go of everything—his peace of mind, his reputation and his good name because he is in love.

What can he do for us? What can make our exhausted, ungrateful, rebellious and corrupt world the object of such love? What enabled the Son to accept the cross? Surely only what the cross was able to become —the body of the beloved Son himself. "I feel sorry for all these people." And God's body is broken so that this earth, which did not even share his hunger and longing, might be filled.

God let himself be stretched out on the wood at Golgotha in order to raise up a mankind that had not even reached the limit of his longing. "I feel sorry for all these people." Only God could really pronounce those words, because only he loved and admired our earth enough. Only he could really know the full meaning of those words, because only he knows man fully—the man he was dreaming of on the evening of the sixth day. Only God could repeat those words without any trace of condescension, because only he could do everything to make that forgotten dream a reality. "I feel sorry for all these people." Only God has the right to pronounce those words, because only he paid the price for mercy and compassion to become resurrection. "Take and eat; this is my body which will be given up for you and for all men."

∎

You who are truly holy,
and the source of all holiness,
    Lord, we bless you.
We praise you for Jesus, your Son,
    your face among men.
He was concerned about our weakness;
he healed our injuries
and raised up our wounded hearts.
He went to the utmost limits of love.
We thank you for his death,
    that unrepeatable gift of himself,
    that act of obedience
    by which we are reborn.
With all those who have believed
    in the words of your beloved Son,
    we bless you.
With all those who have experienced
    your great tenderness,
    we praise the power of your promise,
    God who are our future.

∎

Who will express your wisdom for us?
    It is foolishness!
Who will express your power for us?
    It is weakness!
Who will tell us your name,
    God of tenderness and mercy?
Share with us the bread of your passion!
Fill us with your love!
Then we shall live for ever.

Putting the Sign to the Test

Jesus is in pagan territory. The good news is not simply for those who are "clean." It is for everybody. Even though he did not preach in pagan territory, his presence alone was enough to make the power of Satan draw back. And, in wonderment, creation regained its first youth.

This is what we considered in last week's liturgy. This week, however, we have a completely new situation. Jesus returns to the land of the Jews and is attacked and harassed by the Pharisees as soon as he reappears in public. They put him to the test by demanding a sign.

"This is a wicked generation; it is asking for a sign. The only sign it will be given is the sign of Jonah" (Lk 11:29). Only one sign will be given, then, to all men: the life of Jesus of Nazareth, his words of fire and his acts of tenderness. People were calling for proofs and demonstrations. But all that they were to be given was a poor human life, that of a man condemned to die on the gallows. People wanted to touch God and enclose him within a framework of definite evidence. But they were only confronted with a word that invited them and involved in a relationship that was offered to them.

The sign does not exist for its own sake. If it did, it would simply be magic. No, it exists for the encounter from which it derives its meaning. It takes us back to the encounter for which it is needed. "And leaving them again and re-embarking, he went away to the opposite shore." The sign given is the life of Jesus. And he is only there in order to go "to the opposite shore"—to go back to the Father.

■

God, you keep your word.
May your name be blessed!
Your Spirit enables us to hear
the good news of our salvation.
You want to share your love
and make a covenant with us.
Let us conform to your expectation
and share in the game of your word,
in communion with you and our brothers.
In that way, the power of your promise

and the truth of the signs of it you give us
will be made manifest.

NO OTHER SIGN THAN LIFE

James 1:1-11. Steadfastness when put to the test, prayer for wisdom, poverty and riches—James' tone is lively enough, because he wants to shake his listeners. He begins by exhorting them to perform a "perfect work" by cultivating joy in these trials. There is no place for surliness or defeatism. The trials that we have to endure in life may be hard, but they can also be, for the Christian, an opportunity to test his steadfastness and patience. In this way, the author begins to outline the theme of active faith.

He continues by urging the Christian who feels that he lacks wisdom to ask God for it. God will give him wisdom "simply" and without conditions. But it is important to pray to God for wisdom with faith and without doubt or hesitations. The man who is divided within himself and thinks that a compromise can be achieved between God and the world can expect nothing.

Finally, there is the question of the poor and the rich members of the Christian community. Early Christianity did not do away with the class structure of society, and so the hope of earthly messianism had ended in disappointment. The good things of the kingdom, however, had been given to all. The rich man should not therefore be proud of his precarious riches. His loss of social class had already begun! On one hand, his conversion to Christianity had already banished him from civil society and, on the other, he had sacrificed a share of his possessions for the community.

Psalm 119 is a very long alphabetical hymn to the divine Word.

Mark 8:11-13. See p. 86.

■

He must give us a sign. Mark's Gospel is punctuated with this theme. Even those standing at the foot of the cross wanted Jesus to come down from it, so that faith in his mission would have a firm foundation. Jesus is expected to provide proof for his claims. In asking for a sign from heaven, the Pharisees are demanding proof, given directly by God, that Jesus is the Messiah. As representatives of the Jewish religion, they

---

237

must make a statement based on irrefutable evidence. Their demand is, moreover, in accordance with the general expectation that prevailed with regard to the Messiah. Claims to be able to decipher the signs pointing to the coming of the Messiah were made in numerous apocalyptic writings of the period.

Compared with these apocalyptic expectations, Jesus' life and activity was altogether too modest, too human and too personal for it to be accepted as a decisive sign of the coming of the messianic era. "No other sign will be given." God will give no other proof of his salvation than the life and activity of Jesus, his preaching and his healings.

There will be no other sign than the life of that man. That is the divine act that reveals that God is at work—the life of a man. At the dawn of the universe, God was already known in the life of man—that life which had become the image and likeness of God. And now, in that man from Nazareth, God discovers once again his own first portrait. No other sign will be given than the obedience of the Son—than a life lived unreservedly in the breath of the Spirit.

The life of that man is in itself a speaking likeness. It does not call for proof or demonstration. The signs of the times are present in it—a man who loves, who speaks of forgiveness, who does not break the crushed reed and who, in the confrontation of prayer, calls God his Father.

What is a sign? It is a call to what it shows. A ball is thrown to us. If we catch it, we join in the game. Yes, God gives a sign for us to join in the game. But we have unfortunately reduced that sign so that it has become only a demonstration. But a demonstration creates nothing. It only confirms. A sign, on the other hand, is a call, an encounter. Jesus was asked to provide proofs. But God wanted to disclose a new covenant.

A sign that is a human life, because only the testimony, and by this I mean the life of that man, can be an invitation, a discovery and a promise. God can give no other sign of salvation than the life of his beloved Son handed over to die and in this way going to the utmost limits of love.

A sign—a testimony. Our own human life can also be a sign and a testimony. Our serenity can become a word of hope. Our steadfastness in our search for what is good can bear witness to our faithfulness to the call we have heard. Our simplicity can show that we all share in the same Spirit. Is that sign too modest? We should not forget that God can give no other sign, because he has identified himself from the first day of creation with life.

■

Lord our God,
we have given you our faith.
We ask you:
  may the life of your Son
  not be a sign of contradiction for us
  and may his word be truth and life for today
  and our joy in eternity.

■

May the broken Bread
  be a sign of your promise.
May the shared Word
  not be the block
  that causes us to stumble.
May our life
  bear witness to the power of your grace.

TUESDAY OF THE 6TH WEEK

LACK OF UNDERSTANDING

James 1:12–18. God puts man to the test in order to teach him, as the wise men believed. What, then, about temptation? The author of the letter is convinced that "God does not tempt anybody." He is beyond the reach of the attractions of evil and therefore cannot drive man to commit evil. The origin of temptation is to be found in passionate desire, which "conceives and gives birth to sin" and eventually leads man to spiritual death.

God is the "Father of all light." He not only created the stars, but also made light in man. He is the source of all truth, just as the demon is the father of lies. God is unchangeable and only perfect gifts come from him, such as man's regeneration by the baptism of water and the Spirit. He has begotten us by a word of truth to a new life.

Psalm 94 is composed of two independent songs, verses 7–11 forming a psalm on the theme of wisdom and verses 1–6 and 14–23 an individual lamentation. The verses in today's liturgy express the believer's trust in Yahweh.

Mark 8:14–21. See p. 98.

■

They Have Understood Nothing!
They have been living with him. They have shared the same hopes, have been subject to the same criticisms and have been tired by the same experiences. They were very close to him. They were his family. But, despite this close bond, the signs were still not clear to them. They were still insensitive to the meaning of events. They were incapable of understanding the deep significance of the miracle of the loaves and the importance of the time that they were living through. Like those who were at a distance, they saw without seeing and heard without understanding.

"Be on your guard against the yeast of the Pharisees." Resist the greatest temptation! A sign only discloses its meaning to the loving heart. Love is blind, we are told, because it ventures on ways that reason does not know. If you live by reason alone, how will you ever love? The flowers only speak of love to the one who already loves. A kiss only revives the fire for the one whom it has already burned. So "be on your guard against the yeast of the Pharisees"—against the hardening of the heart that is enclosed within itself. "Never, when you have been tempted, say, 'God sent the temptation,' " for God is totally incapable of breaking the infernal cycle within which you have enclosed yourself. "They have eyes that do not see and ears that do not hear."

Men continue to demand striking signs, but we have no other sign than the cross. Some still dream of a Church that is free of every compromise, but we are a people made unclean by our history, our hesitations and our failures. Some still dream of a powerful light, but we live in darkness, victims of our doubts, incapable of making the Gospel a living reality, dumbfounded by the poor response to the witness that we bear.

"Do you not yet understand?" A little broken bread becomes the sign of man's unbounded expectation. An act of forgiveness becomes the sign of the possibility of a new beginning. Words endlessly repeated tell us what we have always been—beloved sons and loving brothers. Men and women who are trying to love become the bridgehead of a new world in our aging and barren universe.

"Do you still not understand?" God will always be disarming, because he is without weapons. From all eternity, God has "made us his children by the message of his truth, so that we should be a sort of first-fruits of all that he has created." But that word of truth acts in our world secretly, like yeast. Life only grows when it makes the ascent to Golgotha. "Do you still not

---

understand?" God's activity—the work of the Spirit—will always be in signs that have to be deciphered.

■

In a world made deaf by too much talking, Lord,
do not let your word be stifled.
In a world made drunk by too much adulterated love,
do not let your life become degenerate.
Arouse us,
so that we may prepare the ways of the Kingdom.

WEDNESDAY OF THE 6TH WEEK

ENTERING THE DYNAMISM OF THE WORD

James 1:19–27. What are man's duties with regard to the Word of God? Here the author is probably addressing those who have a teaching function in the Church. Before teaching others, he says, they must themselves listen to the Word. In discussion, they must also not let themselves be swept along by anger, since this is never in the interests of love. Welcoming the Word, then, calls for flexibility and generosity. It may also require us to give up an attitude or a way of living.

It is, however, not enough simply to welcome the Word. It has also to be put into practice. The man who does not let the Word penetrate into his being and who does not let himself be converted is like someone who, after examining himself in a mirror, forgets to get rid of the spots and blemishes that he has seen. The man who takes action on the basis of what he has seen in the mirror, on the other hand, will be happy.

The prophets of the Old Testament had denounced the hypocrisy of worship that did not involve man wholly. True religion excludes unrestrained evil talk and ill-timed teaching, but calls for the exercise of justice and charity towards those who are disinherited.

Psalm 15 is part of a liturgy for entry. The priest, whom the believer has just asked if he can enter the temple, replies to him by listing the requirements imposed on those who want to stand in Yahweh's presence.

Mark 8:22–26. See p. 101.

241

■

"I have no one to speak to. I do not know where I am any more." We live in soulless cities, where we have condemned each other to isolation and anxiety. "We cannot speak at home. We watch the TV while we are eating our evening meal. In any case, we have nothing to say to each other." We have consumed the word and have killed personal encounter.

Speaking—we were born to speak. Not to make long speeches, but to wake up to a heard word that expresses the meaning of life. Speaking is listening, because the only true word is the one that we have received in silence. Speaking is first of all listening to what the other person wants to tell me. Speaking is understanding. The true word is sharing. You tell me who you are and I cannot remain cold in the presence of your word. It stimulates me. It involves me. It compromises me. Speaking is also responding. There is no word without a response. There is no word without an encounter. The word is always a word that is exchanged. The word binds us together and forms our communion.

"The Word was made flesh." God became man's word. Faith enables us to enter the dynamism of that word. Faith is listening, because it is only word that has been heard for a long time. It is only recollected word. So James urges us: "accept and submit to the word which has been planted in you and can save your souls." Faith is meditation, because it is only word that has been assimilated and shared for a long time. Faith is stimulation, contestation and conversion. It is wonderment, admiration and gratitude. Listening to the Word without putting it into practice is creating an illusion. Faith is response. There is no word but the one in which "I" and "thou" become "we." As James says, "the word can save your souls." This is because God pronounces his name over your life and you become, in the Spirit, his sons by adoption.

So, brothers, enter into the dynamism of the Word! God does what he says. The word of God is like the rain—it does not leave the earth without having made it fertile. Neither any person nor any thing can prevent God's good news from stimulating men so that they may decide to enter the movement of grace.

The dynamism of the Word! Jesus' adversaries are now attacking him more often and even more fiercely. The people's attitude towards him is becoming even more deeply ambiguous. His disciples are themselves also becoming increasingly incapable of understanding the real meaning of the events that are taking place. Despite this, Jesus still goes on healing—among many others, the blind man at Bethsaida. He is still the man who is not understood, but this does not make him abandon his mission in the world. "I am the light of the world," God says—and neither any thing nor any person can silence that word.

■

God our Father,
tell us again your word of love:
  Jesus, your beloved Son.
He is your eyes and your mouth
and has seen us and spoken to us.
In him we know you
and through him we love you.
We pray you:
  may your word become ours
  and may it be our future for ever.

THURSDAY OF THE 6TH WEEK

THE SIGN QUESTIONED—FROM CONFESSION TO REVELATION

James 2:1–9. No favoritism! But the Christian community is like all other groups of people in the world and the ways of the world are often found in it. The rich are favored, while the poor are left out in the cold. The Bible, however, reveals above all God's preference for those whom the world despises.

It is in order, James writes, if the welcome reserved for the rich is inspired by charity, but not if it is just a question of flattering them; in which case Christians would be acting without discernment and according to a false scale of values. After all, were not the first Christian communities for the most part composed of poor people?

Psalm 34 is an alphabetical psalm. Teaching on the theme of wisdom is contained in verses 10–23, while verses 2–9 belong more to the category of thanksgiving and contain both an invitation to praise God and a reminder to pray to him when one is put to the test.

Mark 8:27–33. See p. 104.

■

The people have ceased for the time being to be attracted by the novelty of Jesus' mission and he has withdrawn into the circle of his disciples and friends. With time, they will come to understand what he is doing.

He is once again "on the way" with his companions. He is between two countries. He has left Galilee, the crossroads of the nations where he

---

243

was born, and is going up to Jerusalem, the holy city. After making what C.H. Dodd has called a "recruiting campaign," he is about to proclaim the good news in the city of the prophets. He has already met with success and has at the same time encountered suspicion. He has proclaimed the kingdom of God that is to change the face of the earth, but he has not yet revealed his identity. He has not responded to a too hasty and excessively enthusiastic reception and has, in such cases, called for silence. Anyone wanting to penetrate to the heart of his secret has had to walk behind him for a long time.

"Who do people say I am?" He might have added: "What do they say about my mission?" The disciples reply: "Some say John the Baptist . . . others Elijah; still others, one of the prophets." His preaching in Galilee has borne some fruit! He is recognized as one sent by God or as a herald of the Messiah, like Elijah, John the Baptist or another prophet. But they are men who belong to the past, whereas Jesus comes from the future.

So he questions his disciples further: "But you, who do you say I am?" Peter replies: "You are the Christ, the Messiah." Has he, then, escaped from his past?

Peter takes him to one side and begins to reproach him, saying that the Messiah ought to be a victorious leader. Jesus' response is immediate: "Get behind me, Satan! I am the one who opens the way. The disciple is not superior to his teacher."

So, Peter, you have recognized something of the sign. Jesus is certainly the Messiah, but not in the way in which you understand the Messiah. He will not liberate the people politically, nor will he give them back their religious purity. If you are to understand his secret, you will have to continue to walk behind him for a long time. Your way will have to be via the scandal of Calvary.

Now Jesus himself replies to the question. Only he is able to reveal the hidden meaning of his life. Only he is able to confess faith. "The Son of man is destined to suffer grievously." The one who is on God's side and whose way of thinking is God's way must suffer, because that is the only possible way of destroying the process of evil.

Jesus begins to speak "quite openly" now. The time of the messianic secret is past, because he is going up to Jerusalem and to contradiction. The day will come when he will in turn be questioned and will reply to the high priest who is putting him on trial: "I am the Christ, the Messiah." On that day, confronted by that despised and condemned Messiah, no one will be able to make a mistake.

So, brothers and sisters, no one can penetrate to the heart of the mystery of Jesus unless the Spirit reveals it to him. The sign can only disclose its meaning when its full dimension is given to it by a word. Flowers displayed in a vase can mean many things: that the home is welcoming or that you went out together during the weekend. But they will only express tenderness if the husband's words reveal their hidden meaning.

No one can confess the name of Jesus unless the Spirit reveals it to him. We do not discover Jesus—we receive him. "But you, who do you say I am?" Jesus asks his disciples and at once adds: "If anyone wants to be a follower of mine, let him renounce himself and take up his cross and follow me."

Our whole life will not be enough for us to say in truth: "You are the Son of God." "Now we are seeing a dim reflection in a mirror," Paul said. We shall have to wait for eternity, when we shall be "seeing face to face," before we can confess, in truth and wonderment, what we have received by grace: "You are God's Son, the Beloved"—you are the one we have always looked for and whom we have at last found today.

■

"But you, who do you say I am?"
  You are the Son of God,
  consecrated to lead men to freedom.

"But you, who do you say I am?"
  You are God's Today,
  here to establish peace and joy.

"But you, who do you say I am?"
  You are the one sent by the Father,
  the servant of mercy
  and the First-born of the new world."

■

Following you, Lord—
there are always days
when it is attractive,
but there are also days
when we are weary and bored.
  Give us a new heart,
  so that we can follow you in truth.

Following you, Lord—
yes, we want to,
but failure and suffering
make us ask:
how can we go on believing in it,
day after day and for ever?
   Give us a new heart,
    so that we can follow you in truth.

Following you, Lord—
what a great risk we take!
What crazy love do we need?
   So, Lord,
    give us a new heart.

■

Lord, you know
   how long it takes
    to make a man and a disciple.
So do not grow weary of our hesitations
and do not despair of us
   when we choose the wrong road.
Take us back,
be our way
and lead us to your light.

■

God of peace,
   your Son Jesus—
   you reveal him to those
   whose hearts are humble and free.
Let us follow him
   in silence and faith.
Keep our eyes fixed on the goal
and let us reach the point
   where your mercy, going ahead of us,
   has already arrived.

THE SERIOUSNESS OF THE JOURNEY

James 2:14–24, 26. This passage brings us to the heart of the Epistle. The debate on the importance of faith and works or "good deeds" underlies the whole of James' letter. The author has touched on this theme again and again, especially in his arguments about the need for steadfastness and patience and about the opposition between faith in Christ and the favoritism prevailing in Christian communities.

The basic idea stressed in verses 14–24 is that, without works, faith is "dead." James does not deny the necessity of faith, but he does denounce the emptiness of a faith that is purely theoretical. He cites, as a concrete example to illustrate this theme, a case that probably occurred in the community: it is useless to tell a needy brother or sister to keep warm without giving that person the means to keep warm!

He then takes a serious objection into account. To those who claim that faith can replace works and who insist that a monotheistic faith is sufficient for salvation, James replies that the existence of faith is proved by works, since even the demons can validate their "faith" in the sight of the one God. He concludes his argument by going back to the Old Testament. Abraham testified to his faith by sacrificing his son Isaac. The patriarch's deep trust in God was the inspiration for this work and this was why God became his intimate friend.

Psalm 112 also has an alphabetical structure, but, as its first verse shows, it can be classified among the psalms of congratulation. It is a song of welcome addressed by the serving priests who have come to the temple for the great feasts of the year.

Mark 8:34–9:1. See p. 107.

■

Jesus is on his way to Jerusalem, the Holy City towards which the hearts of all religious Jews were turned. He is on his way to Jerusalem, the city that kills the prophets. The way of the cross has begun. "The Son of man is destined to suffer grievously."

"If anyone wants to be a follower of mine, let him renounce himself . . . and follow me." Mark provides a detailed estimate of the Christian life

on behalf of Jesus. "Anyone who wants to save his life will lose it."
Everyone has to sit down and think about what this means before
choosing the Christian way. Jesus will take everything. "If anyone wants
to be a follower of mine . . . ." In these words, Jesus communicates the
secret of his life. Risking his life and being ready to die means setting
off on an unknown road and making himself free and available to love.
"Let him follow me. . . ."

Being free to love! Countless men and women risk their lives in one way
or another for other people. In many countries, one can lose one's work
or be exiled or imprisoned for speaking the truth, denouncing injustice
or calling for freedom and respect for others.

Being free to love! We are held captive, both individually and
collectively. We must leave our physical and spiritual well-being, our
comfortable securities, our inevitable compromises which so easily seal
our fate, in order to set off on the unknown road with no more baggage
than the word of the one who claims to be the Way, the Truth and the Life.

Without works, faith is "dead." Being a Christian is more than simply
practising our religion faithfully. What, then, is it? To find the answer to
this question, we have to look for the source of Christian faith within
ourselves and recognize that we cannot be Christians if we do not take
Christ habitually as our model.

It is not just a question of repeating again and again what Jesus did or
said. No, we have to discover, by habitually reading and contemplating
the scriptures, what we have to imitate in Jesus. And what we have to
imitate is the essence, the spirit, the source of Jesus' activity, the heart
of his teaching and the reason for his decisions. Anyone who has learned
how to follow the Master in this way no longer feels any need to try to
define Jesus' spirit. He senses and believes that the Spirit dwells in him.

"A body dies when it is separated from the spirit and, in the same way,
faith is dead if it is separated from good deeds." Whoever listens to the
one who has given up his life in love is already breathing the breath of
life that will not cease even with death.

■

You call us, Lord,
  so that we may follow your Son
  on the way of the kingdom.
We ask you:
let us learn from him
and let the Spirit make us breathe your life.

■

God of unceasing journeys,
*   we bless you!*
Your Son followed the way of the cross
*   to rouse us to life.*
He took the bread of death
*   to become our Bread of life.*
May thanks be given to you,
who have given us the viaticum.
The road will not be too hard
that leads to the ages to come.

SATURDAY OF THE 6TH WEEK

FURTHER—AND HIGHER!

James 3:1–10. In Judaeo–Christian society, teaching was very highly valued as a function. But, even in the infancy of the Church, Paul drew attention to the dangers in the work of certain teachers which threatened the unity of the Church.

"The only man who could reach perfection would be someone who never said anything wrong." James is concerned here with "the tongue." The teacher is, more than anyone else, exposed to the danger of letting his tongue run away. But that is both good and bad—the tongue can be used "to bless the Lord and Father, but we also use it to curse men who are made in God's image." Despite its small size, it can give rise to great prejudices. A little fire can set an entire forest alight. In the same way, the tongue can ruin a man's existence. In a word, the man who is able to tame it is also "able to control every part of himself."

Psalm 12 was perhaps used as a lamentation by a man who had been wrongly accused and had been seeking refuge with God. Unlike human words, God's words are without deception.

Mark 9:2–13. See p. 110.

■

"God, how lovely!" A bud opening into a rose, a beautiful view at the end of a tiring walk, a child smiling through tears, a craftman's finished work. We say spontaneously: "God, how lovely!" and, even used as an expletive, God's name is praise.

Wonderment! The victory of light—there are moments of grace when everything is filled with light and life is transfigured. Love becomes a certainty, brotherhood becomes a living reality and life tastes sweet. There are moments of light that transform our everyday experience. An intense light that keeps us going on our journey through the darkness and leads us to the dawn. The sign becomes translucent and cannot be seen in the presence of the reality that has suddenly become tangible. Love has no need of flowers to express itself at such moments—it is the translucence of two human beings, the communion of two hearts. Solidarity no longer needs to be made manifest—it is experienced in the four hands engaged on the same work.

They are going up to Jerusalem, where the Son of man will be put to death. Jesus takes with him Peter, James and John, the disciples who were with him at Gethsemane. He "leads them up a high mountain, where they can be alone by themselves." There they are caught up in light and, for a moment, the hidden face of things is illuminated. The life of the man they love becomes translucent. Beyond the sign of his existence revealed by love, they are taken into a cloud where they experience contact with the mystery of God. "This is my Son, the Beloved. Listen to him."

The disciples had to be shown the light that is hidden behind death, when death is embraced with love. They had to go up the mountain so that Golgotha would only enter the history of mankind accompanied by Tabor.

This is a momentary spark of light revealing the meaning of the journey. It will not be long before the time of the sign will make itself felt again. Once again love will have need of flowers and kisses so that the communion experienced does not become an illusion. If it is not to be simply a dream of utopia, solidarity will also have to be born again of the long, patient search and hesitant approaches. The light will take us further. We shall have to come down onto the plain, where the end of our journey is hidden.

Your life may often seem indistinct, even hidden. But go on with the journey, whatever happens! The three disciples could not understand what was being revealed to them when they were going with Jesus to Jerusalem. They remained silent until the day of Easter and did not even know what "rising from the dead" meant. Going from sign to sign, we shall come to the end of the road. It will only be in wonderment, when we are face to face, that we shall know the transfiguration of our life and be able to say, finally convinced of the seriousness of our astonishment: "God, how lovely!"

■

God our Father, we bless you!
Faithful to your covenant,
you do not leave us in our poverty.
You lead us up a high mountain,
where we can be alone by ourselves.
You take us away from our muddy paths
    and make us go up to the light,
    so that we can see the new world dawn.
You open the heavens and we know
    the vocation to which you are calling us.
You send your Spirit
    to renew the face of the earth
and our disfigured faces shine
    with the glory of your beloved Son.
Our eyes are dazzled by such a great hope
    and we praise you, God of Jesus Christ.

FROM MONDAY TO SATURDAY

OF THE 7TH WEEK

REBIRTH

Following like a Child

Jesus leads his disciples "up a high mountain" to lift the veil and show them his truth. Below, on the plain, more and more questions are asked and the opposition to him is increasing. He comes down from the mountain and the confrontations begin again. Staying on the mountain would have been putting God outside of the day to day reality of human life. Jesus is now going to Jerusalem and we have to follow him to that other mountain called Golgotha at the gates of the city.

Following Jesus—the evangelist is going to reveal to us some of the thousand and one aspects of the "program" that will take us through death to

---

resurrection. This week, the invitation to be reborn will become an urgent call. We are, after all, being initiated now into a new life. We are being asked to follow, not a condemned man, but the one who is the Way, the Truth and the Life.

Rebirth—no doubt we would like to preserve our old, outmoded ideas. We end by getting used to white hair and wrinkles, but Jesus sets the child on its feet in our midst. The kingdom is in the future. The child is living a life that he has still to receive.

Following Jesus—we have to walk behind him, like a child who has to keep running to catch up with the one who is leading and guiding him on his way. We have to leave all unnecessary luggage behind us and set off with hearts that are light and set free. We have to look ahead, a long way ahead, and we have to look up high, without looking back, like a child who is rushing ahead with his head down.

There is only one condition for following Jesus; that is to let the Spirit work in secret. One day, men and women will find out that they have been begotten by the creative breath, because they have said yes unconditionally to life. "Let the little children come to me." The kingdom belongs to those who are like children, who take the risk and love without any other guarantee than the certainty of being loved and without any other intention than that of waking up to life.

We are certainly not called to take part in a funeral procession. Quite the opposite! It is a procession of children following Jesus to Jerusalem, a merry dance proclaiming the joy of Easter. Georges Bernanos once said that a sad old people was the very opposite of a Christian people.

MONDAY OF THE 7TH WEEK

NOT IN POSSESSION OF OURSELVES

James 3:13–18. Once again "operation truth"! Some Christians call themselves "wise and learned men." That is in order, but it would be even better if these claims were reflected in their lives. If, however, their zeal is full of bitterness or aggressive ambition and if they are jealous and contentious, the wisdom they claim for themselves comes not from God, but from man and even from the animal that exists in every man. Such false wisdom only causes disorders. True wisdom, on the other hand, is the source of peace, tolerance and understanding. It has its source in God and makes man conform to God's holiness.

Psalm 19 is in two parts. The first part is a hymn to the beauty of the heavens, while the second, which was probably written later, consists of a long meditation on the Law.

Mark 9:14–19. See p. 115.

■

No one can come close to him without being touched at the deepest level of his being. Like the light penetrating into the darkness and making it recede, Jesus comes down onto the plain and continues on his journey. He will go on until the very end. Some hard-hearted men he will encounter may well harden their hearts even more when he looks at them, but he will still go on his way. In the desert, a way is being prepared for the Lord. The time has come. The hour is at hand. The days of the Exodus have come. Jesus' face is resolutely turned towards Jerusalem. He sets off on the road to Calvary and calls on us to follow him. A funeral procession? No, because the one who is on that road has the power to heal and to raise up those who are possessed by demons. The procession of death is in fact a procession of life.

We are not invited to follow a man who is condemned to death, and our life is not a series of mortifications or little deaths. Have we perhaps read the Gospel in such a way that "Christian life" has become synonymous with sadness and restraint? We throw ourselves, like the possessed man, to the ground. In despair, we want to tear from the earth its secret. An inner voice tells us: "Raise your eyes and look! I can give meaning to your life!" We grind our teeth, unable to overcome our weakness, and the voice says again: "Come and share your Master's joy! Celebrate and rejoice, because you were dead and you have come back to life; you were lost and are found."

When we become rigid because of our principles, deep within us the same voice tells us that our heart should rejoice with a happiness that goes far beyond the external rigidity sanctioned by the Law. When we are thrown into convulsions and fall into the fire of superficial and fleeting pleasures and false prophecies, the same voice invites us to look into the depths of our own being and return to our inner freedom. The possessed man, it was thought, was dead, but Jesus raises him up again.

Jesus also speaks of selling everything one has after finding a "treasure hidden in a field" or a "pearl of great value." He speaks too of "the smallest of all the seeds on earth growing into the biggest shrub" and of the yeast leavening the whole dough. He is a man who can change life. There is a power in him that recreates the world. "Come out of him!" he commands the spirit that possesses the boy.

A little later, some people will think that they have put out that fire in him by putting him into a carefully closed tomb. Everyone will say, as they said of the possessed boy: "He is dead." But God will take his beloved Son by the hand and raise him up again and with him all those who have been touched by his words.

■

"If you can do anything, help us."

There are so many people, Lord,
who find life painful.
   God who gives peace,
   have pity on them!

"If you can do anything, help us."

There are so many people, Lord,
who find life a burden:
those who are imprisoned by an impossible love,
those who are possessed by money,
those who drag themselves along without hope.
   God who set men free,
   have pity on them!

"If you can do anything, help us."

There are so many people, Lord,
for whom life is without any history.
   God who renews all things,
   have pity on them!

TUESDAY OF THE 7TH WEEK

A NEW ORDER
James 4:1–10. "Wars and battles"—the tone of the letter becomes sharper, because internal quarrels gave the leaders of the early Church a great deal of

anxiety. The author knows that the frantic pursuit of pleasure leads to a disordered life, but he is not simply opposed to the search for material satisfaction. He is much more concerned with the fact that Christians rely more on themselves than on God to obtain what they want. "Why you don't have what you want is because you don't pray for it."

Too many Christians, James is saying, want to combine love of God with love of the world. They cannot make a choice and want both God and money. Man, then, is a divided being and God cannot find in him the breath that he put into him at the beginning of the world. But we are very fortunate—his mercy and his patience are both unlimited. And he will be generous—but only to the humble.

James ends this passage with a solemn call to conversion. We must "give in to God and resist the devil." We must set off on the road to approach God and meet him. "Humble yourselves before the Lord and he will lift you up."

Psalm 55 is a psalm of individual supplication. In today's liturgy, what is stressed is the theme of trust that makes man pray to Yahweh at times of distress. Interwoven into this theme are several accusations made against the enemy.

Mark 9:30–37. See p. 118.

■

Jesus has already set off on the way of the cross. He is taking his disciples through Galilee, but secretly, because the time for sowing is over and the harvest will take place elsewhere. That is the paradox of God's manifestation of himself—that the kingdom is established with power, when everything seems to be lost. "The Son of man will be delivered into the hands of men." The old order is completely overthrown and a new world has been born.

In that new world, the child has the first place. He is central. You must become like a little child again! It is a difficult thing to do, because we cannot rest until our children have grown up. Who would choose to take a child as his model? We do not—we model ourselves on our own image, which is often a grotesque caricature of our faults as adults. And we make children into little adults.

Jesus sets the child on his feet—upright in the middle. He raises him up because he is little. But then the child is also great, because another sets him upright. And he can grow to greatness, because he agrees to receive. The man, on the other hand, believes that he is great and claims the first place, but he goes no farther than the horizon that he can see. He has no future ahead of him. The child is great because of everything that he still has to discover. He is living a life that he has still to receive.

Jesus places the child in the center. Following Jesus is walking behind him, like a child who has to keep breaking into a run to catch up with the one who is leading and guiding him on his way. Jesus invites the man, too, to walk behind him. Jesus is the one who let himself be brought into the world again and again throughout the whole of his life, who let himself be set upright, when God called him out of the tomb, and who experienced being born.

So you too must rediscover your true greatness! You must become like a little child again! You must hold the hand of the one who is leading you —your older brother or sister knows the way of reason to the place where the Father is waiting for you.

■

To whom should we go, Lord?
Without your love, we would be orphans;
without your mercy, we would be condemned.
You invite us to the family table
and we receive our life from your word.
We bless you, our Father:
may you be praised for ever.

■

The old world has passed away.
Justice has been sown in peace.
  Why, then, are we still intolerant?

The old world has passed away.
"If anyone wants to be first,
he must make himself last of all
and servant of all."
  Why, then, do we still scorn our brothers?

The old world has passed away.
"Anyone who welcomes one of these little children,
welcomes me."
  Why, then, do we still reject our fellow-men?

NO RIGHTS

James 4:13–17. "If it is the Lord's will." The author does not criticize merchants for exercising their rights to trade, but he does condemn their presumption. Too many believers behave, in making plans, as though their lives belonged to them. But what are they in fact? They are "no more than a mist that is here for a little while and then disappears" and their riches are, as James has already said at the beginning of his letter, "flowers in the grass" and "the scorching sun comes up, the grass withers and the flower falls." Man, in other words, must recognize his fragility and rely on God.

The final sentence in this passage, "everyone who knows what is the right thing to do and doesn't do it commits a sin," is not part of the context. This aphorism is a condemnation of passivity and it recalls Jesus' golden rule: "Always treat others as you would like them to treat you."

Psalm 49 is a psalm in the form of a refutation about wisdom. After a solemn introduction, it formulates the argument put forward by those who think it is possible to trust in their riches. They are senseless! Do they really think they can take their fortune with them when they die?

Mark 9:38–40. See p. 121.

■

A man who is not one of the circle of disciples is driving out demons in Jesus' name. The disciples react energetically, believing that they have a monopoly in the mission field. They must climb down! Jesus makes it clear to them that the Church does not have a monopoly on the defence of man, even though it may at times think it has. It cannot claim any authors' rights, even though it may be strongly tempted to insist that all those who are living a good and respectable life are "anonymous" Christians and are therefore really members of the Church.

No, there is no need at all to be a Christian to want to build up a more just and human world and to pay the price—sometimes a very high price —to make this dream a reality. The Church is and must always be poor and must always serve, because it is neither the end nor the object of the Promise.

The Church is not the end of the Promise. It is not the end of the history that God has entered into with man. It is simply a signpost, pointing in the direction that God is leading man's life. It is only the bridgehead of the new world. There are others who do not belong to the same army fighting to achieve the same victory. They, too, are striving towards the place where hope will triumph over fortune, where serving others will be victorious over self-interest and where God's new world will be built. "Anyone who is not against us is with us."

The Church is also not the object of the Promise. God's glory is man, living—brought back to life again, recreated and restored. That is the meaning of the promised future! Man's tomorrow will be born where man's face is given again the shape that it had when God conceived it. On that day, countless men and women will be astonished to hear the words: "Come, you whom my Father has blessed. . . . For I was hungry and you gave me food; I was thirsty and you gave me to drink; I was a stranger and you made me welcome; naked and you clothed me, sick and you visited me. . . ." In the meantime, Jesus says: "You must not stop them" because these people are already following God's way.

■

We set ourselves up
  as administrators of your gifts.
Lord, have mercy!

We claim you as our authority
  and want to impose our own laws.
Christ, have mercy!

We forget that everything we have
  comes from you.
Lord, have mercy!

■

Lord, Father of all men,
you do not count your gifts,
  but give abundantly and unconditionally.
We ask you, then:
do not let yourself be imprisoned
  in the cell of our petty rules,
but pour out your grace
  on every man coming into this world
for all eternity.

DECIDING WHEN GOD LEADS THE RACE

James 5:1–6. For the third time, the author criticizes the rich. The first time, he stressed the precarious nature of their fortune and urged them to be humble. The second time, he denounced the vanity of the honors of which they were the object. This time, he is not addressing merchants who are trying to become richer, but great landowners who have their fields harvested by laborers. James is quite explicit about their crimes. They reduce their workers to starvation by paying them very little or nothing at all, while they are enjoying themselves shamelessly. They also make it impossible for justice to be exercised. (This was either because they were often appointed as judges or because they bribed the courts.)

"Start crying, weep!" The author does not invite them to be converted this time—he threatens his readers! His tone is similar to that of the prophets, when they were describing the fate of the guilty people of Israel. The wealth that these landowners has acquired has rotted. Their clothes have been eaten by moths and their gold and silver have rusted. If only these rich men had used their wealth, the "tainted thing," to win friends (Lk 16:9–11) and to store up a "treasure in heaven" (18:22)! But they have not done this and so, when the last days come, they will receive their sentence like a "burning fire."

Psalm 49 is continued in today's liturgy. The author sets out the arguments used by the two opposing sides. Ironically he says: "Look after yourself and men will praise you!" But it is in adversity that one comes to know one's real friends.

Mark 9:41–50. See p. 125.

■

It is useless to sugarcoat the pill. Let us not try to make these words less harsh." If your hand should cause you to sin, cut it off; it is better for you to enter into life crippled, than to have two hands and go to hell, into the fire that cannot be put out." You must decide and then experience the logic of the kingdom. You must decide and then set off. So, you rich people, "start crying, weep! . . . Your wealth is all rotting, your clothes are all eaten up by moths. All your gold and silver are corroding away and the same corrosion will be your own sentence and eat into your body . . . like a burning fire." If anything has led you to sin, you must tear yourself away from it if you are to "enter into life."

So let us be honest—we all want at all costs to tone down such demands and soften the impact of such hard words. We hesitate before setting off on the way that Jesus invites us to follow. We cling to our comforts and, because those who are without them also long for them as much as we do, we are confirmed in our conviction that it would be unreasonable to give them up.

Jesus calls on us to follow him, but he had nowhere to lay his head and was stretched out naked on a cross. He wants to set us free from everything that shackles us. He wants us to be as light and free in our hearts as children who run without worrying about tomorrow but, unfortunately, we have changed the rules of the game. The race has become faltering and the first prize goes not to the winner, but to the one who sits down and hoards wealth. And if anyone leaves the main body of runners and runs on his own, he is left alone and becomes a laughing-stock if he falls and hurts himself.

Jesus calls on us to follow him, but he leads the race. If we want to join, we have to become like little children. And if others run ahead of us, then for heaven's sake let us not try to prevent them! Let us rather be glad they are faithful to Jesus' call and listen to it ourselves.

■

Lord, we are imprisoned in ourselves,
but you call on us to follow your Son.
Give us the strength that enabled him to live
and make us open to the freedom
    that he discovered.
We ask you this through Jesus,
who leads us to you
in the Spirit.

FRIDAY OF THE 7TH WEEK

LOVE GOES BEYOND THE LAW
James 5:9–12. In yesterday's text the author threatened the rich. In today's, he makes a few suggestions to his "brothers." How should they behave, he asks, while they are waiting for the Lord to return? He insists first of all on

the virtue of patience, citing the model of the farmer in verse 7. Then he expresses his longing to see an end to their "complaints against one another."

James' exhortation to patience is supported by two examples, that of the prophets and that of Job. The prophets certainly "spoke in the name of the Lord," but their call to do that did not save them from suffering. Nor did those sufferings prevent them from remaining faithful to their vocation. As for Job, God restored him, after he had suffered, to his previous state. This is therefore, in James' view, a promise of salvation for all those who suffer.

The last verse is surprising. In it, the author denounces the way in which Jews —and Christians—use oaths wrongly. After the exile, Jews had developed the habit of making oaths in season and out of season. Christians, James implies, should not imitate the Jews. Their "yes" should mean "yes" and their "no" should mean "no."

Psalm 103 can be included among the hymns of an individual kind. It speaks of the nature of God, who is tender and loving and who does not remember man's sins, but leads him to life.

Mark 10:1–12. See p. 127.

■

Man and woman were originally one. At the time of creation, God led the woman to the man. He had taken the woman from the man's side and the man had exclaimed: "This is bone from my bones and flesh from my flesh." According to God's heart, man was only able to love totally and freely. Together, they were one.

But man had broken the covenant. He had rebelled in his heart and had learned the meaning of imperfection and limitation. Love had become a muddy source. The life-giving water was still flowing, but it had become darkened by the loss of faithfulness and constancy. "Can a man divorce his wife?" Weary of fighting, Moses had given the people laws on this question and the rabbis had multiplied the number of possible laws. Love itself had become a question of skilfully balancing what was permitted against what was forbidden.

Jesus is asked what he thinks about the indissolubility of marriage. He does not become involved in argument. He does not enter into the complex subtleties of the problem. He does not engage in endless discussions. In him, the new Adam, man can learn how to love as he loved in the first days of creation. This man, Jesus, is totally given to others. He does not discuss what is permitted and what is forbidden. He only listens to the inner voice that sends him to the poor, the lost and the excluded. He hands himself over to all those who long to make a new beginning. In the heart of this man, the last of the prophets, man can learn again how to live. We have become unfaithful and we can rediscover in him the way of tenderness. We have prostituted ourselves and we can rediscover the joy of our father's home. "What God has united, man must not divide." May man rediscover his original beauty!

■

With young people finding, in wonderment,
their power to love,
we ask you:
   give us the enthusiasm of lovers
   when we learn how to know you.

With married couples who, day after day,
discover their love
in sharing joy and suffering,
we ask you:
   make us faithful to the word
   that we have given to you.

With those married couples
who have not been able to stay together,
we ask you:
   let us come back to you,
   who are always waiting for us.

With older married couples
who no longer need words
to live as lovers,
we ask you:
   let us live with you
   in the joy of our acceptance of your word.

■

God of tenderness and mercy,
you bring back the unfaithful heart
and lead us into the desert
to rediscover the youth of our love.
We ask you:
   say your word of tenderness to us again—
   Jesus Christ, our Savior.

LIKE A CHILD

James 5:13–20. The author ends his letter with a final exhortation to prayer. He has personal prayer primarily in mind, believing that the Christian should pray in all circumstances. But there is also the matter of the prayer of the Christian community. If a Christian is sick, he can call on the "elders" of the local church, who will pray for him and anoint him with oil "in the name of the Lord."

This formula is reminiscent of the baptismal formula and it points clearly to the Church's faith in the power of its Lord. The framework is also manifestly eschatological. This is indicated by the use of such verbs as "save" and "raise up again." The healing resulting from this "prayer of faith" is both physical and spiritual. The effectiveness of the "prayer of a righteous man" is based on the example of Elijah.

Psalm 141 is another lamentation. Calls to God for help are mixed with words expressing trust in God. There is a reference in verse 2 to an offering of plants burned for Yahweh.

Mark 10:13–16. See p. 130.

■

What Jesus is outlining in these words today, in the form of an anecdote, is basically the condition of entry into the kingdom of God. It is not so much Jesus' attitude towards children that is at the heart of this passage as the question: How can a man have a share in the kingdom?

"The kingdom of God belongs to those who are like little children." Let us make no mistake about this! Jesus is not giving us as a model of the way children think or the way they feel about things. It is rather the situation in which they find themselves, the place they occupy and their state as children.

Nowadays, the child is treated as a king. Advertisers use children as a means of persuading parents to buy consumer goods. Childhood has become an age with its own values, its own literature and its own fashions. The child really counts today, to such an extent that he has become a tyrant in many households. In the ancient world, on the other hand, childhood was synonymous with insignificance, powerlessness and imperfection.

What an astonishing thing Jesus is saying here! The kingdom of God is given to those who are insignificant and powerless! It is not something that we reach at the end of a difficult search—a kind of prize for our great effort. No, it is grace and it is therefore gratuitous.

The child has no rights in the city of adults, but the kingdom is there for those without rights. The child has the future ahead of him and the kingdom is there for those who let their lives be transformed by a new reality. Again and again the child says: "When I have grown up . . . ." and the kingdom is there for those who have a deep longing to become the new man of God's promise.

"If anyone wants to be a follower of mine . . . ." Jesus is going up to Jerusalem. He is himself already like a child, "without beauty, without majesty," in the words of Isaiah. Again and again he says the same thing, like a child coming back again and again to the same question. Like a child, too, he believed in his own history—to the very end. To the cross!

■

How wonderful a child's hands are!
They are always ready to receive.
But what do we do with our hands?
   You want us to be like little children.
   Lord, give us a new heart!

How wonderful a child's eyes are!
They are always ready to be filled with wonder.
But what do we look at with our eyes?
   You want us to be like little children.
   Lord, give us a new heart!

How wonderful a child's heart is!
It is always ready to love.
But what stirs our heart to passionate response?
   You want us to be like little children.
   Lord, give us a new heart!

■

Lord, Father of men and women,
you have hidden the promise of the world
in the fragile being of a child,
   your Son, Jesus Christ, our Savior.
Let us share in his inheritance

and receive from your hands
the kingdom prepared for the poor.

FROM MONDAY TO SATURDAY

OF THE 8TH WEEK

ALREADY BAPTIZED

Immersed in Jesus' Death

Jesus is on his way to Jerusalem. When he has given God the offering of his life, the Spirit will be poured out on the earth. "Go, make disciples of all the nations; baptize them in the name of the Father and of the Son and of the Holy Spirit."

Peter's letter—a kind of encyclical—is addressed to Christians who are being put severely to the test and are a prey to discouragement. His aim is to reveal to them once again the secret of their hope. They are immersed in Jesus' death and have already seen the inheritance "that can never be spoilt or soiled and never fade away." He has asked two of his disciples: "Can you be baptized with the baptism with which I must be baptized?" and their reply was immediate: "We can." Following Jesus is entering into his baptism.

A baptism of the poor. Jesus presents himself naked—stripped of everything —for his baptism. Being baptized is giving up one's covering of clothes and letting oneself be stripped naked, leaving oneself with no other resource than the gesture of stretching out one's hands.

Jesus goes off. For Scripture to be fulfilled, the Son of man has to go up to Jerusalem. We too have to enter into God's plan and our baptism is in anticipation of what has been promised to us. Baptism in God's faithfulness! The old world has passed away and a new world has already been born. Baptism in a faith that has no justification other than the Word of grace! Baptism in blood—Jesus goes up to Calvary! "If he offers his life in atonement . . . my servant shall justify many" (Is 53). Baptism in love and in a life offered to the very end! Baptism of the grain of wheat that dies to yield a rich harvest! Baptism of the one who offers himself to present to God our earth as a living sacrifice. And we are baptized for intercession, an open house for the suffering of all men, so that hope and love may be made manifest.

"Jesus said to them: 'Can you drink the cup that I must drink or be baptized with the baptism with which I must be baptized?' They replied: 'We can.' Jesus said to them: 'The cup that I must drink, you shall drink and, with the baptism with which I must be baptized, you shall be baptized' " (Mk 10:38–39).

MONDAY OF THE 8TH WEEK

RECEIVING THE INHERITANCE

1 Peter 1:3–9. Hope, being put to the test and baptismal reminiscences—all these themes, which form the content of the Epistle, appear in the hymn with which the document begins, in the manner of most hellenistic letters. The author is writing to the "foreigners in the Dispersion." In accordance with the rest of the letter, this phrase describes Christian converts from paganism rather than Christians from the Jewish world. They form the new Israel and are exiles waiting for the revelation of Christ Jesus, or pilgrims on their way to the fullness of time.

When they were baptized, they were given new birth to a hope based on the resurrection of Jesus Christ. They have been promised an inheritance that cannot be destroyed by death, by sin or by time. That inheritance is God himself. It is entry into the life into which Christ himself has entered, ahead of those who believe in him and who love him without having seen him.

These believers have a living hope that is so real that it cannot be overcome even when they are put severely to the test. The persecutions to which the author refers are, to judge from the peaceful tone of the Epistle, apparently not official ones, but rather a manifestation of the ostracism to which Christians were subjected both by the Jews and by the pagans.

Psalm 111, which is alphabetical, is usually classed as a hymn. It reviews the great actions performed by Yahweh on behalf of his people. Like many acrostic psalms, it also contains the principles of wisdom.

Mark 10:17–27. See p. 132.

■

Jesus continues on his way to Jerusalem. Today, he is approached by a man who is rather like us in that he is an upright, religious man of good will. He is no richer than anyone else. He knows money does not make a person happy, although it does contribute to his happiness. He is looking for something else. He wants to "inherit eternal life."

Jesus "looks steadily at him and loves him." Then he says: "There is one thing you lack." The man is astonished. What can he lack? He already has everything he wants! Jesus continues: "Go and sell everything you own!" Disconcerted, the man goes on his way. How difficult it is to follow the desert road without luggage and without assurance!

"It is easier for a camel to pass through the eye of a needle . . . ." It is a funny story, like so many in the Gospel. Once upon a time there was a rich man who wanted to pass through the door of the kingdom. . . . It is the same story–the same funny story. The disciples were dumbfounded. "Who can be saved, then?" they asked. "Jesus gazed at them," as he "looked steadily" at the rich man. Jesus looks at us in exactly the same way and says: "For men, this is impossible; for God, everything is possible."

For men, it is impossible. What, then, can we do? The rich man who threw himself at Jesus' feet had "kept all the commandments from his earliest days." How futile it would be to practice one's faith for the whole of one's life if one had no right to God at the end!

"There is one thing you lack. Go and sell everything you own." God can only give himself to us if we stretch out hands that are empty—the hands of poor people. It is valueless to capitalize on our virtues and merits. Loving is the only thing that counts. Hands that are full are not loving hands. Loving is always abandoning oneself to the other person and saying: "Look, I am naked. Cover me with the cloak of your tenderness! I am cold. Warm me with your friendship! I have no resources. Share what you have with me!"

So, my brother, you must live in the logic of faith. Faith that is not expressed in life is just a hollow word. You must stand with empty, outstretched hands, like a child who has tried to make a house with his building bricks, but in the end has to ask his father to finish it, because it will not stand firm. Then God will place in your empty hands the eternal inheritance. You will hold in your hands the salvation that is the fulfilment of faith.

■

"Go and sell everything you own;
then come, follow me."
Let us stand before God with empty hands
and what we shall receive
will exceed all our expectations.

No one can serve two masters—
Lord, let us rely only on your grace.

We want to keep what we hold in our hands—
Lord, let us open them and share.

We like to be certain in our hearts—
Lord, convert us
and may your word be our only certainty.

We are always trying to increase
our store of virtues and merits—
Lord, let us be fascinated by your tenderness
and invite us to risk everything.

You have looked at us, Lord,   ·
and your love has penetrated into our hearts
    like a sharp sword.
May your grace be our inheritance.
We believe it
when you say: "Come, follow me."
That is the beginning
    of our eternal communion.

TUESDAY OF THE 8TH WEEK

REBIRTH

1 Peter 1:10–16. Peter outlines in a few sentences a theology of salvation which emphasizes the two covenants. In both covenants, the same Spirit proclaims the mystery of Jesus Christ. Under the old covenant, the prophets examined the light and shade of God's revelation in order to throw light on what had been concealed. Now, Peter suggests, in these last days, the good news has been made known and the Spirit has uncovered profound realities. The whole of this revelation is concerned with Jesus Christ, his passion and resurrection, his way of humility and his ascension to glory.

But, whereas the Jews regarded the angels as the mediators of revelation, Peter affirms in his letter that these very angels also wanted to look into this "message" preached by those who proclaimed the Gospel. What they longed to contemplate were, in fact, the fruits of God's word; in other words, the Church (see Eph 3:10). The Church is the new Israel, the fulfilment announced by the prophets. Begotten by the word of the witnesses, it gives birth to those who are reborn in grace.

Psalm 98 is a hymn glorifying God's zeal for Israel.

Mark 10:28–31. See p. 134.

■

On that day, Jesus was approached and questioned by a rich man and his reply was: "There is one thing you lack. Go and sell everything you own." The disciples had been dumbfounded by this reply. Turning to each other, they had asked: "In that case, who can be saved?" And then, immediately afterwards, they had, through their spokesman Peter, asked the unexpected question: "What about us? We have left everything and followed you." A question with the flavor of a claim!

From "this present time" onwards, there is no one who has risked everything who will not receive a hundredfold. And you have already received this, because you see what the prophets were waiting to see. How happy you are, because it has been given to you to see the secrets of God! You who have left "house and land" and risked following uncertain roads, you who have left security behind and have become nomads, led on by the longing to discover a new country—how happy you are, because God has made his dwelling-place in you!

For you, the new world has already been born. You have been baptized and you have received the seal of the Spirit. The water of that baptism has washed away your mediocrity and God has burned you with the fire of his holiness. You have received a hundredfold, because you have been made holy, reshaped and recreated. You have left "brothers, sisters, father and children," but you have been reborn to a new communion. You belong to a holy people. You are the body of the Lord. You are members of one another.

The road will be very long. You will have to go a long way to become true disciples. The time for renunciation and darkness will certainly come. It will be a long journey before what the Spirit is bringing about in you is fully revealed. The time will also come when your faith is very minimal. But you may be quite sure of this. For you, everything has already been fulfilled and your life is simply the journey that makes you become by grace what you are already by character.

■

You are not offering us, Lord,
  a bad bargain.
When you invite us to set off,
  you always show us the way.

When you call on us to live the Word,
you always give us your Spirit.
Because we have been immersed in Jesus' death,
let us have a share in what he promises us—
your life,
now and for ever.

■

Father of men and women,
you offer the riches of your kingdom
to those who are poor in heart.
Make us open to listen to your word
and make us long to put it into practice.
May we rely on the power of your Spirit
when we decide to follow your Son
wherever he may lead us.

WEDNESDAY OF THE 8TH WEEK

BAPTIZED IN LOVE

1 Peter 1:18–25. Some scholars have described the First Epistle of Peter as a long baptismal instruction and, although it is not necessary to make such a far-reaching claim, it cannot be denied that the reality of baptism is present everywhere in the letter. Peter's aim is clearly to remind those to whom he is writing of the solemn obligation that they have undertaken to live in accordance with their baptism. As C. Spicq has pointed out, this was quite possibly his aim, in view of the fact that, in order to give extra weight to his exhortation, the author has made use of texts taken from the liturgy of baptism, various teachings which bring out its meaning and moral codes in force at the time.

Whatever the case may be, Peter's chief concern is to give the life of Christian believers a deep foundation in the redeeming work of Christ. "You must be scrupulously careful as long as you are living away from your home. Remember the ransom that was paid to free you!" The author cannot prevent his eyes from turning again and again to Calvary, where the "blood of a lamb without spot or stain" flowed. Christ, the true paschal lamb, has set believers free from the slavery of sin. In him, Christians are the fruit of an incorruptible seed, the effective Word of God.

Psalm 147 forms one single psalm in the Hebrew psalter with Psalm 146 and can be included among the hymns. It celebrates the God of divine providence who is always aware of his people's needs.

Mark 10:32–45. See p. 138.

■

The disciples are indignant. They cannot accept James' and John's request for special places close to Jesus. How is it possible to speak of honor and power when the Master has been drawing attention to his passion and death? And then, why should James and John be given these positions and not us? Jesus might have replied, that they are not of the world, but this would not have prevented the disciples from feeling envious. What Jesus does say is: "This is not to happen among you. For the Son of man did not come to be served, but to serve." Have the disciples already forgotten that they have been born into a new world?

We have been born into the blood which was shed as the sign of love given to the very end. God died of loving. Following Jesus is taking up the cross with him. He stripped himself, becoming the very image of the suffering servant. He emptied himself and, in his obedience, went as far as death on the cross. He came to serve and to give his life. He rose from table and washed the feet of the Twelve. "You call me Master and Lord," he told them, "and rightly; so I am . . . . I have given you an example. Do this in memory of me."

We have to be born to love and, for that birth, we must be immersed in the blood of the servant. In the community of the disciples, there is only one title—servant of love. The world is turned upside down! "Among the pagans their so-called rulers lord it over them and their great men make their authority felt. This is not to happen among you." Later, when the cup of the covenant is passed from hand to hand, the Church will, without the disciples knowing it, be founded in the love of the servant, his blood and his life. Leaven mixed into the human dough and overthrowing the dominant powers: "Love one another, as I have loved you." A seed that breaks open the racial ghettos: "There are no more distinctions between Jew and Greeks."

"Now we are going up to Jerusalem and the Son of man is about to be handed over to the chief priests and the scribes. They will condemn him to death and will hand him over to the pagans." "This is my commandment: love one another, as I have loved you."

■

God our Savior,
my heart rejoices in you.
  You have "pulled down princes from their thrones
  and exalted the lowly."
You have turned the world upside down!
Change our hearts too, Lord,
  so that love will spread—
  the love your Spirit has poured into us.

THURSDAY OF THE 8TH WEEK

CALLED OUT INTO THE LIGHT

1 Peter 2:2–5, 9–12. "Destroy this sanctuary and in three days I will raise it up" (Jn 2:19). And the evangelist explains that "he was speaking of the sanctuary that was his body" and adds that his disciples did not understand Jesus' words until after his resurrection. All that they knew at the time was that the stone rejected by men was precious in God's eyes. On Golgotha, the covenant was not sealed "in the blood of goats and bulls," but in the life offered by Christ. His body was able to become the sanctuary in which worship would henceforth be offered "in spirit and truth."

Regenerated by God's word and by the water of baptism, Christians are also "living stones." They can, if they turn away from "the selfish passions that attack the soul," come close to Christ and worship God authentically. From now on, the liturgy is no longer separate from life. The whole of life becomes liturgy!

In response to the argument in First Peter above, the psalmist echoes *Psalm 100*: Jesus Christ is the keystone and Christians are the living stones of the new building.

Mark 10:46–52. See p. 140.

■

"He was sitting at the side of the road." He did not move. He was entirely dependent on those around him. He heard people speaking about Jesus and he heard the movements of the crowd. He heard people walking, running and dancing, but he could not join in. It was a dream. The reality was a severely disabled man, living in darkness and isolation.

According to the voices he heard around him, Jesus was nearby. His wretchedness and the crazy hope that was rising up inside him proclaimed his need and he began to cry out: "Have pity on me!" He might well have shouted hostile remarks, because he had nothing to lose. But he, too, was like a child—he trusted.

Jesus stopped. "It is not the healthy who need the doctor, but the sick." He had set the child on its feet, upright, but in this case, it is the people who "raise up" the sick man by their encouragement and who go with him to the one who is to fulfil the oracle of Isaiah. The blind man throws off his cloak—probably all he possessed was that dirty old covering— jumps up and goes to Jesus. He breaks with his past and runs to the light! "Leave everything you own; then come, follow me!"

So many people are living in darkness, their disabled bodies proclaiming their wretchedness. Look around you and look inward! Open your newspaper! Listen to the long litany of suffering all around you! Hear the heartbreaking cry: "Have pity on me!" It is a call that is often ignored. We prefer to close our ears to it.

But Jesus said: "Call him here." It is your task to raise the blind man up. It is you who have the task of helping him out of his darkness into God's wonderful light. We are here at the heart of the world, with the task of offering the cry of our fellow-men to God.

Yes, we have "tasted and seen that the Lord is good" and, in this world, the only sign that God has in order to reveal his loving-kindness is our human lives transformed by love. Very soon the time of the Son's life on earth will come to an end. Men will put the cornerstone into the tomb and the true dwelling-place of God, the body of the beloved Son, will be thrown to the ground. But on this foundation, which cannot be destroyed by death, the living temple, God's Church, will rise up. In that Church, every living stone dressed and prepared by the Spirit—every man and woman living the Gospel—is present so that the light will penetrate into the darkness.

"Call him here." A temple that does not open its doors to welcome those who are wretched and suffering is not living, but dead. The only reason the Church has for its existence is to give a name to the world of disabled people in God's presence. The time will come when those who have been living in darkness will "give glory to God on the day when he will visit his people."

■

God said: I have "come to save
and seek out what was lost."
Call to me all those who are wretched
and offer to me the world's suffering.
Let me hear the cry of your hope.

Look at the rising of the source of light and fire
that will cleanse your sin.
All you who cry out—
come to the light!

Happy light, eternal splendor of the Father,
blessed and holy Jesus Christ!

Come close to him,
all you who love him,
and you will be filled with light.
All you who cry out,
come to the light!

Keep your lamps lighted,
all you who are seeking,
and you will cease
to walk in darkness.
All you who cry out—
come to the light!

For God takes you out of the night
and wraps you in a cloak of tenderness.
All you who cry out—
come to the light!

Father, we bless you.
We have "tasted and seen that you are good."
We were scattered
and you have made us your people.
We were orphans
and you have begotten us to your word.
We were deprived of love
and you fill us with the Bread of life.
Let us, then, proclaim your wonders,
and praise you, who have called us
out of the darkness into your wonderful light.

STEWARDSHIP

1 Peter 4:7–13. The kingdom is present and grace has been manifested in Jesus Christ. Christians are, in their communities, those who hand on that grace in its many different forms. They may teach or they may serve those in need, but whatever their function is, they should carry it out as witnesses to God's favor. Above all, they should "welcome each other into their houses without grumbling," since, if they love their brothers, they may be sure of benefiting from God's mercy.

Waiting for the parousia made some Christians uneasy, so Peter urged them to pray calmly. This was very judicious advice in view of the fact that Christians were not welcomed either by Jews or by pagans. They should, Peter adds, not be surprised by this. On the contrary, they ought to rejoice, because the Lord had blessed all those who were persecuted for his sake.

"Say among the nations, 'Yahweh is king!' " *Psalm 96* is in the form of a hymn. The verses chosen for today contain elements that refer to divine theophanies—the whole of creation rejoices at the coming of the Lord.

Mark 11:11–25. See p. 142.

■

The leading Jews used to buy God. They imposed human laws on him— payment cash down. Then they offered him sacrifices, so that he could demonstrate his good-will. Appeasing heaven on the strength of the virtues they had acquired by means of the sacrifices offered.

The temple was a house of prayer. It was in the temple that the prayers of the people rose up, the litanies of human misery were heard and the crazy hope for rebirth was expressed. But the Jews had turned it into a robbers' den. They claimed to have rights to God. They had imposed the unbearable burden of the Law on the population and had excluded pagans and underprivileged people from the sanctuary. It was hardly surprising, then, that God had himself deserted the temple and that the Spirit no longer spoke there.

Jesus comes and at once overturns the tables. God takes possession of his house again! That house is no longer a temple made with human hands, but the body of the beloved Son. It is no longer a house with closed doors, but a man who wanders over the earth proclaiming good news that sets man free. It is no longer a place where divine favors are bought, but a sower scattering into the wind a word of grace that is bound to bear fruit.

People had bought God, and faith had degenerated into goods bought and sold. The tree had lost its leaves. The sap was no longer rising to create new life. There was nothing left to astonish in the stereotyped trading relationships. The barren fig tree had "withered to the roots." But Jesus brought the freedom of the Spirit and his word set fire to the house of stone. All you who are hungry, come and eat without paying! God gives everything in his grace. The dead tree was to bear incomparable fruit. The dry wood of the cross would become green and living again and bear the fruit of the Spirit.

From now on, the temple would be made of living stones. No one would be able to buy and sell God, because everyone would be a steward of the work of the Spirit. The sign given by God would no longer be a temple which some privileged people made their home while excluding others and throwing them out onto the forecourt. No, God's house is an immense dwelling-place in which all people are brothers and members of one another, united in the same poverty and enriched by the same grace, because the word of God bears fruit for eternal life. And if the time comes when we are put to the test, the winter's frosts will not be able to destroy the seed. If the frost is too severe, God will sow seed again and the tree will once again bear fruit.

■

Lord our God,
  overturn our securities
  and denounce our transactions.
Show us again the grace of your love.
Be patient with us
  and do not cut down our barren trees.
Give us your Spirit
  and we shall bear fruit,
  thanks to the grace of your mercy.

■

Call us together by the words of your Son,
take us outside ourselves, Lord,
and set us free from our fears and anxieties.
Give us back to the freedom of our dreams
  and to the fascination of your light.

May your mercy be our strength
  and your grace our salvation.
Then we shall be astonished
  by what your Spirit can achieve in us.
We shall be new men and women,
  your Son's disciples,
  children of your tenderness.

SATURDAY OF THE 8TH WEEK

AGAINST DESPAIR

Jude 17, 20b–25. The Letter of Jude is a very distinctive document which was only accepted with great reluctance into the canon of scripture. It is full of ideas taken from the apocalyptic tradition. The author is fierce in his condemnation of certain "impious" men, who, he says, must be "hated even including their tunic spotted by the flesh." The harsh language of the letter resembles that of the Dead Sea Scrolls, which also contain many echoes of the apocalyptic literature.

The author exhorts his readers to be faithful, in view of the dangers that threaten the faith that has been passed on to them. He outlines the attitude that they should have, towards the members of the Christian community who are tempted by the 'impious' men on the one hand and, on the other, towards those who are on the side of the unfaithful. These "impious" men were probably gnostics who claimed exclusive possession of the true knowledge, in the name of which they despised the flesh, abandoned themselves to moral disorders and rejected the incarnation of Christ.

Psalm 63 is an individual lamentation. It contains an allusion to an oracle which was to be proclaimed in the temple at dawn and which was to be favorable to the psalmist, because a promise had already been made to celebrate Yahweh. It also contains a wonderful expression of the feelings of man reaching out to God.

Mark 11:27–33. See p. 145.

■

**"You are a chosen race, a royal priesthood, a consecrated nation. . . .
the People of God . . . . You are living stones making a living house."**

And "you must use your faith as your foundation and build on that" and "keep yourself within the love of God." Let faith be the mainspring of your life! Go on living all the same, hoping all the same and loving all the same, in spite of everything. Because our experience, which does not have to be extensive, very soon makes us realize that life only gives us a little fragment of the hopes we have placed in it. In spite of everything . . . . Because we know very well that we try to love, but never fully succeed. Let faith be the mainspring of your life!

If we were left to our own resources, it would no doubt be more sensible just to give up. But our hearts are so fragile and our actions are so limited and we are so passionately in love with life, and at the same time so conscious of our weakness that we let ourselves be drawn along by life. Let faith, then, be the mainspring of your life! Having faith is living all the same and loving all the same. It is hoping against hope. Urged on by the word of God that we believe is true, we have to run the risk of living.

Let faith be the mainspring of your life! By what authority do we dare to say that daring to live is already a victory? It is because we look at a man who risked believing, with a man's longing, and because the power of his Spirit reassures us that, when we go on living all the same, we make the kingdom of life rise up. We are certain. We believe that a world is already born—a world whose fullness, richness and immensity go far beyond everything we can hope for. The only authority for faith is its own dynamism! When we set that in motion, its only defense is its fruits, which is hope and life.

■

Hear us, Lord,
we implore you,
for who is to be our salvation
if you do not take us to heart?
Subdue the powers
that seek our lives
and give us hope
for the sake of him
who has conquered death—
Christ, your Son,
who lives with you
in the fellowship of the Holy Spirit
for ever and ever.

You are the true God,
but we prefer our own certainties to you.
  Lord, have mercy!

You are all patience,
but we fail to keep your covenant.
  Christ, have mercy!

You are all tenderness,
but we have difficulty in believing in so much love.
  Lord, have mercy!

FROM MONDAY TO SATURDAY

OF THE 9TH WEEK

THE GOSPEL UNTIL THE VERY END

"Proclaim the Good News"

The drama is coming to its end. By this I mean that it is becoming less complex. Jesus is approaching the end of his life and he knows this. Soon the liberator will be bound, ridiculed and put to death. But I also mean that the drama is reaching its fulfilment. Jesus has lived his life throughout in a state of tension and this is now coming to its furthest point of crisis. Everything that has been scattered is becoming tighter and everything that was diffused is being brought together. "The time has come." Jesus has said all that he had to say. This is the final act, when everything that has so far been embryonic will open out. Everything has been fulfilled.

The tenants of the vineyard are of one mind: "This is the heir. Let us kill him and the inheritance will be ours." But men cannot prevent the fire from taking hold and spreading. The Word is at work and Jesus will bear witness to it in season and out of season. He will have to "bear the hardships for the sake of the good news" and he will be obedient to the point of death.

The drama is coming to its end. We must choose. If we want to follow Jesus, we must walk behind him now. The kingdom, which expresses God's good news is here. Jesus is going to continue his passion in order to make God's passion manifest. You have to pay the "tribute" of the kingdom, my brothers, and "keep to what you have been taught and what you know to be true." But you also have to give away everything you have amassed in order to live and present yourself naked and stripped of everything, without any security. Then you will be stimulated to know what can be achieved and the impossible thing to be received. The drama is coming to its end. So let what you receive—God's grace and your brother's appeal to you—be imprinted on your heart and "bear the hardships for the sake of the good news."

You must choose. The Son will be reduced to silence, but the Spirit will continue to stimulate you. God's vine cannot be destroyed. It will continue to grow, becoming an immense tree. Its life-giving sap is love. Will you find your dwelling-place in it? Will the "stone rejected by the builders" become the "keystone" of your life?

MONDAY OF THE 9TH WEEK

IN THE WINE-PRESS OF THE KINGDOM

2 Peter 1:1–7. This document is more like a "testament" than a letter. Testaments, which were common in the Jewish tradition, were a kind of farewell, its words placed by the author in the mouth of a great man. It is therefore doubtful whether the author was in fact Peter, but the letter may have originated in Petrine circles at the beginning of the second century A.D.

The Hellenists to whom the author is writing were familiar with both scripture and the Jewish apocalypses. It is more difficult to identify the "impious" men, because the author uses very conventional language and his portrait of these ungodly men is a stereotype.

After the customary greeting, he defines the Christian believer as a man filled with God. Regenerated by baptism, he has escaped from the "corruption" of "a world that is sunk in vice" and has entered into communion with God. Conscious of what God has given men, he has to learn how to live according to his faith.

Psalm 91 is a psalm that is excellently suited to Compline. It is written in the style of an oracle of divine protection. The first verses are a declaration of principle, expressing the believer's trust in God. Verses 14–16 are God's reply, promising the psalmist that he will protect him.

Mark 12:1–12. See p. 147.

■

Now there is clearly no limit to how far men will go in their hostile treatment of Jesus. At first they simply shrugged their shoulders. He was out of his mind. Then they marginalized him. A man who was so far removed from traditional practice could not possibly be on God's side. But very soon he will be treated as a blasphemer. He will be crucified in order to give glory to God.

The parable of the tenants of the vineyard is a disturbing summary of men's mounting hostility towards the one sent by God. The owner has gone off on a journey and the tenants are longing to seize hold of the vineyard—the inheritance—because then they will be their own masters. Then, they will no longer need to live from what is given to them by grace. They will be able to set up on their own account and create their own fortune and happiness.

The murder of the Son will be an act of liberation. The Son has to be killed, because he has become a rival. He is in the way. But let him be killed and life will then be without grace or favor. The inheritance will become a possession, but without the grace of sonship. A religion without a son and without begetting. A religion in which everyone does his duty. God, like man. But let God send his Son and he will be accused of exceeding his rights.

This may strike you, brothers, as a story about the past, but it is about today. We still prefer to live under the rule of laws and obligations, especially since we can always find ways of bending those laws while still remaining within the bounds of legality. We still want to be tied down to stewardship, so long as God stays outside our life. We try to give him back, without making a profit or a loss, the treasure that he has entrusted to us. We still want to manage the vineyard but we have to kill the son God wants to be born in us, because we would be compromised by love. Let us keep it away from God's grace and attraction, because we can never know where the way of tenderness may lead it.

But we are wrong to think that we can seize hold of the vineyard if we kill the owner's son. The kingdom of God will never be a piece of land that we can possess. It will always be a gift. God's reply to our mounting tendency to confine ourselves to our own land and possessions is to intensify his Word, which urges us constantly to emerge from ourselves. When we enclose ourselves more and more impregnably within the fortress of our own certainties and our own good conscience, the summit of which is Golgotha, God replies by increasing the love that he has never ceased to offer us.

281

The tenants may kill the Son, but God will make him the stock on which he will graft the shoots. They may shed the Son's blood, but God will give him back as life-giving sap. He will give him to us as the Spirit who flows in our veins to let us be born to life. We want to keep the fruit of the vine and God's fruit becomes our food.

"This is the Son! This is the heir!" We may kill him. We may prefer our false freedoms and our illusory possessions to God's grace and to being born to new life. But God's vine cannot be destroyed. It will continue to grow until it becomes an immense tree in which many birds find shelter. The "stone rejected by the builders" will become the "keystone."

■

Good Father, like the grape pressed
* so that the festive wine may flow,*
your Son placed himself in our hands
* so that the time of grace might be born.*
We pray to you:
may he be the sap
that gives life to our withered hearts.

■

God our Father,
blessed are you for the vine—
* Jesus makes us your land.*
Blessed are you for wine—
* leaven of the new time.*

* The Spirit makes our old wineskins burst.*
Blessed are you for the cup passed around—
* it seals your covenant in the blood shed.*
May thanks be given to you—
your love makes us
* the plant that you have always cared for.*

TUESDAY OF THE 9TH WEEK

THE TRIBUTE OF THE KINGDOM
2 Peter 3:12–15a, 17–18. The problem of the delay in the parousia is clearly stated in the Epistle. Sceptics say: "Where is this coming? Everything goes on

as it has since the Fathers died, as it has since the beginning of creation" (3:4). The author recalls the prophecy of Isaiah, who said that the old world would be destroyed to make room for "the new heavens and new earth." What, then, can be said about the delay in the Lord's coming? Two things. Firstly, that the idea of time does not exist for God, for whom "a day can mean a thousand years and a thousand years is like a day." Secondly, this delay is further proof of God's patience. He is keeping his last judgment in suspense to give all men the opportunity to be converted.

Psalm 90 is a psalm of national supplication, characterized by a long description of man's frailty. This frailty is in fact a criticism of Yahweh expressed by the psalmist.

Mark 12:13-17. See p. 149.

■

The Pharisees who are, by way of an exception, joined here by some Herodians, men who openly collaborated with the ruling power of Rome, want to embarrass Jesus. "Is it permissible to pay taxes to Caesar or not?" For the Jews, this was certainly an embarrassing question. Paying a tax was acknowledging the power of the recipient, and therefore compromising with the pagans who made a god of the emperor. Refusing to pay a tax was taking the side of those who wanted to drive the Romans out.

"Give back to Caesar what belongs to Caesar—and to God what belongs to God." There is no question here of setting man up against God or God against man. There is no question of having to choose between one and the other. Jesus' reply is clear: both are chosen! Jesus is going to Golgotha to show that God and man are never rivals. "Give back to God what belongs to God."

Jesus will say solemnly in Pilate's presence: "My kingdom is not of this world." However hard men work to cultivate their gardens, the fruit will come because the sun ripens it. However hard they work, the day of the Lord will always come "like a thief." What God will bring is much more than a mere change of environment. What we are waiting for is a new heaven and new earth. Taking God's side is believing that he is inviting us to be recreated.

"Give back to God what belongs to God." Jesus will be obedient to the point of death on the cross. He will reveal himself on the cross as our servant. God's honor will be saved, because a man will hand himself over totally to the Spirit who sets men free. "Give back to God what belongs to God." Give him thanks for the gratuitous gift of the liberation that he is offering us.

"Give back to Caesar what belongs to Caesar." Take your task as a man seriously. "Insofar as you did this to one of the least of these brothers of mine, you did it to me." This is a very long way from being urged to be indifferent to or to despise the realities of this world, as though they might soil our hands. "So then, my friends, while you are waiting for the Day of the Lord, do your best to live lives without spot or stain, so that Christ will find you at peace."

"Give back to God what belongs to God." Jesus stimulates us to know what we can and must produce, and the impossible thing that we can and must expect from God—what can be achieved and the impossible thing to be received. You are God's vine in this world, so you must bear fruit that will last. The gardener hopes for and expects fruit from the flowers that open as he watches them, but he has to do everything possible so that it will come.

■

Let us pray
for those whose words and opinions
 influence the life of the world;
for those who have political or economic power
and for those who possess the riches of the earth.

Let us also pray
for those who live in the shadow of world events,
for mothers who are caring for their families,
 fathers humbly carrying out their daily work
 and children preparing for their future.

Let us pray too, Lord,
both for those with famous names
 and for those whose names are unknown.

■

God our Father,
you let the earth be born every day
and let us make it a place fit to live in.
May your Spirit fill our hearts,
because only he can teach us
 how to be men and women
 with a new heart
 on a new earth

that will be born
now and for ever.

CALLED TO PROCLAIM

2 Timothy 1:1–3, 6–12. It is difficult to resolve the problem of the authenticity of the "Pastoral Epistles." The most moderate solution is that an important part was played in their editing by one of Paul's secretaries, whose aim was to establish what he regarded as the apostle's spiritual testament.

It is true that the world of the "Pastoral Epistles" is not that of the great Pauline letters, but that of the Church at the end of the first century A.D. That Church was characterized by a strengthening of its organization in confrontation with gnostic teachings.

Strong men were needed to deal with this situation. But Timothy, whose apostolic zeal is not called into question in the letters, appears to have been a timid man. So Paul exhorts him to be faithful in keeping the deposit of faith and even to be prepared to suffer for the sake of the Gospel. To encourage him, Paul reminds him of the grace of his ordination and restates the essential aspects of the good news that he has received in order to pass it on.

Psalm 123 is a very short psalm of ascents, containing the elements of a psalm of national supplication. Only the first verses, which speak of the hope of the man who has risked everything for God, are usually retained in the liturgy.

Mark 12:18–27. See p. 152.

■

"Bear the hardships for the sake of the good news." Jesus is approaching his end. The word that he is proclaiming is fire. It will only become a conflagration of the Spirit when it has consumed him. Jesus is on his way to the cross and God's plan is being made visible. God is bearing the hardships for the sake of the proclamation of grace. Jesus is going to die so that God may appear as the Lord of life—the God, "not of the dead, but of the living." "All this happened to fulfil the prophecies in scripture."

"Bear the hardships for the sake of the good news." You must live, my brother, to the very limit of the call that you have heard. You must give

---

285

body to the life to which you have been reborn. Every day we are confronted with the reality of death. The barrenness of action, the powerlessness of earthly love, fear of the future and a fatalistic attitude brought about by mediocrity—these are signs of death. Each day we have to begin afresh the fight for life, renewal of hope, tightening the bonds of fellowship that have been lost.

"Bear the hardships." With other men, your brothers, you have to commit yourself to the long struggle, resume work on the difficult fabric of tomorrow's world. The promise that has been made to you must take you to the front line of the battle. You have no right to remain in the rearguard of the living forces of history. Man, who has been promised immortality, must go on seizing his victory from the grip of death. He can never give up the struggle to drag out of his existence, which is marked by death, the energies that will give birth to the new world. And in this simple act, and trusting in the life that may be born from his aging body, he will be victorious over that which is always striving to destroy his life. It is in this way that man raises up life again and again.

But this new life will also lead to death. Man's victory will always be partial and temporary. Whenever men and women join forces to give life, they will always have to go back and make a new beginning. But we are all witnesses to what eternity and the fulfilment of the Promise have already given birth to. For we can be quite sure that the day will come when men and women will no longer always have to go back and make a new beginning in order that life may be victorious. On that day, life will no longer be raised up again and again. It will be raised up in a final resurrection and given in abundance.

"Bear the hardships for the sake of the good news." We should never forget the wheat grain that falls into the ground and dies! Our Savior Jesus Christ revealed himself by destroying death and making life and immortality shine forth through the Gospel.

■

God our Father,
may your Spirit wake in us
*   the new man he created*
*   on the day of our baptism.*
Let us remain faithful
*   until the day*
*   when your promise is fulfilled.*

"I HAVE TWO LOVES"

2 Timothy 2:8-15. Confronted with the heresies which were threatening the Church, Timothy is urged to avoid "wrangling about words" and to keep to the rule of faith. He can base his behavior on many good examples: that of Paul, who was imprisoned for the Gospel, and above all that of Christ himself, who made God's faithfulness manifest in a very striking way.

A traditional profession of faith and a liturgical hymn are cited in the Epistle. The first is taken from the common stock of all the churches (see Rom 1). This formula, which is concerned with Christ's resurrection from the dead, is probably quoted in response to the heretics mentioned later, who denied the resurrection of the body (see 2 Tim 2:18) and who did not recognize the spiritual resurrection brought about by baptism. The second half of the quotation, applying the Davidic expectation to Christ, is further evidence that the Epistle originated in Judaeo-Christian circles.

As for the hymn quoted, J. Jeremias believed that it was a hymn of faithfulness sung by baptized Christians who were remaining steadfast during persecution. The hymn stresses the contrast between the martyr's loyalty and the apostate's defection, and the joy of the man who has experienced the faithfulness of God.

Psalm 25 is an alphabetical psalm that can be included among the lamentations. The main theme, which characterizes much wisdom literature, is the antagonism of the ungodly towards the righteous man but the psalm also contains supplications.

Mark 12:28b-34. See p. 155.

■

"Which is the first of all the commandments?" In other words: How can the heart of our faith be defined? A scribe, invested with all the authority of his knowledge, is questioning Jesus. "You must love the Lord your God with all your heart . . . and you must love your neighbor as yourself."

In recalling what everyone knows, Jesus gives the impression of forcing open an already open door. But we should be very attentive to the words that he uses in his reply to the question: "What must I do?" He repeats the opening words of the prayer in which even today all the Jewish people recognize themselves: "Shema, Israel!—Listen, Israel!" At the heart of faith is not a code of laws to be respected, but a vital and profound impulse. Listen! The Christian has always to abandon himself to that dynamic movement of love.

What must you do? You must listen. "Listen, Israel, the Lord our God is the one Lord and you must love the Lord your God with all your heart, with all your soul, with all your mind and with all your strength." You must love unconditionally, both on the days when you are overwhelmed by his presence and on the days when his absence weighs on you like a silence that is too heavy to bear. You must love him because he loved you first. You must turn towards him on the days of grace and on the days of sin. The living fabric of your faith is your heart. It is your heart that enables you to love. Faith is not believing that God exists. It is saying "thou" to him with tenderness and with your whole heart.

"Listen, Israel, you must love your neighbor as yourself." You must let the other speak to your heart. Then he will no longer be a stranger to you, but the one by whom you have let yourself be overcome. As Antoine de Saint-Exupéry said, "he will count for you and you will become responsible for him." You will not be able to be indifferent to anything that concerns him. When you see your brother's suffering, perhaps on the television news, although the pictures are soulless, you will suffer with him. When you are told on the news that men have held their heads high again because tenderness and forgiveness are stronger than deprivation, their joy, even though you do not know them, will also be yours. You will love your neighbor and be a "universal" brother.

"Which is the first of all the commandments?" We too ask the question asked by the scribe, and Jesus' reply takes us further than duty. "Listen!" Let what you receive—God's grace and the appeal made by your brother—be impressed on your heart. Men can increase the number of laws and duties. They can lose themselves in a maze of amendments. But God has only one rule: "Love."

■

God, the source of all love,
  let us love you
    with a burning heart.
Let us long for you
    with a thirst that is always new.
Because you have forgiven us,
let us give you thanks.

■

Father of all men,
let us belong to each other.
May your Spirit be the leaven
    of our communion as brothers.
Because you have forgiven us,
let us live with our brothers
    in your grace.

FRIDAY OF THE 9TH WEEK

FAITHFUL TO THE WORD

2 Timothy 3:10–17. After having suggested to Timothy the way to face
difficulties, the apostle turns towards the future. It is a dark future because the
first communities of Christians are threatened by heresy and moral laxity. But
those who have chosen to believe in Christ must expect to be persecuted. In
contrast with the false teachers, Timothy appears as a genuine believer and,
just as he has been constant and steadfast in following the apostle, so too
must he keep intact the faith which has been handed on to him by his mother
and his grandmother and which Paul is anxious to strengthen.

"The final verses are the most explicit text in the Bible concerning the nature
of scripture. On the one hand, it is inspired by God. . . . On the other, it is
'Christocentric' and therefore leads to salvation" (C. Spicq). Church leaders
have to watch over the moral and religious instruction of believers and
scripture is an essential handbook in this task.

"Permanence is your word's chief trait." Happy is the man who has scripture
to turn to! Once again, the liturgy provides us with a passage of *Psalm 119*
devoted to praise of the Law of God.

Mark 12:35–37. See p. 158.

■

"You must keep to what you have been taught and know to be true."
Because it is faithfulness to a revelation, the believer's very existence
must be obedience to a Word.

Obedience to a Word. We can think of faith, above all, as welcoming.

What are the preconditions for welcoming? Waiting—as vigilantly as a watchman, who lets nothing escape him and as vulnerably as a person who is surprised and overcome. Listening—for a long time and very patiently. "Listen, Israel!" Listening like a lover who gives a name to the step that is hardly audible or who turns round because he has heard someone call him by his name.

Obeying the Word. What is it? It is first and foremost letting it come to you. So many sounds assail us. So many desperate appeals, unanswerable questions, false celebrations and easy hopes reach us from a world in a state of agitation that we become deaf to them. The Word pursues us and we want to escape from it. Listening, after all, is knowing already that a question is being asked and that we shall have to reply to it. Obeying the Word is therefore entering the dynamism of a word exchanged, replied to because it has been welcomed and listened to because it has already been heard. Obeying the Word, then, is entering an encounter that wakes us to freedom. The Word is sharing. Only a shared Word is a word obeyed. Faith enables us to enter into the dynamism of the Word, because it is communication, communion and Church.

"You must keep to what you have been taught and know to be true." You have heard and listened to the Word that God pronounces over the world from all eternity, because of the longing within you to be vulnerable and the joy within you when you find you are loved. You have listened to that voice which has come from elsewhere and embraced it. And you have, to your astonishment, let it rise up within you and have praised it together with all those who have also been roused by it.

∎

We are longing for your Word, Lord.
May Jesus be the secret of our lives.
We exchange your Word.
May the Church be born
listening to your promise.

We pray to you for all those
who, in secret and in silence,
receive the breath of the Spirit
and for all those
who let themselves be followed by your tenderness.

We pray to you for all those
who respond to what they have heard,
for those who give flesh to your Word today

and also for all those
who cannot commit themselves.

We pray to you for all those
who share your Word,
for church communities,
for those who are seeking
and for all those
who let a longing to know you
rise up in them.

Finally, we pray for all those
who are responsible for your Word today.
Let them not keep it for their own profit,
but be the echo of the voice
that comes from elsewhere.

SATURDAY OF THE 9TH WEEK

WE MUST CHOOSE

2 Timothy 4:1–8. Nowadays it is common to produce composite pictures of those holding office in the Church. A very forceful one is provided here. At a difficult time, many believers are turning away from true teaching in search of "myths" and other preachers.

Paul solemnly tells his favorite disciple "before God and before Christ" that his first task is to proclaim the Word. Whether the circumstances are favorable or not and whether those who hear it welcome it or reject it, he must be in the breach to "refute falsehood, correct error, call to obedience." He should never try to imitate the spirit of the times or behave like a sheep in the flock. He is the shepherd and should lead the sheep, not be led by them. It is a difficult and thankless task and has to be done "with patience and with the intention of teaching."

Psalm 71 is an individual lamentation, obviously made by an old man. Faithful to God throughout his life, he continues to profess his faith, even though his hair is white.

Mark 12:38–44. See p. 161.

■

Jesus has been on the way with his disciples for a long time. He has been painfully aware of the hostility aroused by his presence. One has the impression that his sorrow has become deeper as men's hearts have become harder. He has confronted evil of every kind everywhere on his way and now he is in the temple. Soon the hour will come for him to give everything.

While he is watching, a poor woman throws all that she has to live on into the temple treasury. She keeps nothing for herself. She is one of those who hides behind the pillars. "God, be merciful to me, a sinner." Standing prominently on the forecourt of the temple, on the other hand, there are rich men who are ostensibly generous and scribes who thrust themselves forward into the front row. "I thank you, God, that I am not like the rest of mankind."

Jesus is aware that life is slipping through his fingers. He will let himself be stripped and will keep nothing for himself. Lots will be cast for his tunic and his clothes will be shared out. Even his death will be stolen from him. The man who has spoken in the name of God will be condemned for blasphemy. He will be put in the back row. He will be "without beauty, without majesty . . . a thing despised and rejected by men," crucified outside the city walls. And while that is happening, those who are sure of their riches and of their good conscience will continue to believe in a salvation that they attribute to themselves.

The poor woman has given all she has to live on and Jesus recognizes himself in her. She has given everything because she loves. He will give everything so that God's passion may be recognized. God's poor man goes on his way. He will be stripped, but he will make rich those who discover in themselves the heart of a poor man. He will be crowned with thorns to give birth to a race of kings.

He sees the poor woman and she reminds him of the way that God had planned for him. The time will come when men will no longer be able to bear to hear that God forgives and that they will have to sell everything they own to enter the kingdom. The time will come when they will prefer their own illusions to the truth. But he will fulfil his destiny to the very end.

Proclaim the Word in season and out of season, brother! The day will come when men will go in search of other masters to satisfy their itch to hear the "latest novelty." But you just have a Gospel to proclaim. You have to die of loving. People will prefer to be liberated by illusions rather than by the truth. They will want to make use of the Gospel and its spirit of contestation to achieve their own ends. But you have to bear witness to the fact that the liberation offered by the Gospel of Christ is more radical—that it reaches down to the heart.

People will look for easier ways to a less demanding happiness. You will have to live the radical nature of the Gospel to the point of contradiction. The day will come when you will be weary and afraid to go forward, uncertain of the way to follow. Then you must look at the poor woman of the Gospel. She will call you back to what is essential. She will remind you of your need of God.

■

To whom should we go, Lord?
You have the words of eternal life.
Make your good news resound in us
and let us at this time
be the echo your promise.
We ask this through Jesus,
  your word of grace
  spoken for eternity.

■

I have told the Lord:
  You are my God
  and I have no greater happiness than you.
You have made us rich with your bread.
Give us now the inheritance
  that you have promised
  to all those who need you.

NOTES

1. In his *City of God*, Augustine wrote: "Per hominem more hominum loquitur" (*Civ Dei*, XVIII, 6.2; SPL XLI, 537).
2. The idea that God fashioned the woman from a rib may come from a Sumerian play on words. The name of the goddess Nin-ti means "Lady of the Rib" or "Lady of Life." The biblical author may possibly have wanted to

---

293

approximate this play on words in his use of the name "Eve," which means "the living one."

3. See the detailed analysis of R. Lafontaine and P. Mourlon Beernaert: "Essai sur la structure de Marc 8:27–9:13," RSR 57 (1969), 543–561.

4. This text was to a great extent inspired by G. Bessiere, *Jesus est devant*, pp. 84–93.

5. Huub Oosterhuis, *Your Word is Near*, translated by David Smith (Mahwah, NJ: Paulist Press, 1968), p. 19.

The reader who prefers to focus his meditation on the Gospel of Mark alone will find help in the commentaries for both the even and the uneven years.

The following table tells him where to find these commentaries. It gives the week and day, the chapter and verses and the title of the pericope. Pericopes not indicated are those that did not stimulate us to any commentary.

JESUS' MINISTRY IN GALILEE

1 M	1	14–20	Jesus begins to preach
Tu		21–28	Teaching and Healing
W		29–39	Healings
Th		40–45	The Healing of a Leper
F	2	1–12	The Healing of a Paralytic
S		13–17	The Call of Levi and Eating with Sinners
2 M		18–22	A Discussion about Fasting
Tu		23–28	Picking Ears of Corn
W	3	1–6	The Healing of a Man with a Withered Hand
Th		7–12	The Crowds Follow Jesus
F		13–19	The Appointment of the Twelve
S		20–21	Jesus' Relatives Approach Him
3 M		22–30	The Scribes' Accusations
Tu		31–35	Jesus' True Relatives
W	4	1–20	The Parable of the Sower
Th		21–25	The Parable of the Lamp and the Measure
F		26–34	The Parable of the Seed
S		35–41	The Storm is Calmed
4 M	5	1–20	The Gerasene Demoniac
Tu		21–43	The Healing of the Woman with a Hemorrhage and the Resurrection of Jairus' Daughter
W	6	1–6	A Visit to Nazareth
Th		7–13	The Mission of the Twelve
F		14–29	Herod and Jesus
5 Tu	7	1–13	A Discussion about the Traditions of the Pharisees
W		14–23	Teaching about Clean and Unclean

JESUS' JOURNEYS OUTSIDE GALILEE

Th	7	24–30	The Healing of the Daughter of a Syrophoenician Woman
F		31–37	The Healing of a Deaf Man
S	8	1–10	The Second Miracle of the Loaves
6 M		11–13	The Pharisees Call for a Sign from Heaven
Tu		14–21	The Yeast of the Pharisees and of Herod
W		22–26	The Healing of the Blind Man at Bethsaida
Th		27–33	Peter's Profession of Faith
F		34–9:1	The Conditions of Following Jesus
S	9	2–13	The Transfiguration
7 M	9	14–29	The Epileptic Demoniac
Tu		30–37	The Prophecy of the Passion and the Question about Primacy
W		38–40	Using the Name of Jesus
Th		41–50	The Scandal
F	10	1–12	The Question about Divorce
S		13–16	Jesus and the Little Children
8 M	10	17–27	The Rich Man
Tu		28–31	The Reward Promised for Detachment
W		32–45	The Prophecy of the Passion and the Request made by the Sons of Zebedee
Th		46–52	The Blind Man of Jericho

JESUS' MINISTRY IN JERUSALEM

F	11	11–25	The Fig Tree
S		27–33	The Authority of Jesus
9 M	12	1–12	The Parable of the Tenants of the Vineyard
Tu		13–17	The Tribute Paid to Caesar
W		18–27	The Resurrection of the Dead
Th		28b–34	The First Commandment
F		35–37	Christ the Son and Lord of David
S		38–44	The Widow's Mite